THE CHARACTER OF KINSHIP

THE CHARACTER OF KINSHIP

EDITED BY

JACK GOODY

CAMBRIDGE UNIVERSITY PRESS

Published by the Syndics of the Cambridge University Press
Bentley House, 200 Euston Road, London NW1 2DB
American Branch: 32 East 57th Street, New York, N.Y. 10022

© Cambridge University Press 1973

Library of Congress Catalogue Card Number: 73-82448

ISBN: 0 521 20290 6

First published 1973

Printed in Great Britain by
Western Printing Services Ltd, Bristol

Contents

For
Meyer Fortes
on his
retirement
from the
William Wyse
Chair

Introduction

I had two aims in editing this volume. The first was to produce a series of essays by those who have worked with Meyer Fortes, on the occasion of his retirement from the William Wyse Chair in Social Anthropology at the University of Cambridge. The second was to produce a volume of general essays on kinship which would attempt to reconsider some general problems.

Editing a volume of this kind is sometimes like putting one's hand in a barrel of straw dust and pulling out a series of gift-wrapped packages. Some of the contributions may have been lying around in attics for a long time, others may have been hurriedly got together to meet a looming deadline. It was partly to try to avoid such an outcome that I asked contributors to confine themselves to a specific field, namely kinship. But also because in reviewing recently the recent work on kinship I was struck by its rather narrow focus, its neglect of many problems. So within that field I asked for essays dealing with more general themes rather than ethnographic conundrums or descriptive minutiae, in the hope that we would get some reconsideration of certain central problem areas, including those examined by an earlier generation of anthropologists and still raised by scholars outside the discipline itself. For in recent years we have largely abandoned that whole middle-ground that exists between the detailed analysis of single societies and the generalised discussion of concepts, such as filiation and descent, alliance and affinity. Both these other perspectives are necessary, but they do not exhaust the anthropological study of kinship; indeed they exclude what could be its most promising field, the theories of the middle range. Some middle areas such as the study of lineage systems and prescriptive marriage have made progress, even though there has been a marked tendency for the writers in these fields to identify their interest with the study of kinship, even anthropology, itself. It is easier nowadays to see such hallucinations as what they are – the kind of illusion derived from a tendency to blow up work of interesting but limited scope into theories of world-shattering significance. In other words, as delusions of grandeur.

This is not the occasion for an appreciation of the work of Meyer Fortes nor for an account of his career. But the choice of the theme of kinship is clearly related to his own achievements in this field and this in turn to his academic career. Meyer Fortes was born in South Africa of parents who had emigrated from the Crimea. Brought up in a small town in the Cape district, he went to the University of Capetown in March 1923, where he overlapped with Isaac Schapera. On finishing his degree in English and Psychology, in October 1927, he was awarded scholarships to come to do post-graduate work at the University of London, where he began to work on inter-racial intelligence tests with Morris Ginsberg and then with Charles Edward Spearman. Ginsberg also put him in touch with Dr Emanuel Miller who was then working at the East London Child Guidance Clinic, established under the auspices of the Jewish Health Organization. Miller had read natural science and philosophy at St John's College, Cambridge, where he had been influenced towards psychiatry by the Director of Studies in Moral Sciences, W. H. R. Rivers; he therefore had some acquaintance with the wider fields of psychology, psychoanalysis and anthropology. Fortes' job was that of educational psychologist and he was involved in the attempt to devise a non-verbal test of intelligence for inter-racial use, material that was later developed into Raven's Progressive Matrices Test. It was Emanuel Miller who helped him expand his interests in a way that lead him into the field of anthropology. But apart from widening his vision in this general way, Fortes also became interested in some of Miller's more specific concerns, namely the relationship between family structure, sociology and psychology, which was most clearly reflected in his book, *The Generations: A Study of the Cycle of Parents and Children* (1938). It was this work that led Fortes to analyse his own fieldwork material from the Tallensi of Northern Ghana in terms of a developmental cycle, and to study, with such perception, relationships such as those between following siblings, a man and his first born, and other interpersonal situations centering upon the domestic group. It is an aspect of his work that links him to Malinowski as well as to psychology, and one that has received remarkably little comment or follow-up. It is a theme to which he has recently returned in his lecture on 'The Firstborn', the first of the Emanuel Miller memorial lectures given in London in 1972. As the present volume shows, discussion has tended to dwell on the more formal, more inclusive sides of his work on kinship, the organisation of (unilineal) descent groups.

I have mentioned the earlier career of Meyer Fortes because it has always appeared to me that some of the most significant contributions he has made to the study of societies has been at the level of interpersonal kinship. In this he was clearly stimulated by the best of Malinowski, but he also incorporated much from his psychological training. One of the most significant references in the *Web of Kinship among the Tallensi* (1949a) is to Flugel's *Psychoanalytic Study of the Family* (1921). Not that Fortes has been concerned with testing psychological or psychoanalytic theory in a direct way. Rather his examination of the bonds and conflicts, the ties and cleavages, of inter-personal kinship among the Tallensi have set a standard in the analysis of these relationships which no anthropologist has emulated, even twenty-five or more years since the book was written. Again his work in the field of socialisation (especially his essay, 'Social and psychological aspects of education in Taleland', 1938) has had much influence and the position advanced there was commended by Miller and Dollard[1] as 'a very sensible account of imitative behaviour'. This work derives its strength not simply from an acute analysis of interpersonal relations, but also from an understanding of the way these relationships were influenced by the wider structures of political, kin and religious institutions. The connection between the lineage and domestic networks is a central theme in Fortes' work, and forms the basis of one of his best known articles entitled, 'Time and Social Structure', published as his contribution to a volume of essays offered to Radcliffe-Brown (1949*b*). This essay develops the idea of the developmental cycle in domestic groups, and the ways in which differences in structure are related to the process of family change over time. This simple but fruitful idea has been particularly useful in analysing the results of small-scale surveys of settlements, and, more recently, has been used by historians for reconstructing the social organisation of European villages from local records.[2]

The interest in the relationship between the domestic domain and wider politico-jural structures also dominates much of his work in religion, especially on ancestor worship. Here too the interests of psychologists have manifested themselves in his analysis of filial piety as well as of conflicts between the generations. Another aspect of his work on religion to be influenced by his interest in kinship is his analysis of Tallensi concepts of destiny in *Oedipus and Job* (1959*b*), a study of the social and cultural context of beliefs in the different spiritual elements constituting a human being.

It is as well to recall that despite the emphasis he laid on the study of groups (especially unilineal descent groups) that much of the vigour of his analysis comes from his observations of the way that individual (understood here both as a human being and in the Durkheimian sense as physical organism) interacted with such groups (and with the social factor, in the wider Durkheimian sense) in a cultural context, a context that he was able to define in so subtle a manner because of his excellent command of the Tallensi language and his understanding of their concepts. Speaking now as one who has worked among neighbouring peoples, his examination of Tallensi thought (or what is more vulgarly, more superficially and more fashionably referred to as 'the penetration of their code') is more successful than attempts at a facile reduction to a simple formula, such as a table of binary oppositions, or the more elaborate constructions of those others who have failed so signally to distinguish between their own thought and those of their subjects.

In conclusion, I apologise to those potential contributors whom I did not invite. The list of those who have worked with Meyer Fortes includes anthropologists from all continents, and to ask all would have made a volume no-one could afford to buy. I also apologise to those for whom the deadline was too rigid or the field too confined. Max Gluckman and J. Clyde Mitchell had arranged to contribute an essay 'Social factors

Kinship and Descent

Descent and Marriage Reconsidered

Fredrik Barth

A reconsideration of some of the themes from the debate on descent and filiation, so prominently shaped by Meyer Fortes over a number of years (Fortes 1953 *a*, 1959 *a*, 1969) may serve as a fitting tribute to a teacher and senior colleague. My approach in the following departs from the main trend in this debate in two respects: I give greater attention to how native concepts and social groups are shaped by interaction and experience, rather than how they constitute cognitive schemata; and I introduce some further materials, mainly on Middle Eastern systems, into the discussion. By these means I hope to contribute to the debate on the nature of kinship, descent and filiation, and to shed some light on the properties of the Middle Eastern systems.

The intent of Fortes' central original article (Fortes 1953 *a*) was by the examination of a variety of new ethnographic materials to formulate a general understanding of the nature of descent and descent groups. These materials were heavily weighted towards certain African societies; and in retrospect we may see that some of the confusion and disagreement which those early generalizations engendered arose from empirical differences in the descent systems of different areas, i.e. from the common anthropological tendency to transform particular ethnographies to a paradigm of Man. This was first made clear by Leach (1957, last two paragraphs), a lead later developed by Schneider. The basic puzzle was that the classical descriptions (Evans-Pritchard 1940; Fortes 1945) depicted the segmentary structure as a logical entailment of unilineal descent, while later ethnographic accounts (of the 'alliance' systems of South East Asia) reported basic structural differences in such segmentary systems. In Schneider's formulation (1965 *a* : 58)

> Two different kinds of system, each made up of identically structured segments, are really at issue. In [the alliance] system, the segments are articulated into a logically interrelated system by the descent rule, the mode of classification of kinsmen, and the relationship of perpetual alliance between segments. In [the descent] system, segments are defined by the descent rule, exogamy, and the variable bounding of the segments in terms of specific functions (domestic, jural, political, residential, territorial, and so on).

From descriptions of some Middle Eastern societies (Peters 1960, 1967; Lewis 1961; Barth 1959; Pehrson 1966) we may add a further kind of system. Here, segments are defined by the descent rule, but no rule of

3

exogamy relates these segments in marriage exchanges with their social surroundings. Allowed or preferred parallel cousin marriage creates an individuated network of kinship ties within and across segments, and the functions of different orders of segments depend on the variable limits of joint estates. These features have implications so that 'it is erroneous to regard Arab patrilineages as typologically one with the more commonly encountered exogamic patrilineal descent systems, for endogamy not only changes completely the relations between lineal components but alters the very internal structure of these groups' (Murphy and Kasdan 1967: 2).

Problems have also arisen in the application of the descent concept to New Guinea Highlands societies (Barnes 1962; for a summary of the subsequent debate see Strathern 1969). At issue are the mode of recruitment to segments (by cumulative patrifiliation rather than descent according to Barnes 1962: 6), the mode of articulation between segments (by locality; in accordance with descent dogma; by marriage alliance; by ritual exchange), and the ecological prerequisites of the social forms (the effects of density and land pressure). In attempts to accommodate these materials to a general anthropological vocabulary, or vice versa, distinctions have been made between how descent is applied by the actors themselves as (1) a principle of recruitment (2) a conceptualization of group unity (3) a statement of the proper composition of the group, and (4) a statement of the group's relation with other groups (Scheffler 1965; but see also his different treatment of the question in Scheffler 1966).

Where would such wider comparisons seem to bring us? We are faced with an increasing number of types of descent system in which the very concept of descent can imply a range of different things. This outcome is characteristic of a tradition of anthropology which proceeds with each individual society as if it were dissecting an organism, and seeks to depict the morphology of the system by naming its parts, using concepts developed through comparative generalizations. This is the procedure so sharply criticized by Leach (1961 *b*: 2–3); to my understanding it is basic to a structuralism which starts with the empirical epiphenomena of behaviour and works through macro-concepts such as custom and institution to distil an increasingly abstract 'social structure' of which the empirical facts are an embodiment. In contrast to this mode of thinking, I should like to argue very simply that some empirical events are far more pregnant with consequences than others, and that we can construct stratified models of reality where some empirical features are singled out as the sources or determinants of a number of other empirical features. Thus, the practice of using unilineal descent as a principle of recruitment must necessarily produce groups with certain structural properties. Even though the specific consequences of this, on other behaviour, will be affected by additional circumstances such as economic and political context, it remains essential to be

4

able to show how this empirical process of recruitment generates other empirical features. I therefore see the task of analysis as one of locating such identifiable determinants and sources, and explicating the processes whereby their consequences ensue, rather than developing heuristic abstractions for describing structural patterns.

This indeed I feel has also been the intention of Fortes and Leach, among others, in their debate when they turn to the elementary kinship relations of father-child, mother-child, and spouses to find the sources of descent systems. Whatever they might claim to be doing, it has seemed to me that they are turning to real people, in real life contexts, to discover where the factors arise which generate the larger systems. But in wishing to go further and make this a crucial feature of anthropological model-building, I am forced to make clear what remains unclear in the structuralists' representations, viz: the dialectic between the concrete behaviour of persons, groups and categories on the one hand, and the collective institutions of culture and society that persist regardless of changing personnel. I must, incidentally, ask the reader's indulgence for the wide-ranging character of this discussion with the plea that, whenever one seeks to modify a theoretical framework, some previously simple points become unaccustomedly complex while some previously vague but complex questions become disappointingly simple.

To depict the connection between individual behaviour and collective institutions, it is necessary that one construct models with clearly differentiated micro- and macro-levels. I find it reasonable to see social institutions and customs as the outcome of a complex aggregation of numerous micro-events of behaviour, based on individual decisions in each person's attempts to cope with life. This is not to deny the existence of culture as a pre-established framework for choosing behaviour and interpreting experience – on the contrary, it is precisely to depict the interconnection of culture and behaviour that we need the models. Though every actor is dependent on his knowledge and codification, and hampered by conventional blinkers, there must none the less be a dynamic relationship between individual experience and learning, and the socially recognized collective facts which we call culture and institutions. The simplest form of this interconnection would seem to depend on sharing: individual behaviour produces experience, a confrontation with reality which may or may not seem consistent with preexisting conceptualizations and thus may sometimes tend to confirm, sometimes to falsify them. If a number of persons in communication share a similar opportunity situation, experience the same confrontations with reality, and have the same conceptualizations falsified, one would expect them to develop shared understandings and modify their collective culture and expectations in accordance with this. Obviously, this is not a complete theory of culture change, but may be sufficient for our purposes, as will

5

emerge shortly. On the basis of it, we can ask specific questions about how such shared understandings emerge, and what their everyday relevance becomes. It is from this perspective I hope to elucidate the connections between descent systems and actual behaviour.

This simultaneous interest in (native) models and behaviour has been criticized as a 'failure to distinguish the segment as a conceptual entity from its concrete counterpart as a group' (Schneider 1965 *a*: 75). Success in making this important distinction must not prevent us, however, from constructing a model that contains both. I would criticize both Fortes and Leach not so much for being unclear on this distinction as for seeking structure and explanation too exclusively on the *conceptual* side of the dichotomy – the argument about descent often focuses mainly on the question whether it stands in conceptual opposition to affinity or to complementary filiation. Let us rather give equal weight to the aspect of confrontation with *reality* contained in any social experience. Given a certain pattern of membership in a descent group, to what groups and aggregations of actual people can the members of a descent group be counterposed? And how does the social experience thereby produced affect the conceptualization of descent and descent group, and the social uses such group membership will be put to in the future? I am arguing essentially that we should consider the 'we–they' confrontation contained in the social interaction, and inspect how the experience of who 'they' are will mould the actor's conception of 'we'.

Now here is where some essential facts constrain us in our model building: through notions of incest and exogamy man makes an arbitrary and culturally varying, but fundamental, association between descent and responsibilities to dispose of women in marriage. It would be simple to construct a general model of unilineal descent alone, and see its implications of nesting segments, balanced opposition, etc. But people everywhere seem to see 'who they are' in terms of the whole kinship network, i.e. both with reference to relations of descent (or filiation), and marriages. Anthropology has been unable to produce a generally acceptable theory of incest and exogamy: we cannot say why persons everywhere in their choice of spouse must think of whose child they are. But the connection, variable in its particular injunctions as between cultures, is yet ubiquitous. When a group recruited by a rule of descent confronts a 'they' group, who 'they' are will be specified by the connected criteria of descent and marriage; and different marriage systems will therefore imply very different experiences of confrontation, and consequent images of the 'we' descent group.

Let me illustrate this by a straight-forward and extreme ethnographic case: the Marri Baluch (Pehrson 1966). Here, a woman is disposed of in marriage by her closest adult male agnate or agnates. In return for a wife for its member, the extended household gives a brideprice, or a bride, in exchange. At the same time, marriage between close agnates, especially father's brother's children, is preferred. Now imagine the following situation, exemplified in Pehrson's field materials: The children (D–H) of three deceased brothers (A, B, C) form a minimal descent group. Marriage

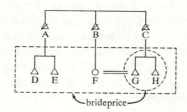

guardianship in the woman F is vested in her closest agnates, D, E, G, and H. G marries F in agreement with the preferred rule of marriage. He receives the bride; he and his brother pay the brideprice jointly. The recipients of the brideprice are his cousins, and he and his brother; i.e. G and H receive half shares in the brideprice which they themselves pay. Similar marriages have high frequency in the population, with a number of confounding effects (pp. 55 ff). The conceptual distinction between parties giving and receiving a woman is clear enough, and where possible it is expressed physically as (the representatives of) two distinct descent groups facing each other (p. 115). But the concrete counterpart of the distinct groups will often fail to emerge, because persons belong equally to both categories; likewise the most elementary distinctions of kinship between agnates, matrilaterals, and affines will be confounded through the practice of such marriages (35 ff., 42). How different such experiences must be from those of the Kachin, where the wife-giving line materializes physically as a distinct group every time and all participants can see them as a corporeal reality, labelled by an unequivocal kinship term – different again from the Tallensi who can experience agreement about the presence of a group, but little agreement about who they are: matrilaterals, affinals, or unrelated.

The main thrust of the following argument is directed to show that this difference is not without effect on the meaning and relevance of descent: it affects the organizational potential of the descent structure, and the kinds of tasks and activities that are pursued by descent groups. Indeed, I shall try to show that this perspective can provide the basis for a comparative analysis of descent systems. This requires (a) concepts whereby one shows how descent rules and marriage networks produce structures with determinate organizational potentials. But despite such potentials one cannot deduce from first principles the behaviour which will actually be organized by the structure in each case, i.e. whether the transmission of rights to real property, obligations in work groups, responsibility in feud, etc. It has been argued (Fortes 1959 *a* in 1970 *b*: 97; Leach 1957 in 1961 *b*: 123) that to understand this, one must consider the political and economic context. But what determines which aspects of politics and economics are relevant? Different structures, as potential frameworks for the organization of activities, are more or less suitable for different tasks. We need to explicate how an aggregate of people come to use a certain structure for the organization of a set of tasks, i.e. we need (b) concepts to show the processes whereby tasks are codified and assigned to status positions in the structure.

This implies a perspective not unlike that of Fortes in his use of the concept of *domain* (Fortes 1969: 95–100), whereby he distinguishes the normative concatenation of activity systems from their positional, structural aspect. I have argued elsewhere (Barth 1966, 1972) that these are always connected dimensions of social organization, which both require systematic attention; and I have sought to identify them on the micro-level by the concepts of situation, occasion and task vs. status, status set and person. In one of Fortes' formulations, 'A social occasion, event or institution is not a hodgepodge of casually mixed cultural and structural elements; it has form and texture – that is, an internal structure. And this is because each element of status manifested in it carries with it (or we can turn this around and say is the outcome of) a specific context of social relations to which given norms and patterns of customary behaviour are attached' (1969: 97). In this light, a preliminary version of our question may be: 'What determines the content of descent relations' – or indeed how is the content of any kinship relation determined?

One is led to pose the question this way because of the way we are used to identify kinship statuses. In most fields of social organization, the bundle of rights which composes a status gives, among other things, command over specific resources that provide the basis for enactment of its characteristic role: the feudal lord his land rights, the director his desk and telephone, the priest his temple. But what resources are given to a mother's brother? We identify a status as one of relevance to political structure because it gives command over political resources; thus we are not led to ask what determines the content of political relations because it is precisely in terms of their content that they are identified as political. But we recognize kinship statuses by a few diagnostic traits only; and so we can ask what determines the (rest of the) content of kinship relations. As Schneider points out in his discussion of the definition of kinship: '. . .it seems self-evident that there is more to kinship than meets the simple prerequisites of regulating sexual intercourse, socializing the young, caring for the baby. There are aspects of any kinship system that are so remote from such problems. . .that it is just not possible to account for them, or to hold them to be necessary, in such terms' (Schneider 1965 *b*: 88).

It looks as if, by dichotomizing status and task and putting our question in this way, we have manoeuvred ourselves into an impasse. I have chosen to do so to provide a basic paradigm of the process of institutionalization – i.e. how individual experience feeds back on cultural standardization – and thereby expose the kind of argument which may also facilitate the comparison of descent group organizations. Let us therefore focus for a moment on real people in an elementary kinship situation in Western society: one where relatively newly married spouses are pursuing the core activities of sexual intercourse, socializing the young, and caring for a baby. These tasks are assigned to a status set of husband/father, wife/mother, and child. This set is obviously for the newborn child the first set that he ever participates in. It can serve as a basis for interaction in a variety of activities, and will indeed tend to do so. If you look at what happens in such a social system of married parents and a child, you will see all sorts of role elaborations emerge as this triad copes with the daily problems of life; and they will organize all these new tasks in terms of the three statuses in the set, because they are what is relevant in the domestic situation. The child is, in other words, trained to participate in this status set; and it is the first he can handle. As he goes out into the world, and meets new kinds of problems, he will continue to appeal to this same status set. Faced with a new problem he will scream for mother, without asking whether it involves tasks organized in terms of kinship; in every community little boys go out every day and try to mobilize this basic kinship triad for new purposes. With growing social experience and competence they will start limiting themselves to doing so only where the status set is adequate or at least not grossly inappropriate. Obviously, the father-mother-child set is no good for organizing a group of boys for an egalitarian operation; for such tasks one must invent or borrow another organizational framework. But where the activity is one that can be adequately handled with the kinship statuses, I would expect them to be mobilized by numerous persons in similar opportunity situations, producing expectations and patterned ways of responding in alters. The roles in the set will consequently become more and more complex, compounded from different kinds of activities that do not have to do with sexual intercourse or socializing the young; and this organization of activities will become institutionalized as common, shared learning of how to cope with life.

What becomes kinship behaviour, in any particular culture, will thus constantly be under pressure of change from two combined set of factors: one of which we may loosely call ecology – the concrete life situations that arise where purposes are pursued under technical and practical constraints, the other of which we may seek in the organizational capacity of kinship sets and relational networks. I do not claim that the full content of kinship relations can be deduced from these determinants; but I do claim to have pointed to mechanisms and processes which act on the tasks and obligations of kinship statuses and change them by cumulative increments.[1]

I should also perhaps point out that the reasoning expounded above bears little resemblance to Malinowski's type of biographical extension theory (Malinowski 1929), since its crucial elements concern the transformation from status to role and the feedback of experience to routinization (see Barth 1966: 1–11) and not the classification of variant cases with reference to prototypes.

Let me also seek to clarify the kind of analysis I am attempting by schematizing it, in contrast to a schematized version of structuralist analysis. This may be useful because my purposes are closely similar to theirs, my language is largely similar, yet some of the basic premises and analytical operations are drastically different. Let us limit ourselves to a simple, and hopefully not unacceptable, distinction between structural premises, social patterns, and individual cases of behaviour, belief, or action. As I understand the procedure of many British social anthropologists, these three are connected in linear fashion. In terms of the anthropologist's model, structural premises explain social patterns which in turn explain, and are exemplified in, individual cases. In terms of the anthropologist's investigation, it proceeds the opposite way, from individual cases to social patterns

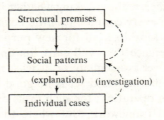

to structural premises, which once they are discovered provide the key to model building. The type of model I am seeking to construct is one based on a micro-macro distinction, as follows: the crucial explanations lie in the transformations between these two levels: (i) how individual cases are generated by choices constrained by empirical social patterns *and*

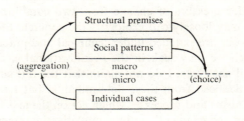

structural, or as I should prefer to say, cultural premises, and (ii) how these individual cases are aggregated through interaction to social patterns and through reality confrontation, learning and sharing to cultural premises. The 'premises' and 'patterns' are only connected through behavioural ('micro') events, not directly in terms of homology and structural fit; the social patterns (e.g. a concrete empirical network of marriage relations) have a primacy in explanation equal to that of structural or cultural premises (e.g. a rule of exogamy).

Let us then pursue the analysis of descent systems in this framework. We have asked what determines the organizational potential, i.e. the structure, of a descent system. This potential derives essentially from the form and scale of the unambiguous status sets defined by descent available for use by the individual actors. We are, in other words, focusing first on the right-hand side of the model: the options presented by the system to the actor. The particular rules of exogamy will obviously have an immediate impact here: within the bounds of exogamy there will be a complete orderliness in the distribution of kin statuses on persons so that only a limited range of consanguines are found within the exogamous descent segment. Positive marriage rules will also create a type of order in patterning the overlap of consanguines and affines. But indeed, since *any* distribution in fact constitutes a pattern, it is the whole concrete network of pre-established marriages to which we should give our attention, not the general rules, since these consummated marriages will determine the total kinship composition of groups to which ego belongs or is confronted, and thus furnish premises for his own actions and understandings.

In Middle Eastern communities with patrilineal descent organization, the ordering effect of exogamy extends only to lineals and first order collaterals; thus no cousin is prohibited. A positive *right* to marry FaBrDa has been reported from many areas; however, since this refers to a specific genealogical relationship it should not be regarded as a positive marriage rule. Whether the explicit right is formulated or not, the actual frequency of such marriages, as a sub-category of descent group and family endogamy, is high. Crude counts vary from around 10% (Ayoub 1959, Khuri 1970) and 20% (Patai 1965), in some communities up to 30% (Barth 1954, Pehrson 1966). There has been some useful discussion of the significance of such percentages (Ayoub 1959, Gilbert and Hammel 1966, Goldberg 1967, Hammel and Goldberg 1971), clarifying how they combine the effects of local endogamy and postmarital residence with the effects of a specific preference for the particular relative FaBrDa. However, in the present context we are concerned with the frequency of the event and its implications, not its causes. These are only exacerbated by its association with rates of descent group endogamy of 40–80%, and even higher rates of 'family' and 'village' endogamy.

As a result of such marriages in the past, paternal and maternal ascendants merge, and numerous affinal relations obtain between fellow descent group members. As noted above, this does not seriously inhibit the conceptual distinction of agnates from matrilaterals, or affinals. What it does, however, is effectively to inhibit any attempt to give this conceptual distinction any systematic behavioural content, i.e. make it the basis for any task organization. If my FaBr is my WiFa, and also a matrilateral relative, it is very difficult to act towards him in terms of these separate statuses, sometimes treating him as a mother's relative, sometimes as father-in-law and sometimes as agnate. The probability of our elaborating behavioural distinctions between these as separate roles is certainly minimal; the probability of our glossing over distinctions is considerable. Thus marginal modifications of behaviour would not lead to the emergence of distinctions in role capacities. And even if we did develop a task organization on this basis, it would not be capable of emulation by my brother, who has not married our FaBrDa, or my neighbour, whose father-in-law is his MoBr, or a stranger.

Considering now the left-hand side of the model, we are concerned with the aggregation of individual experiences and learning to collective and shared cultural premises. In our present case, it is obvious that the actual distribution of related persons in status sets differs so between actors that their opportunity situations are drastically discrepant and they can reach no effective agreement as to what represents useful and workable discriminations. In other words, the standardized organizational potential of kinship, given such a network of marriages, is very limited. The only possible agreement that can emerge, the only collective behavioural solution that is possible in such a system, would be to regard kinsmen of all kinds as essentially similar. And this indeed is true for most aspects of customary behaviour in the Middle East. Specific rights and obligations (inheritance, responsibility for homicide, etc.) are variously allocated, but the general obligations and expectations are of the same kind e.g. as between WiFa, FaBr, Fa and even MoBr[2] (see below) – in contrast to most of the ethnographies in our comparative literature. It is thus possible for Khuri (1970) to detail the basic compatibility of agnate-affine role combinations and conclude that 'given the specifically recognized family relationships in the Middle East, the practice of marrying the parallel cousin contributes to more harmonious relationships between the members of the consanguine group who at once become also the in-law group' (p. 606). Equally, one may reverse the argument in agreement with the view of role formation pursued above, and point out how this codification of kin and affinal roles agrees with what the model would predict from the limited organizational potential of the actors' actual relationship network.

Next, let us consider the political confrontations that take place between the larger descent group to which an actor belongs, and the 'they' group to which it is counterpoised. It is my thesis that the actors' experience of this opposition will affect the cultural codification of the meaning and content of descent. Detailed analyses from different parts of the Middle East document again and again that such political confrontations do not in fact follow a simple segmentary charter of fusion and fission (e.g. Barth 1959, Peters 1967, Aswad 1971). There are limited situations, such as in the allocation of usufruct rights to jointly owned land, when a nesting hierarchy of segments is made tangible; but even then the actual politics is of a more complex nature. In far the most confrontations involving related parties, the opposed units are not unilineal descent segments but *factions*, built on bilateral and affinal relations, friendship and opportunistic alliances as well as a selection of agnatic relations. As shown most clearly in Barbara Aswad's recent study, the main schisms of descent groups occur between close collaterals, in her case even full brothers; and these schisms serve as a focus for the alignment of others – not without regard to segmental position, but transmuted by cognatic and affinal ties created in part by FaBrDa marriage. Thus, twisting an Arab proverb which describes situational fusion and fission, she points out how 'In reality it is more correct as follows: "Me against *some* of my brothers, me and *some* of my brothers against *some* of my cousins, me, *some* of my brothers and *some* of my cousins against *some* outsiders." Another proverb, "The enemy of my enemy is my friend," is closer to the actual segmentation' (1971: 82). The prototypical opponent to which the whole 'we' descent group is counterpoised, is characteristically composed of strangers: armies, caravans, city-ruled police, nomads for the villagers, villagers for the nomads, other ethnic groups, other religious communities, unrelated neighbours. In *this* opposition, the basic essence of agnatic descent, involving as it rightly should close in-marriage, can be fully experienced as an ideal. The words of a Baluch leader summarizes this shifting, ambiguous character of unity and division: 'As close as the nail is to the flesh, so close are the men of our lineage to each other' (Pehrson 1966: 57).

This view also provides us with the key to the other main feedback: how the choices of actors become such as to recreate the social patterns, here particularly the marriage network, that defines some of the features of the system. Unless the distribution of marriages is perpetuated, the premises for role solutions and agreements will change. In the case of exogamy and positive marriage rules, it is sufficient to demonstrate the perpetuation of the rule; in the case of the basically statistical pattern of the Middle Eastern system one needs to show the basis for the perpetuation of a range of choices. If we are not unduly distracted by the large and confusing literature seeking to explain FaBrDa marriage, but retain the wider perspective adopted here, this is not very difficult. In agreement with authors cited above (Barth 1959: 40, Peters 1960: 44, Aswad 1971: 48) it must be recognized that FaBrDa marriage is one of an arsenal of possible moves for securing social position. When, as is inevitable, opposed interests emerge between close collaterals, some of them will seek to align by marriage (whether to close the rift or to bolster themselves by the support of *other* collaterals in the face of the rift), and it is precisely their view of what is involved in descent and in affinal relations that makes this move attractive and effective. At the same time, it is also necessary to establish new alliances, and to renew old ones (i.e. with matrilaterals). Thus the mixed nature of the total marriage network will be perpetuated, and the same premises for experience be provided.

On one point the literature on Middle Eastern societies frequently presents material which seems discrepant with the general argument advanced here, *viz*: the special role of matrikin, and especially MoBr, as indulgent, warm and supportive relatives in contrast to patrilaterals. Informants from many areas give expression to this view, and in the anthropological tradition we might seek to understand it (i) as the result of an extension of sentiments from Mo to Mo's kin or more generally (ii) as the behavioural expression of a basic dichotomy between agnates and matrilaterals. I see no way of refuting such explanations in the present context; but my own argument has been based on the behavioural impracticability of such simple cognitive schemata and so my argument is in danger of falsification unless it can accommodate these data. Rather than appeal to concepts like complementary filiation or generalized exchange, I have to show how the standard experiences of actors could sustain an agreement about these special qualities in matrilaterals, and the feasibility of a specialized task allocation to MoBr.

To see this, we need to consider degree of closeness as a general kinship dimension. If ego's obligations and loyalties to all kinsmen are essentially similar, they will need to be practised with some general rule of priority based most easily on a scale of close vs. distant. Such a scale is clearly formulated by Middle Eastern informants and obtains not only for agnates, but for all kinsmen, to whom it can be applied egocentrically without difficulty also in a disordered system such as is generated by frequent endogamous marriages. The fact of patrilineal genealogies and joint estates for large agnatic collectivities, however, has an effect on this. Persons will know of many more agnates because of standardized genealogies and specific common interests; in cases where both agnatic and matrilateral distant links to a person are known, moreover, the former take precedence over the latter. In effect, a person will 'have' few matrilaterals and many agnates; all the matrilaterals will be 'close' while agnates will be both 'close' and 'distant'. I would argue that statements about the greater degree of intimacy with matrilaterals than with agnates reflect this fact.

Consider next the special position of MoBr. Even where he is also an agnate, he will be a 'close' relative as MoBr and a more 'distant' relative as agnate. In the nesting hierarchy of agnatic segmentation – important because it defines units with joint property, and thus sets of potential rivals – we find the series (1) brothers (2) half-brothers (3) father's brothers and father's brothers' sons, and (4) father's father's brothers' sons – the first possible

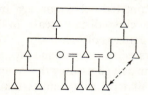

slot that may contain a MoBr. In the schisms that divide close collateral rivals a MoBr will *always* be in a structural position where he can serve as an ally on the pattern 'the enemy of my enemy is my friend'; thus the character of this particular relative (but not 'matrilaterals' or 'cognates') as an elective, close and supporting person can be agreed upon by all actors. Finally, the position of MoBr as politically close by choice (he might align equally with any rival brother, or his other sisters' sons) is consistent with the existence of 'close non-relatives' – friends and allies without kin ties can also choose to establish stable relations involving all the prestations and loyalties of close kinsmen. Thus the politics of kinship merges fully with the politics of non-kin relations in this kind of descent system.

Let us briefly mark some contrasts with other, better known, descent systems in terms of their organizational capacities and implications. In systems characterized by unilineal descent and exogamy, as described from many parts of Africa, one obtains total order and agreement among agnates (to exemplify with the patrilineal case). This affects the organizational potential both of the agnate/matrilateral distinction, and of the segmentary hierarchy. As to the first, it makes possible a clear dichotomy of claims and behaviour towards the two: a number of tasks may be differentially allocated to each, and they can be consummated in behaviour between whole persons without any confounding effect. Thus, a wide variety of special privileges towards matrilaterals, as described for different African societies, is fully capable of realization and general confirmation among actors. However, with marriage scattering in unsystematic fashion outside the descent group, they form, as Fortes emphasizes, an individuated network. Thus while there can be general agreement within a descent group as to *what* the obligations to matrilaterals are, people cannot agree *who* they are. For joint purposes, descent group members must disregard these kinds of relations (or pretend that they are indeed agnatic, when grafting takes place). This means that matrilateral relations can be made a vessel for the organization only of some kinds of tasks, and not for the collective concerns of the agnates. Agnatic relations, on the other hand, will have a greater organizational potential; not merely are they suitable for collective tasks, but the unequivocal organization of persons in a major structure of nesting segments gives a distinctive organizational scheme for such collectivities in situational fusion and fission. The ethnographies describe how this is directly reflected in obligations and in consummated behaviour, e.g. in politics – in contrast to the individuation of the close–distant scale in Middle Eastern systems producing more complex patterns of politics.

The contrast of such systems to the alliance system of S.E. Asia is equally clear. A positive rule of marriage assures the concordance of kinship status and affinal status, the unilateral rule implies that affines are divided into two, each with a categorical relation to ego's descent group expressed, among other things, in kinship categorization. Not only are wife-giving and wife-receiving groups real, tangible collectivities who can appear *en masse* or be represented; since there can be full agreement between all descent group members as to who they are, the relationship can be used to organize collective tasks and collective concerns of agnates. It is this increased organizational capacity, in relation to 'local descent lines', which was so brilliantly demonstrated by Leach (1951); he also makes very clear how the behavioural content carried in such relations is not predetermined by the structure: 'With Kachin type marriage the relationship between wife giving and wife receiving groups is asymmetrical; hence differentiation of status one way or the other is more likely than not. . . (But) one cannot predict from first principles which of the two groups will be the senior' (1961 *b* edition, p. 102). In the absence of such entailment, however, we need to identify the reciprocal influences of structure and behavioural content in terms of the processes whereby these are effected, and this is the focus of my present thesis.

Lévi-Strauss (1966 *a*) provides a discussion of Crow/Omaha systems which invites an analysis along similar lines. He points out very appositely that such terminologies seem to imply marriage patterns whereby new connections must be sought in every marriage, and kinship and affinity become mutually exclusive ties (p. 19). What might be the organizational potential of such systematic discriminations that differentiate members of own descent group, members of the other parent's descent group, and affines? Lévi-Strauss gives a hint by describing the system as resembling 'a pump which requires an external supply to draw upon according to its needs, and an outlet through which to restitute the by-products of its on-going operations' (p. 19). With such a process scattering the matrilateral and affinal bonds and connecting each person in idiosyncratic ways, how much political or other collective content can these relations be given?

On the other hand, it is not clear what empirical cases we have for such a form. Surveying the well-described societies with Crow/Omaha features, and Murdock's classical summary of variations (Murdock 1949: 240, 247), no common gross features emerge that might indicate political implications of an exogamy-based process such as Lévi-Strauss sketches. On closer inspection (pp. 306, 307) even the evidence for a characteristic association of Crow/Omaha systems with these extensive exogamic injunctions seems to fade. Thus the very source which Lévi-Strauss cites on the Hopi (Eggan 1950: 121) reminds us of the contradictory evidence, including the probable positive practice of cross-cousin marriage. It would clearly be premature on the basis of such uncertain evidence to try to characterize the actual operation of descent, and its effects on the actors' codifications, in a Crow or Omaha 'type' system.

It remains for me to suggest how the Middle Eastern concept of descent reflects the gross features of the actors' experience of life with kinsmen and strangers, and the occasions when descent groups are mobilized and descent group identity is activated. Let me emphasize that nothing that is said below denies the existence of a fundamental ideology, which can easily be elicited from informants, of transmission of substance and intangible qualities in the male line, the irrepudiable primacy of obligations between lineal male ascendants and descendants, and the joint fund of honour and shame between males so related.[3] This also provides the ideological underpinning for the transmission of property and other rights and obligations in the male line. But it does *not* provide a sufficient basis for deductions about the ideology involving collaterals, or shareholders in joint estates, and thus the actors' descent concept; it is my thesis that this, like all other concepts, will emerge through a dialectical process of confrontation with the reality it is used to designate With the Middle Eastern codification of all kinship and affinal relations as essentially 'of the same kind', the range of what will be experienced as *distinctive* for agnates becomes limited. One can identify two dominant kinds of precipitate from the flow of experience. (i) Whereas other kinsmen are 'close', many agnates are 'distant', yet tied together in important concerns. Relations to agnates are therefore characteristically formal, jural, obligatory, and limited, often expressed by the concept of *haqqi*, implying 'legal' and 'imperative'. The sanctions behind them are public rather than emotionally internalized; trust is limited in proportion to degree of interdependence and rivalry is precariously controlled. (ii) Descent group affairs focus on property and the control of territory: they relate to a particular joint tangible estate. Among agricultural people, and to some extent pastoralists, this implies common residence and thus local community; but this is an artifact of land tenure rather than a direct effect, or obligation, of joint descent. Thus on the one hand where it dominates land tenure and settlement, descent may be identified as the source of all community life and all kinship, in opposition to outside threats by strangers and unrelated neighbours. On the other hand where joint landed estates disappear (by subdivision, administrative fiat, etc.) as is happening through most of the Middle East, most of the distinctive activities organized by descent are discontinued and descent groups disappear, since there is nothing in the organization of intimate kinship behaviour that sustains or generates them. In contrast to some authors who seek to derive the nature of Middle Eastern political systems from the descent system (Murphy and Kasdan 1959, 1967), I would thus seek the determinants of descent group formation in political, and economic, factors. Indeed, it seems appropriate to characterize the content of descent relations as part of politics rather than kinship; and where the territorial estates at the base of these politics are removed, the whole unilineal organization disappears and kinship and local life take on a highly bilateral character. This would seem to contrast clearly to other unilineal descent systems with exogamy and/or positive marriage rules, which also tend to be sustained by their intimate kinship functions and often other joint concerns.

The main argument of this paper may be summarized as follows: in my view, the very extensive debate on descent and filiation, which has raged among anthropologists of various persuasions, has not produced adequate generalizations or a comparative understanding of descent systems. This is mainly because it has been unjustifiably simplistic in its view of the relationship of native concepts and social life: in part it has focused on these concepts *in vacuo*, in part it has assumed an easy identity between native concepts and their social expression. In a world where actual life often confounds logical dichotomies, falsifies ideological premises, and makes behavioural impossibility of embraced obligations, this is inadequate. We must construct models which capture more of the dialectical relation between concepts and norms, and social reality.

In the preceding pages I have tried to sketch some parts of such a model, focusing on the analysis of Middle Eastern descent systems in a comparative perspective. In analyzing descent and related native concepts, I have consequently asked how they are confronted with reality in terms of the descent groups that emerge and the features of the other groups to which they are counterpoised. In this we find that some culturally important premises, such as the primacy of the common identity of the male line, are retained although their implications for collaterals and the agnatic group are contradicted by the realities of rivalry, schism and factional alliance based on other kinship ties. Other conceptualizations are made ineffectual in real life, such as the dichotomy of agnate vs. matrilateral in a disordered endogamous system. Yet other culturally desired and pursued goals, such as the defence of agnatic solidarity through the retention of the women of the descent group, have unsought and unseen consequences in weakening the distinctiveness of agnatic bonds by generalizing kin obligations.

18

To isolate some of the processes whereby these connections are effected, I gave attention to some different kinds of content, in terms of tasks and circumstances, which may characterize relations, and the organizational capacity of different descent systems for such different tasks. I argued that this organizational capacity of descent groups is determined *both* by the descent concept in a narrower sense, and by the marriage pattern. In this connection it may be important to emphasize that an aggregate pattern of choices represents a structural determinant of the same order as e.g. a rule of descent, since it is a constraining 'given' in every person's life situation and canalizes his choices (*pace* Schneider 1965 *a*: 76). Our perspective in analysis must be one of elucidating feedback (and consequent stability or change) in ongoing systems, and not the genesis of society from *logos*.

In conclusion, I might suggest that attempts to clarify and refine the anthropological concept of descent as a central analytical concept will hardly meet success, since it straddles so many analytical levels and encloses so diverse feedback effects. We might do better to regard it as an important member of that large vocabulary of concepts which we employ in our efforts to make adequate cultural translations, and rely on terms of greater specificity as analytical tools.

Notes

1 It might be noted that this form of reasoning is reminiscent in some respects of marginalism in economics or selection in evolutionary theory, though based on different mechanisms in each case. The force of such reasoning in explaining also the gross features of form in a system should not be underestimated.
2 See Peters 1967, who, while he emphasizes the distinction between agnates and MoBr gives material consistent with the view expressed here: a MoBr gives access (on request) to the same resources of water and land as do agnates; he contributes voluntarily to bridewealth where agnates are obliged to; he gives support in revenge for homicide; the killing of a MoBr is as sinful an act as killing a close agnate; a case is even cited where revenge is wrought against a MoBr rather than an agnate.
3 This is clearly not a question of mere 'filiation', as it is visualized by informants as a *line*, reaching back to the creation of Adam, and forward into the future.

Kinship, Descent and Locality:
Some New Guinea Examples

Andrew Strathern

'What is the irreducible fact about fatherhood?' After worrying at the problem unsuccessfully for some minutes we would be faced with the reply: 'fatherhood itself'. In this way at undergraduate seminars students in social anthropology classes were introduced to the quality of Meyer Fortes' ideas on kinship. His position in the debate on the nature of kinship was, and is, clear. It is re-stated in his book *Kinship and the Social Order*, where he refers (1969: 52) to 'the irreducible genealogical connections, the given relations of actual connectedness, which are universally utilized in building up kinship relations and categories'. And with regard to kinship terms: 'Their distinctive character arises from the generally recognized fact that the relations they designate have their origin in a distinct sphere of social life, the sphere which, for both observers and actors, is demarcated by reference to the base line of genealogical connection' (p. 53, cf. 251–2). Fortes refers to these points as anthropological commonplaces; yet, of course, they are not ones which are unchallenged, even within the school of British social anthropologists of the 1940s to 1960s. Beattie, in arguing against Ernest Gellner's suggestion that an ideal language for kinship structure theory should be developed, based on various possible kinds of biological relationship, states that 'kinship as it is studied by social anthropologists is not a set of genealogical relationships, it is a set of social relationships. This is so even though these relationships may (or may not) be denoted by terms having a genealogical reference, and even though they may (or may not) overlap with "real" genealogical links between the parties concerned' (1964: 101). Both Fortes and Beattie go on, in the works I have cited, to stress that the business of the social anthropologist is to elucidate the relationship of kinship to social structure, which involves, in Beattie's words, an investigation of the 'jural, ritual, economic or other social or cultural content' of kin relationships and of 'the manner in which they are related to other co-existing complexes of social inter-relationships in the society being studied' (1964 *a*: 103). The difference between Beattie and Fortes lies rather, it would seem, in the definition of the basis of kinship itself. Beattie professes disinterest in this question, arguing that it is irrelevant for the social anthropologist's enquiries; yet in so doing he is less than clear about his own fundamental position. Thus he writes: 'to say that a social relationship is a kinship one is to tell us nothing at all of its content... Kinship is the idiom in which certain kinds of political, jural, economic, etc., relations are talked and thought about in certain societies. It is not a further category of social relationships. . .' (1964*a*: 102). If kinship is an idiom, the idiom must have some kind of basis, and Beattie does not tell us what that basis is or how we might be able to recognize labels employed in particular cultures as ones denoting kinship, unless we set up a prior formal definition of kinship (see Schneider 1964: 180–1). Fortes, by contrast, both decides for genealogical connection as the basis for kinship relations and argues that there is also in kinship relations a universal essential content, that is 'amity' or 'the axiom of prescriptive altruism' (1969: 110).

Some of the problems involved here can be handled in the light of distinctions made by British and American anthropologists between the concepts of society and culture. In the 1940s British social anthropologists, concerned to define the area of their subject matter, declared their main interest to be the investigation of social structure, which they isolated out from 'the total body of traditional custom and usage to which the label of culture is usually attached' (Fortes 1957: 162). What social structure itself was might not be too easy to say, but investigation of it clearly covered the constitution of groups in a society, focusing on the roles and statuses chiefly important in maintaining continuity in the society. More recently, Scheffler, Keesing, and Schneider have all found a culture/society distinction to be useful to them in looking at problems of kinship and descent theory. Scheffler, while picking his way through what Leach in his reply called 'the minefields of Cambridge anthropological scholasticism' (Leach 1966: 546), found it helpful to make a distinction between 'cultural or ideological constructs and the social processes they may regulate or validate' (1966: 542). He went on to distinguish from one another the *processes* of group affiliation, succession, and inheritance, *descent-constructs* which are employed in any of these contexts of status – transmission, and *descent-phrased rules*, the norms which employ such constructs (p. 543). His distinction is thus between 'ideational (cultural) forms and social transactional structures or processes'. Interestingly, Keesing, who employs a similar set of distinctions in his analysis of Kwaio social organization, does so in the context of a supposed criticism of Scheffler's discussion of Choiseul island social structure, in which Scheffler himself actually employs the distinctions I have mentioned. Keesing's formulation is based on 'a radical distinction between the conceptual world of our subjects and the pattern of events and transactions in which they engage. . . The conceptual order includes shared codes I call culture. . . The realm of events. . .also has order and structure; but that order is primarily *statistical* in nature.' The relationship between the two orders, he says, is rarely one of neat congruence, it is characteristically dialectical. In the cultural order he further distinguishes between things and relationships that are posited to exist and normative rules which specify how people should behave. He adds that 'we distinguish centrally between *categories* of people (in the cultural realm) and *groups* of people (in the social realm)' (Keesing 1971: 125–6).

In the terms of these distinctions, a cultural study of kinship would tell us how categories and relationships were defined and what norms were supposed to be applied to them, while a social study would tell us how such definitions and norms worked out in the actual behaviour of people. A 'social' anthropologist would concentrate on the latter task – but note that it presupposes knowledge of the former. Beattie, while arguing that a social anthropologist is concerned only with the jural, political, ritual, economic etc., content of kinship, refuses to concern himself with the question of the cultural definition of kinship itself, beyond making the rather unhelpful observation that it may or may not involve genealogical reckoning. He excludes the 'actual' biological realm of facts from consideration, but ignores the *tertium quid* of cultural constructs 'about biology'. It is precisely this *tertium quid* to which Schneider has in recent years directed his attention. He too begins by making a culture/society distinction: 'culture consists in the system of symbols and meanings of a particular society, and a social system consists in the manner in which social units are organized for various purposes' (1972: 40). Within 'culture' he includes 'the basic premises which a culture posits'. He says that 'culture' can be abstracted from the normative system and is separate from it. It is concerned with the stage, the setting, and the cast of characters whereas the normative system 'consists in the stage directions for the actors and how the actors should play their parts' (p. 38). As he points out, this conception of culture is a narrow one, but useful, he thinks, because it yields a 'more concentrated and homogeneous body of materials than many other definitions' (p. 38). It is, for example, much narrower than that suggested by Fortes in the passage I have quoted earlier, in which 'culture' becomes almost everything that is left after 'social structure' has been abstracted from the processes of social life.

All three American theorists, then, as one might expect from the prominence of the study of cultural anthropology in the United States in the past (see Bidney 1967), point up the importance of paying attention to the cultural definition of kinship, the question which Beattie sidesteps. From that point on they diverge. Scheffler explicitly and Keesing implicitly through his ethnographic writings propound a view that kinship is based on genealogical reckoning. Scheffler and Lounsbury have proposed this in sturdy opposition to alliance theorists who allegedly argue that kinship terms denote social categories which are not defined genealogically (Scheffler and Lounsbury 1971, see also Lounsbury 1965). In their argument, which corresponds to that of Fortes, kinship relations are defined by genealogy, and extensions from the genealogical grid are made by means of

23

metaphor. Kinship terms do not denote social categories in a monosemic way; they are polysemic indicators of particular sets of kin types. Schneider, by contrast, questions the theory of the genealogical basis of kinship and throws it out, although rather quaintly one of the cultural premises of American kinship which he elucidates is the notion that kinsfolk have shared biogenetic substance ('blood ties'), and his other criterion, that kinsfolk are supposedly held together by a norm of 'diffuse, enduring solidarity', corresponds closely to Fortes' 'axiom of prescriptive altruism' which Fortes claims as a universal cultural component of kinship. Schneider identifies in American kinship exactly the same components as Fortes appears to identify in kinship everywhere, but denies that these components *are* necessarily found everywhere (Schneider 1968). For him, then, it would not be right to say that the irreducible fact about fatherhood is fatherhood itself.

The anthropologists who have worked since the 1950s in the Highlands areas of New Guinea have come predominantly from the American or British traditions of anthropological research. Most of them have been social anthropologists, concerned, in the manner posited by Beattie, with the political, jural, or economic content of kinship relations and less with the cultural realm. They have been largely engaged in mapping the major lineaments of social structure in Highlands societies, and in the 1950s, as Barnes (1962) pointed out, the most obvious model to apply in the Highlands was that of the corporate, segmentary lineage systems described for uncentralized African societies in the 1940s. The model began to break down on all three fronts of definition: it was not clear in all cases whether groups were corporate; their modes of segmentation and political recombination did not appear often to follow the patterns established for Africa; and, worse, it was unclear whether Highlands groups could justifiably be called lineages at all. Each ethnographer of the Highlands peoples has emerged from confrontation with this problem with a slightly different solution, and all are agreed that there are identifiable and explicable variations between Highlands societies in terms of the corporateness of groups, segmentation patterns, and the degrees and contexts of emphasis on unilineality, as also that explanations of variation may be sought in terms of ecology, alliance patterns and aims of warfare, and the phenomenon of leadership by big-men who seek for followers as part of their aim of maximizing exchange transactions. The sociology of Highlands societies is now fairly well understood (cf. de Lepervanche 1968–9 for a statement of the main themes), but some problems remain. Why was the African model applied at all? Was it just a mirage, as Barnes (1962: 4) maintained? And if it was a mirage, what was it that made the mirage appear? Had it no connection with Highlands realities? An early approach to the problem was to see in the Highlands material a discrepancy between ideology

24

(propounded by Highlanders themselves about their groups) and actual social processes. Thus groups might be ideally but not actually corporate, ideally but not actually unilineal, and so on (cf. Langness 1964). 'The' ideology could thus be taken as read and sociological explanations advanced for the discrepancies between it and 'actual' behaviour. This early formulation has now given way to a more complicated set of approaches. Barnes has continued to question whether we can identify a unilineal ideology at all in Highlands societies (1962, 1967 *a*), even among the Mae-Enga, described by Meggitt as having a 'lineage system' (Meggitt 1965); and he has been followed by others who have declared that we must look carefully at the diversity of prescription and idioms in each case (Langness 1968; A. J. Strathern 1972). Second, there has been something like a consensus that descent dogmas, if not rules of unilineal descent applied to group-membership, are found in a number of cases, but they do not function exclusively as rules giving entitlement to membership in groups, instead they must be looked at as charters for or assertions of male in-group solidarity and inter-group alliance (e.g. de Lepervanche 1968–9, A. J. Strathern, 1969, 1972, Glasse 1971, Watson 1964, Sahlins 1965). Third, the overviews provided by Scheffler and Keesing support the view that descent-constructs may be posited culturally by a people but need not always be applied by them in the same way, for example they need not be determinants of group-membership as we would expect from lineage theory. In any case what they define culturally, when they do relate to membership, is a set of categories rather than groups. We should reserve the term group for our (abstraction from?) the statistical social realities of behaviour, which are shaped by numbers of factors and principles, not simply by a descent rule. Moreover, in the transactions of social life, governed in practice by a pursuit of self-interest and power over others (the 'big-man' complex), we may expect to find inconsistent norms promulgated, and set against each other in competition, according to the dictates of convenience ('expediency', as Reay 1959 puts it). Hence, as Evans-Pritchard pointed out for the Azande so long ago (Evans-Pritchard 1937), we should not expect to find consistency in the use of norms and the expression of attitudes. Fourth, processual models of the growth and decline of groups have been offered, which attempt to explain the circumstances in which groups are *de facto* more or less 'agnatic' in their composition (e.g. Meggitt 1962 *b*, Vayda and Cook 1964, Reay 1971, Watson 1970).

One important feature of Highlands societies is that it is usually possible to identify within them major territorially-based political units, mostly described by ethnographers as 'clans' (clan-parishes, parishes, clan villages etc.). There is usually also a well-marked higher level of grouping, termed variously phratry or tribe, which in some instances (e.g. Enga, Melpa, Meggitt 1965, A. J. Strathern 1971) carries political functions and in others does not (e.g. Daribi, Wagner 1967). It is most often the 'clan' which is identifiable as the salient corporate group in respect of land-holding, war-making, ceremonial exchange and exogamy. When the group affiliation of persons is changed, they are usually said to be moving from one clan-group to another. 'Clan' here is best understood as an 'archetype' term by analogy with the archiphonemes which some linguists posit (Lyons 1968: 116). It refers both to the world of process in which local groups actually interact with one another and to the world of constructs in which men posit common descent from ancestors, common substance in the form of semen or blood, and so on. Confusion can arise in our handling of terms because, as Scheffler has pointed out, the terms used by indigenous speakers are often polysemic and designate both '(a) classes or socially significant categories consisting of agnatic or uterine or cognatic descendants of a specified "founder", and also (b) the operant groups (sometimes "localized") which form around some of those category members' (Scheffler 1966: 550). The fact of polysemy is used by speakers themselves to draw various kinds of boundaries on a we/they basis in accordance with transactional contexts. Persons included in the local group may be excluded from membership in the clan category, and vice-versa. If we look at the matter in this way, our task becomes one of sorting out the various meanings of polysemic terms as a preliminary to describing the use of ideology in action. The constructs or categories are likely to turn on concepts of kinship and descent; whereas the operant groups will contain many members who do not belong in ideal terms to the categories.

Such a viewpoint is essential if we are to avoid initial confusion, but it is important also, I believe, to recognize the possibility that there is some feedback between the cultural and the social domains, or, as both Scheffler and Keesing have stressed, that the relationship between ideological and transactional domains is dialectical (Scheffler 1966: 550, Keesing 1971: 126). Given the importance of territoriality and co-residence in the definition of 'operant groups' in many Highlands societies, we should expect to find some kind of locality ideology in the cultural sphere, as well as a descent or kinship ideology. One possibility indeed, as I have argued for the case of the Melpa or Mount Hagen people (A. J. Strathern 1972) would be for a partial fusion of descent and locality ideology to develop, which would bring ideology more closely into alignment with transactional patterns. To investigate this possibility it would be helpful to proceed at least as if one gave credence to Schneider's view that we should forget about our 'pre-conceived' definitions of kinship and examine closely the statements people actually make. The use which can be made of such a perspective is illus-trated in Silverman's study of Banaban kinship, in which he posits that both 'blood' and 'land' act as symbols to stand for concepts of common identity and a code for solidary conduct (Silverman 1971). The field of

26

'kinship', in this extended sense, includes the symbolism of blood and land and the ways in which these two symbols are related to each other. Thus: 'If a child has been adopted by another and has received no land from his natal family, he has "gone away". It is recognized that he may have strong feelings towards his natal family ("the blood loves its own"), but the normative code is not there any more... That child is a child to his natal parents by identity but not by code' (Silverman 1971: 233). Rephrasing this, one might argue rather that the moral aspect of the child's relationship, based on filiation, remains, but the jural aspect (based on what? locality or descent?) has been removed.

How, then, do we find locality and the ties of locality expressed in the Highlands? Are there parallels with Silverman's Banaban material? Is the question of ideology illuminated when we place symbols of the sharing of substance and symbols of the sharing of place together?

My introduction of this question was based on the fact that there is in the Highlands a considerable apparent divergence between descent dogmas and local group composition; and it is clear both that persons play on the discrepancy for particular purposes (cf. Ploeg 1969: 13: 'Thus a Wang-gulam may say: "xy has become a Penggu" and then in the next sentence "xy is not a Penggu, he has come from afar and Penggu is the section his mother belonged to"'), and that ethnographers have been forced as a result of it to establish categories of members of local political groups which take the discrepancies into account (e.g. the category of 'associate members' employed by Reay 1959 *a* and Ploeg 1969). The discrepancies most often play on a duality between locality and descent (or kinship). To take the example from Ploeg's study of the Mbogoga Dani which I have quoted above: the play here is on the polysemy of 'Penggu'. In the first sentence the speaker refers to Penggu the local group, in the second to Penggu as an agnatically defined descent-category. The polysemy of the term tricks the ear, and we are tempted to consider that a kinship unit is referred to in both cases, whereas this is not so. Many other Highlands examples could be cited, indeed almost any definition of 'the clan' in Highlands societies tends to show up the problem (e.g. Newman 1965: 35, Lowman-Vayda 1971: 322).

But the recognition of polysemy is not enough. What is it that mediates between locality and kinship? If the facts of local-group composition in the Highlands are well-known, it is also well-known that in many cases there is a conversion process, whereby over a variable period of generations persons can be transferred from membership in one category to another. To handle description of this process adequately it is necessary, of course, to define aspects of membership and to show how these aspects are progressively taken on by immigrants and their descendants. The process is usually said to require two to three generations. It is undoubtedly continued residence and participation in group affairs by the sons and sons' sons of immigrants that fixes and converts affiliation in this way. How is the conversion conceptualized or symbolized?

Since, as I mentioned earlier, most of the anthropologists who have worked in the Highlands have concentrated on the social realm, they have not all reported carefully on this matter. From what they have reported we can say that in many cases processes of conversion are facilitated by a lack of interest in maintaining long genealogies, coupled with significant breaks in genealogical chains relating to group ancestors (e.g. Kuma, Bena Bena, Melpa). In these cases the outside origins of the predecessors of group members are forgotten after three generations or so, although within those three generations there is always the possibility of moving back to one's predecessor's original place. (Schwimmer 1972 has stressed the importance of dual affiliations in providing avenues for communication across social boundaries between groups; at the same time, once ambiguity in affiliation emerges, strains are set up within local communities, as Glasse and Lindenbaum 1971 demonstrate.) But in addition to the processes of genealogical amnesia, locality concepts are also involved. For example, among the Mendi, while it is true that 'all non-agnatic members of a sub-clan are related, either cognatically or affinally, to one or more members of the agnatic core', it is also true that the process of converting affiliation is spoken of in terms of links with clan *territory*. Thus 'the Mendi recognise non-agnatic affiliation in the use of three terms: *shu moria* ("born to the land") *ol ebowa* ("having-come-men"; i.e. "new-comers") and *ebowan ishi* ("sons of a new-comer"). The sons of *ebowan ishi* become *shu moria*' (Ryan 1959: 265). It would seem that both patrifiliation and the place of birth are important in determining the potential membership status of persons in this case. In the Melpa area the place where a person's navel-string is buried is sometimes cited as a symbol of identification with his group. It is ordinarily a father's duty to bury the navel-string, plant a banana-tree or cordyline on the spot, and throw the child's faeces at the roots of the plant. He should maintain a fence around the place, to keep out pigs which might eat the faeces. The growth of the child is matched ideally by the growth of the plant in the soil of the father's land (cf. the Maring concept of *yu min rumbim*, 'men's soul cordylines', Rappaport 1967: 19). This example suggests that the notion of 'growth from soil' is important in establishing identity, and a complex of terms in Melpa supports this interpretation (A. J. Strathern 1972: 19–20, 46–7, 100–1, 217–18, 221–2, 246). Food, in fact, we may suggest, is a mediator between locality and kinship. A clear case is found with the Maring, among whom: 'First-generation non-agnates in residence are usually considered members of other clans. Their children, however, appear to be considered members of the clan with which their father resides. The rationalization for this is that these children have been nourished by and grown on the products of local land and therefore may be claimed as members of the clan' (Lowman-Vayda 1971: 322). I interpret the rationalization as follows. Clansmen are felt to share identity. One way of symbolising this is in terms of descent-constructs (see Lowman-Vayda 1971). Such constructs posit that clansmen share substance in some way through their descent from an ancestor. Another way in which they share substance is through consumption of food grown on clan land. Food builds their bodies and gives them substance just as their father's semen and mother's blood and milk give them substance in the womb and as small children. Hence it is through food that the identification of the sons of immigrants with their host group is strengthened. Food creates substance, just as procreation does, and forms an excellent symbol both for the creation of identity out of residence and for the values of nurturance, growth, comfort and solidarity which are associated primarily with parenthood. In cultural terms what we often find in the Highlands, I would suggest, is a combination of filiative rules and ideas based on upbringing, nurturance, and consumption of food. It is only such a combination that can explain, for example, the Bena Bena case mentioned by Langness (1964: 170): 'a man might hold rights in the group into which he was born, equivalent rights in a group in which he was raised, the same rights in a group in which his father was raised, his mother's group (either her natal group or one she happened to be raised in), and so on'.

The notion of shared substance has been found useful by at least two further Highlands ethnographers, both, it may be noted, influenced by Schneider: Roy Wagner and R. F. Salisbury. Wagner, in his elegant study of the Daribi, who live on the fringes of the Eastern Highlands, is largely bent on proposing a reversed version of an alliance model for his society, based on the axiom 'exchange defines; consanguinity relates'; however, his account of Daribi kinship concepts makes it clear that Daribi speak of internal relations between members of clans as one of shared paternal substance deriving from a putative founding ancestor. Appropriately, Daribi, who traditionally practised a form of cannibalism, were allowed to eat the flesh of their deceased father's brothers, for in doing so, I suggest, they would be reinforcing their own paternal substance, but not that of their mother's brothers, since this would increase the maternal substance present in them and Daribi appear concerned to oppose and ward off the influence of the mother's people, channelled through the tie of substance, by making extended payments to maternal kin (Wagner 1967: 66–7).

A concern, in cultural terms, with paternal and maternal substance is shown most clearly in the work of Salisbury on the Siane people of the Eastern Highlands. Salisbury refers to Siane clans as 'corporate groups possessing a stock of land and of ancestral spirit'. Non-agnatic clan members may include sons of sisters of the clan (i.e. those who have a filiative tie with it), and also other men, whether kinsmen or not, who have been brought up in the clan-village. These categories of persons can be members if they have eaten the food of the clan, or had their initiation or their bride-price financed by the clansmen. As Salisbury neatly shows, such multiple criteria of eligibility leave room for manipulation in the world of choice and transactions. Groups can argue about their claims on an individual, and the individual can maintain dual claims at least for a while, until he decides where his best advantages lie. However, here I am concerned with the cultural criteria themselves. The 'mediating symbol' which I have cited so far, that of food, is included, in Siane concepts, with that of *korova* or 'spirit'. In life an individual's spirit is called his *oinya*, which after death becomes his *korova*; later at a special ceremony the individual spirit is made to join the undifferentiated body of clan ancestor spirits. When another child is born within the clan a part of the body of ancestral *korova* enters the child to become its *oinya*. Children are accordingly named after dead ancestors. Ancestral *korova* are also identified 'with the land from which they originally emerged and to which they are relinked by mortuary rites. They make the land fertile and in return receive portions of all crops' (Salisbury 1965: 57). Siane clan ceremonies of initiation have the purpose of infusing paternal spirit into boys and young men of the clan. It is by this means that their identity is fixed. A child at conception is composed of paternal spirit (semen) and maternal spirit (blood). Ritual is performed to remove maternal spirit and infuse paternal spirit. Techniques of doing so are to play flutes before young male novices – the flutes represent the ancestors – to give them flying-fox meat to eat (i.e. they eat creatures which also represent ancestors), and to expel maternal spirit in the form of blood through their noses. Novices must avoid having contact with 'female things', for example rats and opossums, for to do so would impede their adult male growth. In addition to the flutes, each Siane phratry possesses a 'horn three feet long, made of telescoped lengths of bamboo joined to a curved gourd' described as 'the old man'. This, too, is a symbol of the ancestral *korova* (Salisbury 1965: 66, cf. Salisbury 1956). Paternal spirit, Salisbury explains, may be introduced into a person in many ways. It may come from 'the father's semen, *food eaten during childhood which contains spirit from the land on which it is grown* [my italics], from pork, from a name, or from proximity to objects such as sacred flutes which symbolise *korova*... The individual has a direct relationship with the original clan ancestors, sharing their material essence...most of which is acquired through ceremonial or growth' (Salisbury 1964: 170). Food in the Siane case is thus clearly one of the media through which paternal spirit is instilled into clan members as they grow up. Girls also, incidentally, are held to share the paternal spirit of their natal clan. Their first menstruation is described as a 'birth' of this paternal spirit, and it must take place on their natal clan territory. A special ritual captures a girl's paternal spirit before she is sent away in marriage to another clan (Salisbury 1965: 72 ff.).

Salisbury's excellent discussion enables us to pinpoint not just one but a range of symbols defining clan identity. The Siane make explicit certain connections of ideas which are latent in other Highlands cultures, for example the Melpa. Siane *korova* are directly identified with clan territories and make the land fertile. Food grown on the land is thus impregnated with ancestral spirit. Locality and descent are in this set of ideas exactly fused. A Siane non-agnate who grows up on the land of his host-clan might thus expect to partake of that clan's ancestral spirit to a degree approaching that of agnatic members, especially if he is a second-generation, and thus patri-filial, member. Possibly a similar set of ideas is, or was, entertained by the Bena Bena, of whom Langness states 'that *the sheer fact of residence in a...group can and does determine kinship*' (Langness 1964: 172).

This last statement brings me back to the definition of kinship, the question with which I began. The topic is much too large for me to handle, but here I merely want to stress its relevance for New Guinea Highlands studies. Langness's point of view is tenable if we are prepared to abandon the definition of kinship in genealogical terms. In Highlands studies it has been very tempting to do so, because of 'the problem of non-agnates', the lack of genealogical documentation of relationships between segments of clans or phratries, and the stress on co-residence as a basis of co-operation. But such a step may be too hasty. Proponents of the 'anti-genealogy' view of kinship (see for two recent discussions Bloch 1971 *a* and Southwold 1971) perhaps are in danger of forgetting that the 'pro-genealogy' theorists are quite willing to admit that kinship terms, and similarly terms for kinship units, may be polysemic, and that their meaning may be extended within the genealogical grid, or beyond it by metaphor (see, e.g., Lounsbury and Scheffler 1971). A pro-genealogy theorist might thus agree with Langness, but would place 'kinship' in inverted commas in his statement, to indicate that metaphorical extension is involved. It must be admitted, however, that the idea of metaphor has to be worked hard to subsume all Highlands examples of kinship usages. Pro-genealogy theorists point out that in many languages it is possible, and customary, to distinguish between 'true' kin and others, with the implication that by true kin are meant those who are genealogically immediate. This tends to hold especially in relation to parenthood and sibling ties. The difficulty is that it does not always hold in all other relationships. Glasse, for the South Fore, reports on a survey of 'matrilateral cross-cousin marriage' which he conducted with the aid of assistants from the South Fore area itself, who were impressed, he says, with the necessity of distinguishing 'between actual and classificatory kin'. Nevertheless, 'when the genealogies were assembled it became apparent that classificatory and *kagisa* ("fictive") kin were often listed as true

MBD. . . Even the daughters of MB's age-mates were sometimes counted this way' (Glasse 1969: 33). Glasse explains that the South Fore refer to 'true' and 'tenuous' relationships, 'but their distinction refers to the importance and solidarity of the bond and not necessarily to its genealogical closeness'. He generalizes further that 'in New Guinea those who behave towards one another in a positive reciprocal manner regard each other as kin, whether or not they are known or believed to be genealogically connected' (Glasse 1969: 33, 37). Slightly earlier, in dealing with *kagisa* relationships, which he translates unwillingly as 'fictive kin ties', he argues that 'it is better to view kinship as a broader spectrum of relatedness in which genealogical connection, actual or putative, is one important element. Then *kagisa* relations would have a place under this wider rubric of relations of solidarity and reciprocity' (p. 31). We need to be sure here whose viewpoint we are following. In discussing the meaning of 'true' as opposed to 'tenuous' relationships Glasse is clearly translating South Fore ideas. The superclass of 'relations of solidarity and reciprocity' which he sets up may, however, be his own construct, devised to include both genealogical kin and *kagisa*. Since he defines *kagisa* (p. 30) as 'a category of genealogically unrelated people who are treated as if they were consanguines', it is clear that South Fore do distinguish between persons genealogically related to them and others, and it is thus open to a pro-genealogy theorist to argue that *kagisa* are metaphorical kin. He would have at the same time to admit that, if so, the South Fore may nevertheless call such *kagisa* their 'true kin', if exchange relations between them are well established. What is, in terms of the genealogical theory of kinship, a connotation of a kinship term is thus, by means of metaphor, taken as criterial instead (Scheffler 1972). We could call this an example of a 'persuasive definition', in which over-emphasis is placed on one element of definition (or in this case connotation) for a particular purpose. Glasse's example is similar to statements Melpa speakers sometimes make. Thus at a Melpa exchange ceremony a ceremonial speech-maker declared 'I call you my sister's sons, my cross-cousins. I am your true cross-cousin, living close to you. My sisters' sons, my cross-cousins, you say you see big pigs, big shells, well, now I have given you large pigs. . .' (A. J. Strathern 1971: 241). The speaker says he is a 'true' cross-cousin because he lives near to his kin and is their regular and generous exchange-partner. He selects the role-component or 'code for conduct' aspect of the meaning of the Melpa kin term *pel* ('cross-cousin') in order to persuade his hearers that he is indeed close to them. While this is acceptable Melpa usage, it is also the case that in other contexts speakers will say that 'X is not my true (i.e. immediate genealogical) cross-cousin, we call each other by this term only because we exchange pigs and shell valuables'. In the latter context the genealogical component is selected as indicating the 'true' relationship. The pro-genealogy theorist would recognize this as the standard mode of definition and look on the other instance I have cited as a metaphorical usage (see Scheffler and Lounsbury 1971: 5 fn. 5, where Schneider's view of American kinship is criticised).

If we abandon the pro-genealogy view, the solution to the problem of the relationship between local groups and kinship constructs is as simple as Langness in his early article (1964) declared: residence creates kinship, 'kinship' being understood here in some special cultural terms for the Bena Bena, the South Fore, and so on. If we retain the pro-genealogy view, we must recognize that residence can create 'kinship' only in a metaphorical sense and are then left with the task of elucidating the ideas behind such a metaphorical usage. It is here perhaps that the most interesting point (for those interested, that is, in symbolic anthropology) lies. I have suggested, following Salisbury's discussion of the Siane and some ethnographic material on the Mount Hagen Melpa speakers, that the concept of 'food' may be an important mediator between the concepts of identity through locality and identity through descent (as a special case of kinship). Comparative investigation of this assertion would take field-workers more deeply than I have been able to go into the realms of both culture and psychology, as a supplement to their concern with sociological questions. At any rate the hypothesis can be taken as an attempt to explain a statement made to me by the leader of the group with which I am associated in Mount Hagen: 'Yes, you were born in England and your father is there, but now you have come to live on our ground and have grown up on our food and so you belong to us.'

Descent in New Guinea: an Africanist View

Jean La Fontaine

This article[1] is written as a tribute to the man whose name is inextricably linked with the study of kinship in Africa. It takes its point of departure from that classic article, 'The Structure of Unilineal Descent Groups' (Fortes 1953 *a* [1970 *b*]) but is concerned with the strictures made upon it by anthropologists working in other parts of the world, particularly New Guinea. The origin[2] of the debate was the article by Barnes (1962), 'African Models in the New Guinea Highlands'. It refers to the 'African Mirage in New Guinea' which prevents ethnographers from perceiving the distinctive characteristics of the societies of the New Guinea Highlands (Barnes 1962: 5). Despite Salisbury's articles (1956, 1964), the impressive refutation by Sahlins (1965), and documentation of the importance of other forms of kinship by Kaberry (1967), articles repeating Barnes' criticisms continue to be written. Perhaps the latest and most detailed is that of de Lepervanche in *Oceania* (1968 *a* and 1968 *b*) in which she calls for 'a model suitable for New Guinea' (1968 *b*: 181). The implications are very serious; if, as some New Guinea ethnographers claim, Fortes' concept of unilineal descent is not applicable in New Guinea because it derives from African ethnography (Barnes 1962: 8, 9, de Lepervanche 1968 *b*), the whole status of anthropology as a generalising discipline, aiming at statements of universal validity is at stake. Clearly this regional parochialism was not what Fortes intended: his article devotes several pages to developing the point that the concepts he is elaborating have general validity. Many anthropologists would accept this and the utility of the concept of lineage has not been questioned in studies of Chinese or North American Indian kinship. However the claim that New Guinea lineages are qualitatively different from those studied by Fortes, Evans-Pritchard and their students in Africa, is still common enough to make the investigation of New Guinea ethnography rewarding for the Africanist. Some of the results are offered here.

The most important characteristic of unilineal descent groups is that they are corporate groups (Fortes 1970 *b* [1953 *a*], p. 77). To define corporate groups Fortes draws on the theoretical statements of Maine and Weber. The essential characteristics are:

(a) a single legal personality, that is 'all the members of a lineage are, to outsiders, jurally equal and represent the lineage when they exercise legal and political rights and duties in relation to society at large' (p. 79);

(b) perpetuity in time, that is the group has perpetual existence regardless of the deaths of individual members (p. 79);

(c) an estate consisting of joint rights in material or immaterial property or differential privileges (pp. 80, 84). Barth (1966) argues that in relation to one another members of a descent group hold joint rights which may or may not be exercised but they can never form the basis for transactions. Relations within a descent group are relationships of incorporation or sharing. (Nuer use the term *buth* to refer to this relationship, a word which also has the connotation of calves sharing the milk from a cow.);

(d) a 'structure of authority' based on the succession of generations and the principle of seniority which is defined by an individual's position in terms of generational strata (p. 86).

It is clear that the principle of descent defined here is a means of allocating membership of segments of society. That is, an individual is placed within the society into which he is born by reference to his membership of a segment of it. It underlies the allocations of status, including political privileges and liabilities, and often legitimises rights to various forms of property. Most clearly of all descent is not an observable reality but an analytical construct.

The ethnographic manifestation of this underlying principle is variable. As Leach has claimed (1961 *b*) and Lewis has documented (1965) the particular significance of descent in any one society cannot be deduced from the statement that this structural principle is present. Variations seem to me to be of two kinds: first, variation in cultural manifestations of the principle and, secondly, variations which have to do with the context, economic, ecological and social, within which descent operates as a principle. An example of the first can be seen in the wide variation of marriage rules in relation to descent groups. Among the Nuer the clan is the exogamic unit and Nuer may not marry anyone with whom there is common patrilineal descent (Evans-Pritchard 1940); such corporate ties preclude the establishment of ties of affinity. Among the southern Somali (Lewis 1965: 103), by contrast, as among many peoples of the Middle East, marriage with the patrilateral parallel cousin, a close agnate, is a preferred pattern. Exogamy is a manifestation of jural identity among the Nuer but not among the Somali. As for the second source of variety the point can probably best be made by comparing the nature of political identity among the Nyoro of Uganda (Beattie 1970) and the Nuer (Evans-Pritchard 1940). Among the Nyoro, legal domicile in a particular locality is obtained by offering allegiance, in the form of tribute and obedience, to the headman. The political unit is bounded by association with the territorial jurisdiction of the office to which all residents owe allegiance. Among the Nuer such a unit is bounded, not by the jurisdiction of an office but of an ancestor, the founder of the patrilineal descent group whose territory it is. In both societies membership of a patrilineal descent group is a feature of the social organisation: only among the Nuer does it confer status in a system of politically significant units.

It is important to note what Fortes says on the relationship between descent groups and local communities, for that is an important source of the argument with which I am dealing. He states (1970 *b*: 91): 'I think it would be agreed that lineage and locality are independently variable and how they interact depends on other factors in the social structure. As I interpret the evidence, local ties are of secondary significance, *pace* Kroeber, for local ties do not appear to give rise to structural bonds *in and of themselves*' (my emphasis). Thus it would appear that Fortes is suggesting that co-residence is not a structural feature, it has no juro-political significance, except in so far as it is legitimised in other ways, as in the case of Bunyoro. It follows that descent refers, not to collectivities of real people but to social constructs.

Finally, and this is crucial, descent is an aspect of the kinship system whereby interpersonal, as well as intergroup, relations are categorised. A major error, in subsequent anthropological writing, has been the separation of descent from kinship (Smith 1956). Kaberry's 1967 article shows clearly that allegiance to a local group may result from the affinal or matrilateral links which may be utilised by individuals seeking to change residence or encourage dependants to settle with them. The statuses defined by the kinship system denote roles, of which any member of the community may assume a number. They are identified, as are the constitutions of descent groups, by reference to the process of physical reproduction. In the case of descent groups the charter of legitimacy is a genealogy and Fortes emphasises: (this is what) 'Malinowski called a legal charter and not an historical record'.

I turn now to the criticisms of Fortes' conceptual scheme. Barnes lists eight characteristics of Highland New Guinea societies which he argues makes their categorisation in terms of descent 'less certain' (Barnes 1962: 6). I prefer to group them under three main headings which seem to me to represent the critical areas of dispute. They are: (1) the fact that local groups are heterogeneous with respect to the lineage affiliations of their members, and there is mobility of individuals between local groups (points a, b, g). (2) Secondly, there is considerable choice available to an individual as to where he will give his allegiance, and individuals resident in a locality are not disadvantaged by belonging to alien lineages. Indeed descent group membership, it is said, may be easily changed (points c, d, b). (3) Finally, genealogies are unimportant and non-segmentary (points e, f) and there are no common religious or other activities which represent lineage membership (g, h). The argument might simply stop right here, for as Kaberry says (1967: 114) most of the characteristics also describe the Nuer and the other characteristics may be found in other societies in Africa. Indeed it is an error to assume the existence of an 'African' model, for the social significance of descent varies widely in Africa. However, the claim I am examining is that the *nature* of descent differs in New Guinea, it is thus necessary to examine the arguments for this point of view.

What is at issue is: first the composition of the local community, then the question of individual choice of allegiance and the acquisition of leadership within the political community and last, but of more importance than most writers have considered it, the question of ideologies of descent. I shall treat them in this order, drawing on material primarily from the Kuma, Bena (Korofeigu), Chimbu, Siane and Daribi. The Mae-Enga, who figure prominently in the debate, I shall not make a primary subject for treatment since it is generally admitted that they, of all Highland New Guinea societies, fit most easily into the 'African mould' (Meggitt 1962 *b*).

Barnes describes the situation in the Highlands as follows: 'In each generation a substantial majority of men affiliate themselves with their father's group and in this way it acquires some agnatic continuity over the generations. It may be similar in *demographic appearance* and *de facto* ties to a patrilineal group. . .' (Barnes 1962: 6, my emphasis). It is clear that group here means locality, not descent group to which all man's sons are affiliated by virtue of their birth. Sahlins has pointed out this confusion between descent and residence (1965: 106), but since de Lepervanche persists in the same vein (1968), perhaps a more fundamental confusion is involved. It would seem that in some of the New Guinea ethnography, 'group' has an implicit spatial reference. Indeed Langness makes this clear: in summing up his discussion of the composition of Nupasafa local group and the location of members of Nupasafa clan, whose members do not all reside in the locality associated with it, he remarks: 'more than 50% of its (Nupasafa's) members, both male and female, are probably resident elsewhere. But does this constitute a group? The answer, of course, is no, not by any standard of definition. The members never come together for any purpose. They do not participate as a group in *any* activity' (Langness 1964: 168). By thus defining group in terms of common residence or common action, the analytical concept is confused with ethnographic appearance and the actions of particular individuals.

In Fortes' definition, a unilineal descent group is corporate, the concept refers to formal jural criteria and it is quite clear that these do apply to Langness' data. A community is described as a clan (Langness, 1964: 46) and the same name applies to both units; rights of residence do not lapse if a member lives elsewhere (p. 169). Moreover it was possible for the ethnographer to discover the kinship identity of residents of the local community who were not members of the associated descent group, showing that aliens, in descent terms, are not immediately absorbed. He cites a quarrel in which someone is insulted by reference to his alien origin; the man replies: 'Yes, *my place* is' so and so (p. 169, my italics). This remark makes the relation between jural rights conferred by birth and political allegiance quite clear. The corporate rights of a lineage refer to rights in a territory expressed as political authority. Langness refers frequently to the fact that non-members of a descent group must obtain 'permission' to reside in their territory (pp. 164, 169, 170, 171, 174). Residence in the territory implies political allegiance to the descent group in whose name the political community takes action. The same situation occurs among the Siane (Salisbury 1962: 14), Kuma (Reay 1967: 4), Chimbu (Brown, 1967), Daribi and Enga (Meggitt 1965: 26–7). Indeed among most Highland peoples the political identity of locally-based communities is expressed in terms of descent. Even Chimbu tribes, which are defined by local contiguity, are named by juxtaposing the names of the allied clans which dominate them.

There is much further evidence on the nature of the jural identity of descent groups in the New Guinea Highlands. Among the Bena Bena, pig exchanges, although undertaken by individuals, are coordinated on a group basis and bring prestige to the descent groups involved (Langness 1964: 175); women should remain with their husband's descent groups even after they are divorced or widowed for they 'are fundamentally clan property' (Langness 1969: 48). Marriages are arranged by subclans but must be paid for by contributions from the whole clan (p. 41). Among the Daribi marriage payments for women form a 'pool of wealth on which their clan brothers may draw for payments for their own brides' (Wagner 1969: 58–9). In addition to the evidence on the significance of marriage for interclan relations, ceremonial or ritual activities represent various genealogical levels of descent group. Brown (1967) presents in tabular form the levels of group organisation and associated activities of thirteen Highlands societies; what is striking is the degree to which ritual or ceremonial activities are organised at the higher levels of descent: that is they appear to be periodic restatements of the association of segments, which are regularly involved in the day-to-day prosecution of affairs, into a larger unity. The material amply exemplifies Fortes' statement: '. . .every person belongs to a hierarchy of lineage segments lying between the minimal and maximal limits of his maximal lineage. Different orders of segmentation become relevant for his conduct in different degrees and in accordance with variation in the social situation. . .grades of segmentation vary in dimensions from one maximal lineage to another and from one generation to the next in the same maximal lineage. They cannot be precisely defined by morphological criteria, for they are distinguishable only in functional terms, by the incidence of jural, ritual and economic rights and duties' (Fortes 1949 *a*: 9 f).

The perpetuity of the descent group is everywhere assumed in the Highlands. Clans are seen as having been created once and for all and it is a major duty of living members to increase their strength and wealth. Even though Highlanders are aware that warfare may disperse or annihilate the existing clan members, the mythology maintains the structural existence of all known groups even if represented by one or two individuals. I do not propose to go further into this aspect but turn instead to the question of the internal structure of authority of the corporate group.

In his discussion of the unilineal descent group Fortes associates authority with the relation between successive generations within the descent group and it is here that his distinction between lineage and clan is important. A clan, according to Fortes, is the unit in which common descent is postulated but not demonstrated.[3] Hence the lack of genealogical precision does not permit a differentiation of members according to kinship status, particularly with respect to recognised generation differences. We find indeed that the kinship term 'brother' is widely used in New Guinea to denote cooperative relations of equality, particularly where common descent is assumed. Thus the founders of Korofeigu level III units are 'brothers' as are the founders of level II units. The Siane refers to other members of his clan as 'brothers' but usually addresses them by personal names, teknonymy or as child of their mother's clan, unless a request is imminent, when the term brother is also used in address (Salisbury 1962: 23). Meggitt states that members of one phratry refer to each other as brothers, and the term may also be used to refer to two phratries (Meggitt 1965: 5–6). It is significant that Enga clan members are referred to as father-and-brother, and Meggitt comments: 'That is to say, they recognize generation levels among living clan agnates in a way that phratry "brothers" do not' (p. 8). Similarly the Chimbu 'visualize parallel segments (of a phratry) as "brother groups"'; (Brown 1960: 26–7). An alliance unit is referred to as *angigl-angigl*: brother brother (p. 31). The term used to emphasise agnation is father-brother, and 'older men are addressed as "father" within the clan' (p. 31).

Information given by Meggitt and Salisbury's description of the lineage office of *yarafo* (elder brother, Salisbury 1962: 20–3) would seem to indicate that with a narrow span lineage senior kinship status carries the connotation of authority. Within the group within the wider descent group, age determines the use of kinship terms but genealogical reckoning is absent or unimportant.

There is little evidence on the relation between descent and interpersonal kinship in New Guinea.[4] Only Salisbury gives a complete list of kin terms and discusses their application.[5] However, in describing local units among the Bena, Langness states: 'everyone who resides in Nupasafa group is called by a kinship term and all are brothers and sisters, mothers and fathers, sons and daughters and so on' (Langness 1964: 43). Earlier he has stated that the group's personnel 'are ordered according to a system of kin-ship terminology and attendant rights and obligations'. In the New Guinea literature young men are frequently pictured as irresponsible, their marriages are arranged for them, even in opposition to their wishes, and it is implicit that they cannot be Big-Men, since such a position takes time to build up. Thus authority within the lineage may relate to its genealogical structure. A Tallensi is unable to take independent political action while he has a father alive; we do not know how far Highland New Guinea kinship ideo-logy structures the relations of agnates.

The 'African model' seems to be useful in ordering certain aspects of data concerning Highland New Guinea societies. There are certain aspects with which it does not deal successfully: namely the nature of leadership in these societies and the particular form of intergroup relations. De Leper-vanche, following Barnes, Langness, Brown and others, attributes this to the distinctiveness of the New Guinea scene: warfare and the stress on killing and the particular ecology of the Highlands are the most usual features cited (de Lepervanche 1968). However, warfare was no less a part of the traditional African scene and some at least of the characteristic features of New Guinea economy are duplicated in Africa. What is involved here is a difference in emphasis which can be explained in terms of the history of anthropological theory rather than the geography of anthro-pological field-work.

The concept of unilineal descent was first developed in the context of political systems, as Smith has pointed out (M. G. Smith 1956). A segment-ary lineage system formed the basis for the identification of political units and the specification of rules for the allocation of rights and duties. Clearly, for this purpose, the work of jurists such as Maine and the concepts of Durkheim were of prime significance. The same concerns: the definition of political units, their interrelations, and the definition of offices with political jurisdiction, can be seen in contemporary analyses of primitive states, as any reading of Fortes' and Evans-Pritchard's *African Political Systems* will serve to demonstrate. In a discussion of a system of legitimacy (in Weber's terms) or of jural rules (Maine) the actions of individuals were necessarily obscured.

Dissatisfaction with the limitations of this approach was early expressed by a number of anthropologists, among them Leach (1954), M. G. Smith (1956), Barth (1958), who pointed out that the formal principles of descent did not, in many cases, provide the means whereby men were mobilized for political action. As Barth puts the objection: 'One may describe a pattern of kinship organization and a pattern of political organization and no necessary interconnections are postulated other than the supposed fit between them – a fit with respect to mutual consistency as structures' (Barth 1966: 23). In the form which it took the criticism obviously stems from an assimilation into anthropological theory of Weber's approach to the study of political systems: an emphasis on the distribution of power and a distinction between power and authority, that is between the *de facto*, statistical distribution of power, mobilisation and recruitment of followings and the means by which political units are defined. The starting point for a new approach, then, was the perception of a distinction between the formal bounding of social units and the constitution of groups mobilised for action. The basis of Barth's analysis is a distinction between the rules allocating rights and the action of individuals in choosing whether to exercise those rights. Implicit in it is the factor common to all four societies he discusses: leadership is achieved not ascribed, and it is based on the accumulation of wealth and influence over persons. The point here is that the situation he describes very closely parallels that of New Guinea, although the cultures of the Middle East, from which Barth draws his examples, and of New Guinea are widely divergent.

Almost without exception, New Guinea ethnographers point to the distinctive features of New Guinea leadership. In all these societies leadership is achieved by the manipulation of relationships and the accumulation and distribution of wealth. De Lepervanche (1968 *a* and *b*) gives a useful summary of the characteristics of the New Guinea Big-Man, so I can confine myself to noting a few important features. First, 'Big-Men are the foci for local groups' (de Lepervanche 1968 *b*: 176). I have established that local groups are identified by reference to descent; it is also clear that they may be referred to by reference to their leaders and that their affairs are directed by these leaders. While a man may achieve the position of Big-Man in a community other than that in which his own descent group is dominant, there is evidence that generally not to belong to the agnatic core is a disadvantage. Meggitt shows that non-members of the descent group have fewer pigs and are rarely leaders (Meggitt 1967: 25; 1965); Brown emphasises the necessity for a man to have attached dependants in to achieve a position of leadership (1967: 45). Since it is only agnates who can award rights to residence it is fair to assume that it is more difficult for a man living outside his natal clan area to build a following. There is intense rivalry between agnates for leadership and it is clear that a position of leadership depends on a man's building up ties with groups other than his own, by lending pigs and land, contracting many marriages and attracting young kinsmen and affines as dependants.[6] What Sahlins (1963) calls the internal and external sectors of a Big-Man's following are mutually reinforcing. It is because of his influence within his own group that outsiders take refuge with him in it, initiate exchanges with him and give him their daughters as wives; it is because of his usefulness in directing external relations that members of his group support him. This process could be duplicated from many areas in the world; it is the essence of the acquisition of power by an individual. Certainly one can find evidence for it occurring among the Nuer and the process was the means whereby ambitious men of the people I studied in Uganda, the Gisu, achieved political influence. The competition for power occurs within an arena defined by cultural norms and values. Descent refers to properties of these ordering and evaluating concepts not to the events of political manoeuvre.

It is true that in some societies the genealogical structure of the lineage confers authority on senior kinsmen. Fortes' account of succession to the custodianship of a Tallensi shrine shows how kinship seniority defines political office. It is a mistake to assume that lineage systems determine the distribution of power. Descent does not define political or ritual offices in the New Guinea Highlands – nor does it in many parts of Africa.

Later research has made clear that specification of the qualifications for political office does not remove competition between individuals for that office. Middleton's study of the Lugbara shows incontrovertibly that although leadership within the family cluster (a shallow lineage plus non-agnatic accretions) is in principle transmitted in a line of seniority from eldest son to eldest son, rivals for an elder's power may attempt to invalidate his authority by accusing him of sorcery. Some lineage heads may exercise little or no *de facto* power. Competition between agnates may, and often does, cause fission of the group and the emergence of new autonomous groups, without thereby invalidating the succession rule. The rule legitimising authority in terms of seniority of descent is thus distinct from the action surrounding the appointment of a particular individual, although it remains an important component since factions must justify their candidate for office in terms of his descent status. Seniority is a claim to authority with a variety of possible applications by interested parties.

Fortes is quite clear on the analytical status of the concept of descent. He writes of the Tallensi. These varying rights and duties and interests alter from running a common unit of production and consumption at the lowest level, to sharing a common interest in patrimonial farmlands and joint rights of inheritance, to definitions of marital prohibitions and provision of assistance of various kinds at different higher levels (Fortes 1949 *a*: 7–10). Gluckman, citing this passage in his Introduction to Meggitt's book on the Mae-Enga, remarks 'The Tallensi, Fortes stresses, do not make these distinctions' (Gluckman, Introduction to Meggitt 1965). This is what is crucial: the ideology of descent serves to legitimise in a single system a variety of social phenomena – economic, political and ritual. The rationale for this is the agnatic genealogy which presents all the phenomena as dependent on certain kin relations: between fathers and sons and between brothers. We are in grave error if we inject our own notions of historicity and biology into this legitimising scheme. Patrilineal descent groups are not the proliferation over time of relations between begetter and begotten.

In Highland New Guinea, descent is the principle of recruitment to corporate groups. Descent groups give political identity to the territories associated with them and command the allegiance of those who live within the area of their jurisdiction. Rights to cultivate the land, as distinct from sovereignty over a territory, may be acquired in a variety of ways: by patrifilial inheritance, by loan or gift from various kinsmen. Such cultivation rights may necessitate residence in another community; even where they do not, they require cooperation with members of it. All these rights may be transmitted by patrifilial inheritance. Residence in a community through the inheritance of usufructory rights of this sort may be claimed, by members of the local group, to 'prove' a man's membership of the descent group that controls it, or to justify calling a resident brother. Where land is plentiful and men are needed to augment the fighting force of the community, recruitment to the local group is easily accomplished and may be quite distinct from the allocation of descent group status allocated by the father-son tie. Where land is scarce and manpower relatively plentiful, as Meggitt, Brown and Reay have shown, the political dominance of the descent group extends to the control of cultivation and residence rights. In the latter situation cultivation rights and residence can only be legitimised in terms of prior membership of the descent group. Descent is thus a means of exclusion as well as inclusion. In neither case is the unit that lives together and goes to war a descent group: it is an assembly of men.

If then kinship, and particularly descent, are not 'facts about people' but ways of conceptualising social phenomena, where do we start to understand these ideas? According to the African prototype, the genealogy enshrines the myth which legitimises descent. An important part of the New Guinea critique refers precisely to this area; African genealogies are said to differ from New Guinea ones and hence the nature of descent in the two areas is different. This claim is worth investigating further.

Genealogies are of two kinds. In terms of known persons, genealogies chart the kinship status and living and dead individuals vis-à-vis others in such a way that antecedent marriages and births pinpoint the position of Ego in relation to others within and outside his community. This may be called a personal genealogy since it charts personal relations. Such genealogical reckoning is bilateral and the categories of kin it establishes order the social universe of individuals. Genealogical knowledge of this sort is used to prove the possibility of projected marriages or substantiate claims to assistance or gifts. In Africa, and indeed very generally, the depth of these genealogies rarely exceeds four to five generations, but the classificatory nature of such kinship systems allows for the inclusion of a large number of individuals. Recent publications (Sharman 1969, Bloch 1971 *a*, Gulliver 1971) have demonstrated the flexibility they permit.

On the interpersonal aspect of genealogy we have virtually no information for New Guinea. Various authors give information on the relations between matrilateral kin, affines and agnates but in the context of relations between groups. The only systematic discussion of kin terms and their social significance is that of Salisbury for the Siane (Salisbury 1965: 18–25). A partial exception is Cook's (1970) article on the conversion of cognates to agnates among the Manga, but in general studies of 'kinship' are dominated by discussions of descent.

The politically significant genealogy, what I shall call a descent genealogy, is that which relates groups by reference to a hierarchically ordered series of ancestors. It is the nature of these genealogical formulations which appear to give rise to the doubts of New Guinea ethnographers. Thus Brown says, of the Highlands in general: 'Genealogies are rarely precisely kept' (Brown 1967: 37) and writing of Chimbu: '...while the closest patrilineal kin are known by a genealogy extending to the fathers or grandfathers of present-day adults, the connection between this small genealogy and others is not known by most people'. Among the Bena Bena 'Each clan group is named and the group members believe they have a common ancestor although they cannot state specifically how they are all related to him nor are they concerned to do so', but 'level III groups have shallow but precise genealogies' (Langness 1964: 164). Reay writes of the Kuma: 'It is expedient for the Kuma to be uninterested in genealogies, because the lack of strict reckoning facilitates the assimilation into agnatic descent groups of people who are not *in fact* agnatic kin' (Reay 1959 *b*: 35, my emphasis). In many of these discussions there seems to be an implication that the shortness and 'imprecision' of genealogies is a *consequence* of the people's lack of interest or knowledge. The underlying assertion is that the long, 'precise' genealogies attributed (somewhat inaccurately) to Africa are the result of more accurately preserved *knowledge*. Indeed Cook's article (1970) is devoted to showing how the Manga come to confuse non-lineage kin with agnates. Kinship is identified with the biological, so that, it is implied, kinship exists whether the people know it or not, just as blue eyes are transmitted through consanguinity regardless of a person's knowledge of the laws of genetics. This is patently not so; if it were not explicitly stated in Fortes' formulation, the article by Sahlins, which I cited, demonstrates it conclusively.

As has been shown by Bohannan (1952), Peters (1960), Middleton and Tait (1958), the length of genealogies relates to the span and, to some extent, size of the segments concerned. Gulliver has claimed that the nature of Jie genealogies are related to the small scale of social units and to a static overall population (Gulliver 1955: 103–5), a conclusion which can also be drawn from Salisbury's discussion of the Siane material. The size of New Guinea descent groups is very much smaller than most African ones; the most significant group rarely exceeds 400, with some exceptions, such as the Enga, Chimbu and Melpa.[7] There are rarely more than four levels of segmentation in the genealogical hierarchy. The simple genealogies of the Highlanders must be related to this. Corroborative information comes from the Mae Enga and Chimbu where the mean population of the largest recognised descent group is 2,290 (Meggitt 1965: 6) and between 1,000 and 4,000 (Brown 1969: 78) respectively. Among both these peoples the reckoning of genealogies involves greater generational depth and detail than is the case elsewhere. Further, in both these cases land is felt to be scarce and, as Meggit and Reay have argued, where land is short the agnatic credentials of would-be residents are more closely scrutinised. That it might also produce a greater genealogical complexity is indicated by comparative material from Africa, where, for the Bemba among others, Richards (1950) has related the much longer genealogies kept by the members of the Crocodile clan to their corporate claim to chiefly office.

A further characteristic of Highland New Guinea genealogies is that they present two distinct aspects: a relatively fixed ascription of ties between higher level groups referred to as phratries, clans and sub-clans in which the subordinate units may be described as founded by the sons of the ancestors of the more inclusive unit. The ancestors may also be characterised as affines or exchange partners. Below this fixed hierarchy is a level of uncertainty until the relatively limited range of precise genealogical knowledge which refers to living men is reached. Reay gives what seems to be an accurate explanation of this phenomenon when she writes: 'Genealogical shallowness is useful to them (the Kuma) for it allows recruitment by assimilation'. Langness, citing this passage, comments: 'This fits the Bena material beautifully' (Langness 1964: 173). Peters, writing of the Bedouin noted a similar functional gap in genealogies (1960). Gulliver (1955) indicates how the lineages remain stable in form by assimilating distant agnates to the pattern of descendants of a common (recent) forebear. This genealogy in no way links with the clan ancestor. It is clear that genealogies are multifunctional: at the more distant levels they serve to chart divisions within the wider tribal community, while at the lower levels by tracing the genealogical relations between living members of a corporation, they serve to relate individuals as kin of certain categories, distributing a variety of claims – to property, political allegiance and the exercise of authority of men of senior generations. An examination of a rare case of the analysis of discrepant genealogies in the literature, that of Salisbury's examination of two Siane genealogies, given by a man and his classificatory grandson, shows this clearly (Salisbury 1956: 4). The genealogy given by the younger man differs from that of his senior in that he gives only three members of the paternal generation where the older man gives eight brothers. Salisbury notes that the older man derives the eight brothers from three men in the preceding generation, that of *his* grandfather. He relates the pattern of reducing antecedent generations to three members to the existence of three roles in the Siane lineage authority structure: these are referred to by Siane terms which Salisbury translates first father, second father and other father. Hence what these genealogies demonstrate is a view of the authority structure of the lineage and the informant's place relative to it. The younger man's genealogy relates his perception of persons to this authority structure by allocating brotherhood in a manner that demonstrates the allocation of authority at the generation of his grandfather; a member of that generation does the same, but designates a more remote generation as the source of authority. 'Brother' in this context is the designation of an office, and the descent genealogy a political ideology.

A descent genealogy then expresses a variety of ideas which have many different connotations: linguistic divisions, geographical distance, political alliance, exogamic, ritual and other ties may all be expressed in this way, as Fortes noted. A patrilineal genealogy is built up of father-son ties and brother-brother ties which stand for relations of hierarchy and inequality on the one hand and relations of equality and identity on the other, for it is these structural principles that underlie the varying cultural 'meanings' of fatherhood and brotherhood in such genealogies. A kinship terminology displays the full range of such principles and is based on distinctions between the generations and between the sexes (Radcliffe-Brown 1949). In the absence of detailed information on this aspect of kinship among Highland New Guinea peoples, let us look at the biological beliefs associated with it.

New Guinea ideas of procreation show a balance between the maternal and paternal principles. Siane believe 'that an individual at conception is composed of spirit material from his own clan, located in the semen of his father and in spirit material from his mother's clan, located in her blood' (Salisbury 1962: 34). Throughout life the maternal contribution must be diminished and the maternal spirit driven out by various ceremonials, each of which entails a payment in compensation to the maternal clan. Among the Daribi 'a distinction is drawn between paternal substance (*kawa*), semen (transmitted by males and forming the outer envelope of an embryo and *pagekamine*, mother's blood) transmitted by females and making up its blood, bones and internal organs' (Wagner 1969: 58). A father recruits his children to his own group by making payments to his wife's clan, who are regarded as the 'owners' of the child. Again, among the Enga, a child is the mingling of semen and maternal blood animated by the spirit it receives through its father from the ancestors of the clan (Meggitt 1965: 163). Any physical injury to an individual entails compensation to the maternal clansmen for damaging 'their' substance. These compensations are paid for hair-cutting and other physical changes which accompany the life-cycle. We can see a general pattern in these beliefs. An individual's incorporation into the paternal group, with which he shares part of his being, is achieved by exchanges with his maternal kin. From the point of view of the group, then, increase in members is acquired by exchange with non-members. The implications of this belief ramify widely.

At the level of kinship between siblings there is a general and sharp distinction between ties relating men as brothers and ties relating brother and sister (or her husband). The former relationship epitomises identification and sharing; the latter difference and exchange. Burridge, discussing 'Siblings in Tangu' (1959) shows that these two types of relationship remain as social principles after the complete disintegration of the descent systems that once existed among these people. They are, so to speak, the irreducible principles of unilineal descent and the lowest common denominator of matriliny and patriliny. Elsewhere, the implications for descent group organisation are clear: identity and sharing are characteristic of relations within the descent group, relations with non-members are those of distance tempered with exchange. Mother's brothers and affines are exchange partners with whom only gifts can maintain the amicability of kinsmen. As Wagner puts it: 'Exchange provides the criterion by which clans exist as discrete units' (Wagner 1969: 64), by setting apart non-members from members, with whom no exchange is possible. Of course the external relations which I have characterised as exchange need not all be of the same nature: marriage, ceremonial pig-feasts and fights are all different manifestations of exchange and may be given different significance in each society.[8] Moreover, in any one society, the state of relations between particular clans may be demonstrated by the form of transactions they are currently engaged in. In Africa inter-descent group relations are typically those of the exchange of cattle as bridewealth for wives; in New Guinea the more typical exchange is the pig-feast.

In New Guinea exchange is closely linked with leadership, in that individuals promote their own careers by engaging in their clan's exchanges with others. Successful exchanges may result, not only in the enhanced status of their own group but the achievement by individuals of the acknowledged status of 'Big-Man'. Such a status is not an office but a position of power which is not transferable. The absence of political office is characteristic of Highland New Guinea and consistent with what has been referred to as the 'egalitarian' nature of New Guinea Highland social organisation (Forge 1972). In some, but by no means all, African societies offices defined by descent criteria exist. The Tallensi provide perhaps the most famous example but there are many others. Among the Gisu the office of lineage head was achieved not ascribed, although the arena of political competition was circumscribed, being limited to members of a lineage. Here too an individual acquires power and prestige through his affinal and other exchanges outside the lineage (La Fontaine 1963), exchanges which were part of a system of inter-group relations. The major differences between such a system and that of New Guinea seem to relate to the nature of the exchanges rather than the fact of exchange itself.

An important characteristic of the New Guinea societies we are discussing is the fierceness of interpersonal competition and rivalry; it is this which strikes the Africanist even more than the lack of specialised political office. A Big-Man must constantly validate his position in order to keep it. Moreover occasions for him to do so are provided by the relatively frequent ceremonial pig-feasts. It seems likely that a more close examination of Barnes' suggestion of the different forms of animal wealth, the pig and the cow, might provide some insight here. As Rappaport has shown (Rappaport 1967) pigs[9] compete with humans for both food and time[10] and there is considerable pressure on resources just before a pig-feast. Moreover their destructive foraging habits results in a higher risk of disputes within the neighbourhood, the greater the pig population. Cattle on the other hand usually require different resources and are herded away from cultivation; the increase in their numbers is less destructive and can be maintained for longer periods. Pigs increase very rapidly compared with cattle but do not provide elements of diet, such as milk or blood, until they are killed. They must be killed in public, both in order for the wealth of the pig-keepers to be demonstrated and to facilitate the consumption of the massive amounts of meat. Periodic pig-feasts thus seem to relate to the characteristics of the pig as a form of wealth. The cycle of accumulation of wealth and its dissipation is thus one of very short-term with the further concomitant that permanent wealth differentials are also impossible to establish. The competitive growing of yams has similar short-term characteristics. The emphasis on, and ceremonial elaboration of, exchange in Highland New Guinea communities can thus be seen as dependent on competition for leadership within descent-based communities plus the absence of any form of storable wealth. This formulation goes some way towards explaining the apparent paradox that in such egalitarian communities massive efforts are made by individuals in order to demonstrate their superior power. To paraphrase Orwell: all men are equal but all strive to be more equal than others.

In this paper I have been concerned to demonstrate the continuing vitality of the concept of descent. Further, I have contended that kinship is a system of symbols denoting fundamental relations between individuals, categories of persons and groups. This conceptual structure is not a 'grammar', a set of rules generating categories by extension from the biological existence of genitor, genetrix and offspring but a use of the perceived 'facts' of biology to create a powerful symbolic system by which to represent social relations.[11] Beattie (1946 *b*), among others, has emphasised the flexibility of kinship as an organisational system, pointing out that kinship relations can have a wide range of relevance, political, economic and ritual. What I have emphasised is that the idioms of kinship and descent give a cultural unity to fields of actions that are analytically discreet. Too often we are led into supposing that because a relationship between offspring of the same pair is referred to by the same term that denotes a relationship between the founders of two groups, i.e. brotherhood, the full range of implications of the term is the same in both cases, or that one is a metaphorical extension of the other. In the latter case we are guilty of ethnocentricism in supposing that the biological components in one relationship make it 'primary' and 'real'.

Fortes' recent work (1969) underlines the moral quality which characterises kinship. I would suggest that kinship carries moral weight and a quality of inalienability by virtue of the powerful symbolism with which it is expressed. No human power surpasses the power of life itself, no quality is so unalterable as the source of a man's existence. By equating kinship with biology, culture makes it a powerful and ineluctible force.

This paper has been an attempt to show the continuing relevance of African models for the New Guinea Highlands and to go further, to show the value for anthropology of the broad comparative aim which Meyer Fortes has done so much to advance. Such a dedication is hardly necessary but it gives me great pleasure to offer my contribution to this volume in his honour as a means of expressing the gratitude of a student who came into his department by chance and remained fascinated by anthropology as it was taught there.

Notes

1 A first draft of this paper was given at a seminar in the Anthropology Department of Brown University, Providence R.I. I am grateful to Professor P. Leis for inviting me to give it and to members of the seminar for their helpful discussion of the points it raises. The opportunity for reading in the ethnography of New Guinea was afforded by the generosity of Ohio State University who appointed me Visiting Professor (1971–2). I would like here to record my appreciation of their hospitality. Thanks are also due to Linda Kimball who assembled much of the material and to Professor Lucy Mair and Dr M. Bloch who commented on earlier drafts. However, responsibility for the contents of the paper is mine.

    There are two major omissions below of which I am conscious. I did not hear J. A. W. Forge's Malinowski Memorial Lecture for 1972 since I was abroad. For the same reason I did not obtain a copy of A. J. Strathern's important book, *One Father, One Blood* until after this article had gone to press. It thus suffers from the fact that I had read neither of these contributions to the subject under discussion.

2 Leach had made a somewhat similar criticism earlier distinguishing 'two entirely different categories of unilineal descent systems' one of which includes 'most of the African lineage systems', although it is also clear that the criterion he uses to define this category is not that it is 'African'. (Leach 1957 [1961*b*]: 123.)

3 Evans-Pritchards' use of the term differs from that of Fortes' but both his and Fortes' definitions would make the largest descent groups in New Guinea Highland societies clans, not lineages.

4 Kaberry (1967) discusses the importance of extra-descent group ties.
5 Gluckman in his Introduction to Meggitt (1965b) notes the lack of interest in kinship terms and relations.
6 See Kaberry (1967: 117, 118, 120).
7 See Kaberry (1967) and also Forge (1972).
8 See the very common dictum: we marry those whom we fight.
9 I am discussing domesticated village pigs, not the use made of wild pigs.
10 Rappaport's argument concerns the timing of pig-feasts – the wider conclusions drawn here are mine.
11 The influence of Leach's *Pul Eliya* is obvious here, but I do not accept the definition he gives to kinship in his concluding chapter. To me, kinship is much wider than mere economics and the moral component is axiomatic. In a recent (1972) lecture on kinship in England he, however, broadened his definition of 'property'.

Complementary Filiation and Bilateral Kinship

Edmund Leach

This very short essay is simply a token of respect to my one time teacher and long time colleague. I offer my apologies to the Editor and to the Reader and to Meyer Fortes himself that pressure of other concerns should have compelled me to contribute such a cursory effort.

The concept of complementary filiation which was such an important and seminal feature of Meyer Fortes' writing and teaching during the 1950s was developed out of Fortes' own field experience among the Tallensi. As a result, both his followers and his critics, and perhaps Meyer Fortes' himself, have tended to assume that complementary filiation only has analytical value within the general framework of a unilineal descent system. It is I think a moot point whether this is really so.

Bilateral kinship structures are incompatible with the empirical existence of true unilineal descent groups but, where such structures are associated with well developed notions of individual property, it is not uncommon to find that the practice of marriage and the rules of inheritance among the property owning sector of the community have been so contrived as to create notionally permanent property owning corporations which are conceived of as patrilineal descent groups even though, in detail, they are nothing of the sort. Two examples of this are the 'landed gentry' class of eighteenth and nineteenth-century England and the Radala, the ruling class upper elite of the *goyigama* caste in Kandyan Ceylon at much the same period. The basic kinship structure both in England and in Kandyan Ceylon is unquestionably bilateral but, in both cases, in the property owning sections of society, devices were introduced which greatly restricted the possibility of a female heir who had male siblings from inheriting property in land. These devices were of various kinds and patterned in different ways; they included primogeniture, entailment, and dowry payments in cash and jewellery (rather than land).

Because of such procedures the members of the property owning class in such societies come to think of themselves as members of a particular 'family' associated with a particular ancestral landed estate of which the owner is the 'head of the family'. The actual structure of such 'families' is not easily determined since, at the limits, it becomes an arbitrary matter whether any particular descendant of the founding landowner is or is not included, but the general ideology is strongly patrilineal. The use of patronymic surnames is an important feature here and it is notable that in

Kandyan Ceylon the aristocratic 'family name' (*vasagama*) was transmitted in accordance with conventions very similar to those found among the English.

These are very general statements but it seems to me that an empirical instance may be of some interest. The point I want to make is that, once a bilateral structure is so distorted for ideological reasons that it is made to appear 'as if' it were a patrilineal structure, then it will automatically follow that the pseudo-patrilineal descent is complemented by a mystical reverence for a less pseudo principle of matrilateral filiation. Here is my example. In essence, no community could be more 'bilateral' in their kinship arrangements than the English Quakers. From their beginnings in the mid-seventeenth century the Quakers maintained a strict rule of sectarian endogamy coupled with elaborately preserved genealogy books. In principle, all Quakers were deemed of equal social status and everybody was related to everybody else. In later times prosperous nineteenth-century Quakers were proud of their humble saintly beginnings but they also needed to adapt to the ideological conventions of the aspiring English industrial middle class of which they were an important sector.

The socially upstart English industrialists modelled themselves quite blatantly on the life styles of their social superiors, the 'landed gentry'; they aspired above all else to be accepted as members of 'the County'. The Quakers had similar aspirations and it may be that because of the powerful role that they played in the banking institutions of the City of London they were more successful in this game than many others, (Barclays Bank is now the largest of all English banking agglomerates and it is still headed by a Seebohm!). In the nineteenth century this social climbing went along with entry into the professions and even the Peerage.

The Quaker 'families' of Rickman, Godlee and Lister were among those who achieved this kind of social success. Rickmans were notably successful as large scale farmers in and around Sussex; Godlees were particularly prominent in the legal and medical professions; several Listers, including Lord Lister, were eminent scientists. They were all closely intermarried. Sir Rickman John Godlee (1849–1925), the eminent surgeon, was sister's son to Joseph Lord Lister (1827–1912), whose fame derives from his recognition of the need for sterile conditions in surgery.

Among his other notable achievements Sir Rickman John Godlee wrote a major biography of his uncle Lord Lister. It is a work of 670 pages devoted, in the main, to Lister's professional career. The rather surprising fact that only four lines are devoted to Lord Lister's entirely satisfactory marriage to Agnes Syme was evidently influenced by other factors. From Sir Rickman's point of view Lady Lister had a double defect; she was not merely female, she was not a Quaker. The first chapter of the biography, as might be expected, sets out to establish Lord Lister's family background and for this purpose the author had evidently studied Lister family records. The book does not contain a family tree, but if the recorded facts had been put onto a diagram by a social anthropologist they might have appeared as in Fig. 1. Notice the tremendous emphasis on male as distinct from female

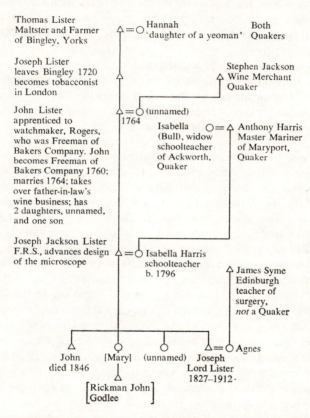

Fig. 1.   Lister genealogy as implied by Rickman John Godlee's biography of Lord Lister.

links. Spouses are ignored except as links of complementary filiation. And indeed Sir Rickman's text makes it clear that his thinking on these matters was distinctly 'Fortesian'. Here is a quotation which is a summary comment on the data illustrated in my diagram:

It is thus clear that the Bingley Listers lived in the very depths of the country, and were not 'renowned by intellect, by action or by station'. The usual paternal family tree is preserved with a few isolated facts which are useless in seeking for indications of hereditary genius. Possibly the first spark prompted Sir Joseph Lister in the early part of the eighteenth century to seek his fortunes in London. If he had not done so, it may be supposed his descendants, if any, would have resembled the humble residue at Bingley after two generations had passed away. It is interesting to speculate upon the question whether it was the influence of London alone that made his son a well-educated merchant, his grandson an accomplished scientific man, and his great-grandson a genius, or how much of this advance may have depended on maternal influences.

Sir Rickman is writing about 'hereditary genius' and, in a formal sense, as is appropriate to a medical man, the argument presupposes that 'influence' means 'genetic influence', but it is noteworthy that the patrilineal line from the humble Quaker farmer of Bingley in Yorkshire is seen as 'descent' while the economically significant ancestors are seen only as 'maternal influences'.

Quite recently Sir Rickman John Godlee's great nephew (brother's son's son) Nicholas Godlee made available to me a number of Godlee genealogies compiled by various members of his family from around 1850 onwards. Down to 1914 they all have characteristics very similar to those of the Lister pedigree shown in Fig. 1. There is a very marked emphasis on the 'chain male'; so much so that it is only individuals who were entitled to the patronymic Godlee who were really thought of as 'ancestors' at all. According to this somewhat contrived pedigree Sir Rickman John Godlee was descended from an 'original' Godlee ancestor, Peter Godle (c. 1645–1719). As in the Lister case, Peter's virtue lay in the fact that he was a humble but saintly Quaker. In this case the territorial base was near Lowestoft. One of Peter Godle's patrilineal descendants expressly attached value to the fact that he was a fisherman and likened him to Saint Peter. Peter Godle's son Burwood moved up in the social world and married a London merchant's daughter. This was the start of the family fortunes. If we examine the detailed evidence (see Fig. 2) it is quite apparent that Sir Rickman John Godlee's prosperous upbringing owed far more to the (financial) 'influence' of collateral females and 'complementary filiation' than it did to the chain-male of fishermen-sailors descended from the saintly Peter Godle.

My point is simply this. In bilateral structures the practical economic significance of descent through females is usually at least as significant as descent through males, but the introduction into such a system of the kind of semi-patrilineal ideology that is associated with inherited patronymics (surnames etc.) generates an ideological differentiation, among the people concerned, between the value that is to be attached to patri-filiation and that which is to be attached to matri-filiation. In such circumstances, surname groups can come to be credited with many of the characteristics of patrilineal descent groups even though these attributes are largely fictional.

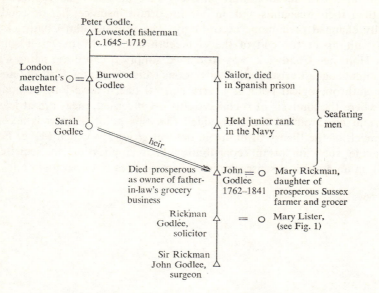

Fig. 2. 'Patrilineal descent' of Sir Rickman John Godlee.

In this brief essay I have drawn attention to one such characteristic; the appearance of a differentiation between patrilineal descent and matrifiliation in an endogamous, bilaterally structured, community. But other features of patrilineal descent groups can also appear in 'pseudo' form in comparable situations. It was Fortes who first effectively explained why patrilineages the world over tend to terminate at the top in an apical ancestress rather than an apical ancestor; the argument is related to that concerning complementary filiation and again derived in the first instance from Tallensi materials. But this feature too can appear in 'pseudo'-patrilineages of the kind I have been describing.

My own ancestral origins derive from Rochdale in Lancashire and a complex of closely intermarried surname groups all of which were involved in the Industrial Revolution and the rise of the textile industry between 1770 and 1850. As in the Quaker case, these 'families' thought of themselves as patrilineal corporations associated with a particular piece of physical property, in this case a textile mill and an associated family mansion. But the point I would make here is that, in every case, the founder of the family fortunes, the beginning of the line, is a woman. It does not appear that these ladies actually provided the original capital; the 'firm' is created by the lady's sons and grandsons by hard work and entrepreneurial enterprise.

But the ladies in question were in every case of somewhat higher social class than their husbands and, in one important instance, her descendants actually changed their name accordingly. The firm of John Chadwick and Sons, built up at the end of the eighteenth century by the grandsons of Sarah Holt, née Chadwick, was so named simply because the name Chadwick might suggest aristocratic associations which the name Holt did not.

My anthropological point is a very general one. I have long maintained that, where the analysis of social systems is concerned, ideas are at least as important as empirical facts. Provided that this point of view is accepted then much of the theory of unilineal descent groups to which Meyer Fortes has made such important contributions has application to societies in which, in an empirical sense, unilineal descent does not operate at all.

The Nature of Kinship

Genetrix: Genitor : : Nature: Culture

J. A. Barnes

We salute Meyer Fortes for his achievements not only in the intensive investigation of the Tallensi and Ashanti of Ghana but also in the comparative analysis of diverse social and cultural systems, notably in his Lewis Henry Morgan lectures published as *Kinship and the Social Order* (1969). Although he has long remained a steadfast defender of the strategy of concentrating anthropological field resources on the study of peoples whose material artefacts are simple (Fortes 1958 *a*), he has always been sensitive to the light these studies shed on patterns of living found in industrial societies. It is therefore appropriate in the present context to discuss some of the issues that arise in kinship studies when we endeavour to compare social and cultural patterns in many different societies including our own. My thesis is that this comparison suggests a reformulation of the relation between kinship and nature. I focus on putative physical relations rather than on relations of social parenthood.

It can be argued that in anthropology and sociology comparative analysis is impossible without including, either explicitly or by implication, the society to which the analyst himself belongs and the culture whose concepts and categories he uses to think with. This view has been expressed by Schneider (1972: 47–8) who, in recent years, has appealed forcefully for the study of kinship as part of a cultural or symbolic system and who has provided the most uncompromising account of such a system in the Western tradition. He says:

> The next problem. . .is the old one of how comparison can be conducted on a cultural level if it is assumed that each and every culture may be uniquely constituted. . .our own culture. . .always serves as a base-line for cross-cultural comparison. Without some comprehension, however botched, distorted, biased, and infused with value judgments and wishful thinking, both good and bad, our own culture always remains the baseline for all other questions and comparisons. In part, this is because the experience of our own culture is the only experience which is deep and subtle enough to comprehend in cultural terms, for the cultural aspects of action are particularly subtle, sometimes particularly difficult to comprehend partly because they are symbols not treated usually as symbols but as true facts.

Schneider implies, so it would seem, that even when we are comparing, say, unilineal systems found in different parts of Africa, as in Fortes' classic paper on 'The structure of unilineal descent groups' (1953 *a*), there is an implicit comparison between the various African notions of unilineal descent and filiation and similar notions current in the Western tradition. In the passage cited however, Schneider is talking about cultural symbols, and it is not clear whether he would argue that in comparing, say, forms of social organization we are similarly forced to begin our analysis with forms prevalent in our own society. Indeed, at other places in his paper he draws a distinction between, on the one hand, 'the scientific facts of biology' and 'biology as a natural process' and, on the other, the cultural symbols that may perhaps (or perhaps not) be derived from these scientific facts. This suggests that he sees science as the study of nature, i.e., as natural rather than social science, and that he makes a distinction between 'science', dealing with facts, and 'culture', dealing with symbols. But if there are facts of nature and biology that can be demonstrated scientifically, as he maintains (he seems to have the processes of human reproduction in mind), then presumably there are other scientifically ascertainable facts about where people live, who they work with, who commands whom, and so on which can provide a framework for a comparative analysis of social organization that is not linked distinctively with any particular society, not even our own.

The distinction Schneider draws is widely used in social science. It is somewhat akin to the contrast between objective and indexial meanings used by the phenomenologists, and to that between 'objective' and 'subjective' social class by students of stratification. The same distinction is presented in another form in what Naroll (1964: 306) calls Goodenough's rule: what we do as ethnographers is, and must be kept, independent of what we do as comparative ethnologists (Goodenough 1956: 37). The closest analogue to Schneider's contrast is found in the distinction between etic and emic categories, labels which some social anthropologists have taken over from linguistics (see Goodenough 1970 *b*: 98–130). In Pike's (1960: 37–72) formulation the etic–emic contrast is unashamedly positivist. The scientific linguist observer, with his objective categories, is contrasted with the speaking actor who uses subjective categories to produce and decipher meaningful utterances. Inter-language comparison is implicit in Pike's scheme. As used in anthropology the cross-cultural and cross-societal emphasis has been retained but the positivist implication of the contrast has been played down. Instead we have the emic categories of thought of the actors contrasted with the etic categories of analysis of the observer, neither set necessarily more real or true than the other.

I have argued that this contrast can be applied without modification only in the 'colonial' or laboratory situation such as Pike had in mind (Barnes 1967 *b*, 1970). If the actors speak only their own language, think only in their own terms, and draw only upon a locally-generated stock of 'knowledge' of their environment, then the flow of information is only one-way.

The observer may well modify his etic analytical categories in the light of what the actors do and say, but they do not alter their ways of thinking and acting because of assertions made about their behaviour by the observer. This is the paradigm situation of inquiry in natural science, the principle of indeterminacy notwithstanding. Until a couple of decades ago anthropological fieldwork in distant colonies approximated to it, though even then there were substantial and critical differences from the typical scientific laboratory. These laboratory-like conditions have not persisted and, following the end of colonialism in its classic form, they are probably now gone for ever. Instead there is two-way communication between actors and observers, so that the actors begin to take over not only the material artefacts brought by the observers and their compatriots but also their languages, concepts and social institutions, changing them in the process. In particular they take over and adapt some of the jargon and some of the content of science. Once this happens the observer in the remotest jungle begins to face the same difficulties as his colleagues working in the metropolis have always faced: the facts that the language of science, and of social science in particular, is also to some extent the language of the people and that the findings of science, and even its techniques of inquiry and verification, are continually seeping into popular consciousness. In general, then, though his reasons are different from mine, I accept Schneider's point that the categories and concepts of the observer's own culture are the starting point for comparative analysis in social science.

If this is so, how does it affect the study of kinship? There are many issues we might take up but I want here to consider just two related matters: how valid is the distinction Schneider draws between culture and natural science; and how does kinship, in contrast to other aspects of social and cultural life, relate to nature? I use the standard triple distinctions between genetic or carnal father, genitor and pater, and between genetic or carnal mother, genetrix and mater, stressing that the statuses of genitor and genetrix are defined, if at all, in terms of local doctrines about the process of human reproduction (Barnes 1961: 297–8; 1964: 294; Goodenough 1970 *b*: 27). Fatherhood and motherhood are used as cover terms.

At first glance Schneider's position seems to be paradoxical. He seeks to establish science as distinct from culture and yet to insist that a comparative science of cultures has to be rooted in a particular culture, the culture of the investigator. He appears to make natural science free of culture but to query the possibility of meta-categories for analysing cultures. But this apparent paradox can be quickly disposed of by referring to his book on American kinship, where he makes a fourfold contrast between (1) what he calls biological facts, (2) formal science, (3) informal ethnoscience and (4) 'certain cultural notions which are put, phrased, expressed, symbolized by cultural notions *depicting* biological facts, or what purport to be biological facts' (Schneider 1968: 114–15). I find it confusing to use 'biology', the name of a science, for phenomena that exist independently of efforts to study them, and therefore re-label (1) nature. Category (4), of which 'broken heart' and 'heartache' are examples from American culture, need not detain us. This category contains what in more traditional language might be called extensions of kin usages that are perceived by the actors as being metaphorical, figurative, symbolic; all the parishioners know that the village priest is not 'really' their father. We can concentrate on categories (1) (2) and (3).

Formal science, category (2), is part of American culture as much as categories (3) and (4). Indeed Habermas (1972) argues that the salient diagnostic feature of contemporary culture in industrialized societies is the belief that science is the only authenticated form of knowledge. Though both are part of Western culture it is possible, at least for classical times and since the Renaissance, to draw a fairly clear distinction between professional scientific assertions and lay beliefs that, rightly or wrongly, are perceived as based on formal scientific inquiry (see S. B. Barnes 1969). Informal ethnoscience embraces more than the latter category but it certainly includes it. Weber (1946: 139) notes this distinction, and it is well put by Evans-Pritchard, in a discussion of the views of Lévy-Bruhl.

> The fact that we attribute rain to meteorological causes alone while savages believe that Gods or ghosts or magic can influence the rainfall is no evidence that our brains function differently from their brains. . .It is no sign of superior intelligence on my part that I attribute rain to physical causes. I did not come to this conclusion myself by observation and inference and have, in fact, little knowledge of the meteorological processes that lead to rain. I merely accept what everybody else in my society accepts, namely that rain is due to natural causes (Evans-Pritchard 1934: 21).

Our yardstick, then, is our own culture, which contains a vast number of propositions perceived as science. Against it we compare other cultures, noting in what respects they resemble one another and how they differ, and endeavour to discover why this is so. How does a comparison of this kind work in the field of kinship?

It is reasonable to expect that data from category (1) will impinge in special fashion on kinship data from categories (2) and (3). Despite the recent efforts of some ethologists to postulate a pan-primate basis for political order, and for much else as well, kinship remains the aspect of human culture with the closest links to the natural world. Indeed, in American culture, we are told, 'kinship *is* biology' (Schneider 1968: 116). Apes and monkeys may have dominance hierarchies and territories but, unlike men, they do not have representative government nor, as far as we know, do they believe in God. Like us, however, they copulate, conceive and give birth, activities with which kinship has a close connexion, however problematic the qualities of the connexion may be. These activities, when performed by humans, are perceived as natural rather than cultural. Part of the basis for a comparison of ideas of kinship has then to be our own cultural notions about the reproductive process, some of which are derived directly from formal science but which include others that belong solely to ethnoscience.

The inevitability of beginning cross-cultural comparison by matching alien cultures against our own is well shown by the discussion in *Man* a few years ago on virgin birth (Leach 1967; Spiro 1968; Douglas 1969 and references therein), and by earlier controversies about the ignorance of physiological paternity. The diverse beliefs about non-miraculous human reproduction found in pre-scientific cultures have been described many times and need not be repeated here (Ashley-Montagu 1937, 1949; Ford 1945; Leach 1961 *b*, 1961 *c*, 1967; Malinowski 1963; Meyer 1939: 1–16; Spencer 1949–50). The point I emphasize is that when these beliefs are compared, the yardstick used is falsely presented, for we tend to assume that for ourselves no distinction between formal science and informal ethnoscience is needed. We present our own view of conception as a single event, in which only one man and one woman are involved, and which triggers the whole sequence of gestation, as scientifically validated. We contrast this view with theories that the foetus forms and grows in the womb by receiving contributions via many acts of coitus not necessarily all performed by the same man, a view held, for example, by the Azande (Evans-Pritchard 1932: 410); or with other theories, found for example in Aboriginal Australia, whereby the process of gestation is neither initiated nor sustained by coitus; or with intermediate theories. These indigenous ideas are recorded in the ethnographic literature, but where do ours come from? From formal science, or informal ethnoscience, or from a cultural heritage in which natural substances like blood and semen serve as symbols in statements that have nothing at all to do with natural science? Even if we prune away metaphorical ideas in Schneider's category (4), a moment's reflection shows that ideas in categories (2) and (3) are not as easy to pin down as may seem at first sight.

At this point we can come to grips with a distinction between fatherhood and motherhood. Consider first fatherhood. Nowadays most educated people in the West have heard of genes and chromosomes and know that the embryo draws its stock of chromosomes equally from its genetic father and mother. I guess that, in the sex-conscious culture of contemporary Britain, almost all adults believe that conception occurs when a spermatazoon penetrates an ovum. But what sort of knowledge is this? Surely most of us know as little about the physiology of human reproduction as Evans-

Pritchard knows about meteorology. We believe these processes to occur because we believe also that at some point in the past long-forgotten scientists discovered that this is what really happens. We assume that though the discovery of genes and chromosomes is post-Darwin, the fact that conception is a unique event and not a prolonged process has been scientifically established for a long time. The view that conception and gestation can follow a single act of coitus is indeed consistent with Aristotle's account of reproduction in *Generation of Animals*, Book 2, and is implied in his statement in the *History of Animals* that 'if the second conception take place at a short interval, then the mother bears that which was later conceived and brings forth the two children like actual twins. . . The following is a striking example: a certain woman, having committed adultery, brought forth the one child resembling her husband and the other resembling the adulterous lover' (585[a]). Thus the doctrine of 'one child, one genitor' has been part of the Western tradition for more than two thousand years. Yet although the presence of physical resemblances between some, though not all, children and their mother's husbands calls for an explanation, it does not necessarily demand a theory of universal monopaternity. The dominance of a monopaternal theory cannot have been determined by the weight of evidence, for apart from resemblances there was little material evidence available until the seventeenth century. Spermatozoa were discovered accidentally in 1677 by Ham, though their connexion with fertilization remained unknown. Mammalian ova were discovered, also accidentally, in a pregnant bitch by van Baer in 1828 and in 1853 Newport claimed to observe spermatozoa entering an ovum. Not until 1875 were the male and female pronuclei in spermatozoa and ova identified by Oscar Hertwig, who described how they combine (Meyer 1939: 123, 137–8, 189–192). Thus for most of the historic period in the West, the uniqueness of physical paternity was a cultural construct for which there was very little conclusive evidence.

Even so, this doctrine was modified by a belief in 'maternal influences', the idea that events experienced by a pregnant woman are reflected in the constitution of her child. The belief forms part of several indigenous theories of procreation (e.g. Lévi-Strauss 1966 *b*: 76) and is certainly still present in contemporary Britain. It is exemplified for animals in the story told in *Genesis*, chapter 30, verses 25–43, about Jacob changing the colour of the lambs borne by Laban's ewes. 'Maternal influences' may always have been restricted to ethnoscience, old wives' tales, but orthodox formal science long entertained the related idea that Weismann (1893: 383) calls 'telegony', the notion that the physical characters inherited by an individual are influenced not only by his (or her) own father but also by other men by whom his mother may previously have had children. Dobzhansky (1970: 420A) attributes this belief to Aristotle and it was supported, for plants and animals at least if not for humans, by Darwin (1875: 435–7; see Morton 1821; Zirkle 1935: 117 and 1946: 119; Parkes 1960: 242) in conformity with his thesis of pangenesis. Thus whereas most pre-scientific beliefs about multiple physical fatherhood identify as genitors men with whom a woman has had intercourse during a given pregnancy, telegony ascribes physical paternity to her earlier mates as well as to the man who initiates the pregnancy. The doctrine of telegony lives on among animal breeders but has been abandoned by orthodox science, as has a later suggestion of a naturally-occurring polypaternal process called 'somatic fertilization'. According to this hypothesis, substances may be absorbed in the female genital tract after copulation; these evoke the production of factors which may exert an influence on the embryos of subsequent matings (Austin and Walton 1960: 393; Parkes 1960: 242). In the laboratory, however, the fusion of two embryos at the eight-cell stage has been achieved, producing tetra-parental mice. Chimeric mice with even more complex constitutions have been bred and studied (Tarkowski 1961; see Wegmann 1970; Mullen and Whitten 1971 and references therein). Indigenous assertions of human polypaternalism in nature have thus been vindicated for some mammals in the laboratory. Indeed there is evidence that double fertilization sometimes occurs naturally in humans (Benirschke 1970: 40–5). Human polypaternalism seems therefore to be compatible with the available scientific evidence.

Tetraparental mice and other chimeras produced in the laboratory receive their diverse constituents before the implantation stage, long before birth. A belief in the post-natal physical transmission of information and attitudes is implied in the expression 'He took that in with his mother's milk.' An earlier belief in a more specific and selective form of located transmission is suggested by Dobzhansky's (1970: 420A) statement, made in the context of an article on heredity, that 'An ancient English law holds a man who seduces the wet nurse of the heir to the throne guilty of polluting the "blood" of the royal family.' I have been unable to trace this law. The closest comparable laws seem to be those listed during the reign of King Æthelberht of Kent about A.D. 600, whereby a man who seduced a maiden of the king's house-hold had to pay fifty shillings in compensation, compared with only twelve shillings for the seduction of a girl occupied on menial tasks (Attenborough 1922: 5; Liebermann 1903: 3 and 1916: 7). These laws give special recog-nition to the king's entourage but make no reference to suckling or pollu-tion. It may well be that the ultimate source for the alleged ancient law is merely the *Mirror of justices* where it is said that one of the ways in which an adulterer may commit the crime of lese-majesty, 'a horrible sin', is by seducing the nurse suckling the heir of the king (Whittaker 1895: 15). The *Mirror* was at one time regarded as a true account of the laws of England before the Norman conquest but in Maitland's view was largely fabricated by Andrew Horn, fishmonger and Chamberlain of the City of London, in about 1289; it contains many wilful falsehoods and misstatements of law (Maitland 1895). The Anglo-Saxons may never have held the doctrine that some kind of malign influence can be transmitted from a man by adulterous copulation to a lactating woman and thence through her milk to her royal foster-child. But if the law never existed, at least the doctrine formed part of the imagination of a thirteenth-century fishmonger.

Despite these contrary notions, the main stream of Western popular belief has clearly been 'one child, one genitor'. If there was no compelling scientific evidence for this belief the reasons for its persistence must be sought elsewhere, in the organization of social life and in other parts of Western culture, rather than in nature. As far back as we have knowledge, Western society, like most other human societies, has been organized on the premise of one child, one pater. Likewise the Christian faith of the West stresses the uniqueness of God the Father. The Holy Ghost impregnated Mary through her ear and was manifest in, or symbolized by, a dove at Christ's baptism, but neither act makes the third person of the Trinity co-pater with the first (see Jones 1951; Swete 1909: 28–9, 45, 365–6; Gudeman 1972: 54). If we encountered this constellation of facts in a tribal society, surely we would have no hesitation in saying that the organization of society and the major premises of religion are reflected in myths about unique physical parenthood.

Motherhood is different. Conception is an internal and microscopic event that we laymen believe scientists have investigated, whereas gestation and birth, and with them the relation of physical motherhood, are macroscopic processes that, in principle, anyone can see for himself. Hence the descriptions of physical motherhood in diverse cultures do not vary as greatly as with fatherhood. The so-called denial of physical maternity is not homologous with the denial of paternity, except when applied to special myths for uninitiates, as for example in our own tale for children about storks bringing babies (cf. Spiro 1968: 260, n. 11). The denial of physical maternity usually means merely that the mother is thought to contribute nothing of importance to the foetus during pregnancy, as for example was believed in ancient Egypt (Needham 1959: 43) and is stated by Apollo in Aeschylus' *Eumenides* (lines 657–61), when defending Orestes against the charge of matricide.

This lack of symmetry between the notions of genitor and genetrix is emphasized by Goodenough (1970 *a*: 392) who says that 'procreation associates children directly with women but only indirectly with men' and that 'Motherhood and fatherhood cannot be defined in the same way for comparative anthropological purposes'. Fathers are not self-evident as mothers are. 'Genitor' is a social status, and societies vary greatly in the rights and duties, privileges and obligations, if any, that they associate with this status. If the status exists, there must be a rule for identifying genitors.

But for the status to exist at all there must be a theory of procreation that calls for one, or for several, and, for all cultures prior to the physiological discoveries of the late nineteenth century, this theory cannot be supported by scientific evidence. Even though Aristotle wrote his *Generation of Animals* in terms of a unique and necessary genitor, who might be the wind rather than an animal, he misunderstood the significance of menstrual blood, which he thought was coagulated by semen just as milk is coagulated by rennet, thus forming the foetus (739[b]). It is scarcely surprising that Australian Aborigines and many other pre-scientific peoples should have developed theories of human reproduction which do not require a genitor or which allow for the possibility of several. What calls for explanation is why in the pre-scientific West the dominant folk theory happened to be in one particular, though not in many others, more or less in accord with evidence from nature later to be disclosed. In this light, the debate between Leach, Spiro and others about ignorance of physiological paternity is cast in the wrong mould, for their arguments are all about how to interpret correctly apparent ignorance of a fact that everyone should know. Against the participants in this debate, on both sides, I contend that physical paternity is a fact that, until recently, nobody can have known scientifically. Our proper task is to explain the fabrication of flimsy hypotheses as well as the denial of material evidence.

Schneider (1972: 62, n. 9) queries the assumption that American cultural symbols like blood and shared bio-genetic substance, and perhaps even coitus, derive from the facts of nature. Beliefs centring on these symbols presumably belong to informal ethnoscience, where the predominance of cultural rather than natural influence is not surprising. For example, in the fourth century B.C. Anaxagoras stated that sperm coming from the right testis produced males, and from the left testis females, an assertion repeated in the sixteenth century by Melanchthon, Luther's supporter, with the rider that males were born from the right side of the womb. What is more impressive is the effect that cultural influences, usually in the form of adherence to unproved theories, have had on formal science as well as on ethnoscience in blotting out the evidence provided by nature. The most striking examples are given at the end of the seventeenth century by the homunculi, minute but fully formed human beings, which Plantade and Hartsoeker separately asserted they had seen through their magnifying lenses inside human spermatozoa (Meyer 1939: 69–70, 133, 152, and Figures 16 and 17). Even Leeuwenhoek, who reported Ham's discovery of spermatozoa to the Royal Society of London, wrote about the 'nerves, arteries, and veins' he saw inside his own spermatozoa: '. . .I felt convinced that, in no full-grown human body, are there any vessels that may not be found likewise in sound semen' (Cole 1930: 12). The history of popular and professional scientific beliefs about monsters, malformed foetuses, provides further proof of the difficulty we encounter in recognizing the evidence of nature when this challenges doctrines we cherish (Meyer 1939: 212–7).

Kuhn (1970) and many other writers have drawn attention to the way in which fresh evidence from nature is moulded as much as possible to fit existing scientific theories. Without necessarily accepting Kuhn's notion of a paradigm, we can apply to the scientific quest for physical fatherhood in general Needham's comment on Aristotle's account of human reproduction: 'The whole matter affords an excellent illustration of the way in which an apparently academic theory may have the most intimate connections with social and political behaviour. . .' (Needham 1959: 14).

From this standpoint we can easily resolve the paradox that Aboriginal Australia, the major locus of so-called ignorance of physiological paternity, is also the home of what Fortes (1969: 101) calls a kinship polity (Barnes 1963: xxiii–xxvii). For if of necessity physical paternity is prescribed or denied culturally without the constraint of the natural order, the way is open for the elaboration of rules of fatherhood for any social or cultural purpose whatever. Aboriginal cultures seem generally to have managed without human genitors, while ascribing a relation of social fatherhood to the mother's husband (see Fortes 1969: 106, n. 10). Indeed, Hiatt (1971) analyses secret pseudo-procreative rituals performed by Aboriginal men in terms of the contrast between the uncertainty of the male contribution to reproduction and the certainty of the contribution made by women. In this perspective we might see all assertions of physical paternity as examples of what is fashionably called male chauvinism.

In some Aboriginal societies where many marriages are unorthodox, and also among the very orthodox Walbiri, the required relations between sections, lines and generations are maintained by applying rules of indirect matrifiliation rather than patrifiliation. The unorthodox affiliations of an individual's father are ignored and he acquires the category and group memberships he would have had if his mother had made an orthodox marriage. A rule of indirect matrifiliation in a 'kinship polity' of Australian type reduces the range of contexts in which an individual needs a specified social father; a dependable prospective mother-in-law may be a more important requirement (see Warner 1958: 119–20; Meggitt 1962 a, 1972: 74; Shapiro 1969, 1971). He needs a single human genitor even less. It is perhaps possible that the lack of interest in nominating a physical father may have been facilitated for Australian Aboriginals by the predominance of marsupials in the fauna. The process of marsupial gestation remained a mystery long after the beginning of White settlement in 1788. Although the unaided passage of a kangaroo embryo from the vagina towards the pouch was recorded in 1830, more than a hundred years later many Australians firmly believed that marsupial young develop on the teats 'like apples on twigs' (Collie 1830: 240; Troughton 1965: 13–21). Only recently has there been a satisfactory explanation of the phenomenon of embryonic diapause, whereby the interval between copulation and birth may increase up to ten or more times its normal value (Sharman 1955; Sharman and Berger 1969). Thus the evidence available from nature for Aboriginal would-be scientists was confusing. There is no reason why Aboriginals should have based their ethnoscience of human reproduction on the eutherial dingo or bat any more than on the kangaroo or other ubiquitous marsupials. Seligmann (1902: 300–1) mentions that in Papua a community he visited knew little about the reproductive organs of a wallaby he had dissected.

Where the local theory of reproduction does call for one or more genitors, another problem arises. Copulation may be thought to be a necessary pre-requisite for conception or foetal growth, but it is a compelling fact of nature that it is not a sufficient condition. We do not need to be scientists to discover this. To be complete, a theory must specify sufficient as well as necessary conditions, and in the absence of clues from nature these must be generated by the culture rather than derived from observation. Even in the scientific West not all the causes of infertility are known. To fit the facts the actors' causal model has to contain a substantial error term, and it is scarcely surprising that this is labelled God or spirit, beyond human control. Thus for example Evans-Pritchard (1932: 400, 402, 408) reports that the Azande believe that conception results from copulation, and that subsequent acts of intercourse are beneficial in that semen assists foetal growth. But they stress that conception cannot occur unless it is the will of the Supreme Being, Mboli. Likewise according to the Talmud, there are three partners in every human birth: God, father and mother (Abrahams 1924: 150, 176). In the exchange of views on virgin birth in *Man*, the contributors seem to have forgotten how recently this tripartite doctrine has ceased to be current in Britain. In the days before our present fertility clinics, the only advice available to barren couples seeking a child was: Prayer and perseverance.

One last point. Whatever may be their ideas about physical parenthood, virtually all cultures attach symbolic value to both fatherhood and mother-hood. I suggest that fatherhood is the freer symbol, able to take on a wider range of culturally assigned meanings, because it has a more exiguous link with the natural world. One striking instance of the use of the symbol of fatherhood is in the charters of organization of polysegmentary societies. There are certainly good social reasons why matrilineal societies never achieve segmental hierarchies with as many levels as are found in patrilineal systems of widest span (Schneider 1961). But it can also be argued that the pedigrees that describe the relations between the major components of polysegmentary societies have nothing whatever to do with domestic kin-ship, whether patrilineal or matrilineal. I have suggested for the Mae Enga that the idiom of agnation is used to describe simply relations of inclusion; that the statement that A, the apical ancestor of one group, is father of X,

Y and *Z*, the apical ancestors of other groups, means in the higher levels of the hierarchy merely that the groups associated with *X*, *Y* and *Z* form part of the larger group associated with *A*. In describing the structure of the United States of America to a Mae Enga I might say that Uncle Sam is father of California who is father of San Francisco; but this statement would imply neither that my mother's brother founded the United States nor that St Francis of Assisi is his grandson (Barnes 1971 *a*: 8–9). In other words, the kin-like relations postulated between high-level taxa in segmentary hierarchies belong to Schneider's category (4) rather than (3).

But why in these cases are *A*, *X*, *Y* and *Z* all taken to be men rather than women, so that *A* is father and not mother of the others? The organizational arguments about the limited possibilities for polysegmentation in matrilineal systems are irrelevant, for at this level explanations of present-day group dispositions in terms of some historically remote differentiation between brothers and between sisters are equally implausible. We can appeal to Fortes' notion of organic societies, in which 'social organization is governed by the same principles at all levels' (Fortes 1949 *a*: 341; see Gluckman 1963: 73–83), though I would recast this to assert that in these societies social organization is described by the same symbols at all levels. In this case, the Mae Enga organizational plan is written in agnatic symbols at the top because agnatic principles of organization, even if in modified form, are actually at work at the bottom (Barnes 1967 *a*). Fatherhood is certainly not the only kin term that can be used to indicate relations in set theory; in our own culture we speak sometimes of daughter churches and of sister Oxbridge colleges (consisting originally of celibate male dons), while second and third generations of computers seem to be born asexually. In pre-scientific cultures agnatic idioms appear to be more widely used, and as we move up an agnatic pedigree the symbol of fatherhood is switched imperceptibly from referring to the connexion between individual men and their wives' sons to the connexion between taxa in adjacent levels in a segmentary hierarchy. I suggest that this switching occurs partly because of cultural and social parsimony but also because the symbol is largely a cultural construct, unfettered by evidence from nature.

My argument can now be summarized. The relations of nature to fatherhood and motherhood are different. The difference is expressed in the title of this paper: physical motherhood is to physical fatherhood as nature is to culture. Some writers have argued that kinship is based on the cultural and social recognition of physical relations, while others have stressed that kinship, as a social and cultural system, has nothing directly to do with genetic linkages (Beattie 1964 *a*; Levy 1965; Schneider 1965 *b*). I take an intermediate view that will please neither camp (see Gellner 1963; Barnes 1964). I argue that the mother-child relation in nature is plain to see and necessary for individual survival. An infant may be free to form attachments to mother-surrogates, but most scientists would agree that a woman's response to an infant after she has given birth is at least in some degree innate or genetically determined. Hence a relation of physical as well as social motherhood is always recognized culturally and institutionalized socially. On the other hand the evidence for the human father–child relation in nature has been, until the last hundred years in the West, slight and inconclusive. There seems to be no evidence that a man is programmed genetically to act differentially towards an infant merely because he has sired it. The processes, necessary for collective survival, of socialization, economic and political mobilization, transmission of offices, power and resources, have facilitated, though they may perhaps not have determined, the institutionalization of social fatherhood in some form or other. Combined with the institution of marriage, this role of social father has provided a basis for the possible development of ideas about physical fatherhood.

Thus cultural motherhood is a necessary interpretation in moral terms of a natural relation, whereas the relation of genitor is an optional interpretation, in the idiom of nature, of an essentially moral relation. Speaking more generally we may say that there is a real world we call nature which exists independently of whatever social construction of reality we adopt. The relation between nature and culture is contingent; some aspects of nature impinge more obviously and insistently on the human imagination than others. The constraints on the construction we make of fatherhood arise from our social lives as adolescents and adults; our concept of motherhood is more closely constrained by our lives in the womb and as young children while we are still largely creatures of nature.

ACKNOWLEDGEMENT

I am much indebted to Frances Barnes, Les Hiatt, Mervyn Meggitt, David Schneider, W. Ullmann, W. K. Whitten and D. E. C. Yale for suggestions I have used in this paper.

The Long Term and the Short Term: the Economic and Political Significance of the Morality of Kinship

Maurice Bloch

There have been few aspects of Fortes' views on kinship which have been so often criticised as his insistence on the 'morality' of kinship, its 'irreducibility' or its 'prescriptive altruism'. His insistence has been that socialisation, and perhaps also instinct in a very wide sense, means that individuals are willing to forego their political and economic interest for the sake of the good. His critics, Worsley (1950), Leach (1960) and others, have refused to recognise, or have minimised, the notion of morality as having a force of its own and have chosen to see the kind of ethnographic facts referred to by Fortes as a front for 'what it really is all about', that is, the interest of the parties concerned. In this, these writers have adopted the traditional assumption of functionalist arguments that the cause of social facts is the result of the uses to which they are put. However, if we chose to abandon such a teleological position which confuses effect with cause (see Jarvie 1965) then the two sides of the polemic stop joining. For if motive and effect are not identical, there is no problem in seeing 'morality' as an essential aspect of the actor's motive while the effect is entirely other, an observation of the scientist whose value depends on his methods of observation and his categories of measurement which when dealing with such facts as the distribution of goods and services is not likely to include 'morality'. We then realise that we are faced with a different – and to my mind much more interesting, question: what are the effects of 'morality' on economic and political organisation? A question we can ask without having to doubt the existence of an independence of morality in the motivation of the actor which sound ethnography illustrates again and again. The problem becomes therefore how is the economy, how is the political system, affected by the fact of the moral character of certain links between individuals, which are due to socialisation and indeed perhaps instinct? However, to put the question like this and to examine certain examples, a common technique of analysis of much recent British anthropology must be avoided. This has been labelled following writers in other disciplines 'transactional analysis' or 'game theories', meaning by this a metaphorical comparison of games and society (Bailey 1969: 1 ff.) or certain logico-mathematical procedures which assume such a comparison. In fact the perspective stressed in such writings is the functional one in a rather extreme form[1] which were the basis of Leach's and Worsley's criticism of the explanatory value of

75

'morality'. Analysing situations as though they were the result of a 'game' played by individuals seeking to maximise their satisfaction assumes that the observed advantage gained by an individual is his motive but it is precisely by distinguishing the motive for the actor and the effect of the action (as recorded by the observer) that I propose to proceed. This will not allow such a simplification of reality which is no doubt the virtue of game theory.

There are many other difficulties in the use of game theory or similar 'formal functionalist' frameworks but they seem to have been little discussed directly in anthropology. In economics, by contrast, where such analyses were first introduced in the social sciences, similar models working on the assumption that the economy can be understood as the interplay of individuals maximising their gain have been repeatedly criticised, and although many of the criticisms would apply to the cognate anthropological formulation, very few of these have been carried over. For example, the distinction I am stressing above between the motives of action and the potentially totally different effects of action is at the basis of the distinction between macro and micro economics. Even more relevant here is the criticism that such a theory collapses the time scale either to a state where all actions begin and end simultaneously or all end in a very remote but identical long-term (Robinson 1971: 32ff.). Actions in real life have a variety of time scales and it is this variety of term existing concurrently which is the basis of social and economic life.

It is in this perspective that I want to show the economic and political implications of 'moral' social relationships of which kinship is a prime example. Such implications independent of the motives of the actors would inevitably be excluded from analysis by the way some social anthropologists have fused motive with effect. Fortes' 'functionalism' would lead us to expect that he too would collapse time but in fact his, possibly inconsistent, stress on morality avoids this. Fortes stresses as the essence of kinship morality 'sharing' without 'reckoning' (Fortes 1969: 238). He contrasts this relationship with debt repayment within a specified time. These notions, Fortes stresses and most anthropologists would confirm, are extremely common, but it is worth considering what they imply. Sahlins (1965: 147 ff.) has called the relationship which follows from such relationships 'generalised reciprocity'. It is clear that an implied aspect of this is that balance is not sought in the short term because the relationship is assumed to endure – in Fortes' terms it is 'unconditional'. In fact of course it is reasonable to assume that in the very long term and on average the exchanges will be balanced but this is an observer's conclusion. The actor sees himself as forced into imbalanced relationships by morality. We therefore can conclude that the crucial effect of morality is long term reciprocity and that the long term effect is achieved because it is not reciprocity which is the motive but morality. The link up of morality and long term relationships with delayed reciprocity, that is with relationships with great tolerance of imbalance, is not new in anthropology. It was made by both Malinowski and Mauss who stressed how immediate reciprocity is tantamount to the denial of any moral relationship between the parties while delay between gift and counter gift is an indication of the moral character of the relationship. The fact that morality carries the inevitable corollary of 'long-term' means two things. First that we can, however imprecisely, estimate the amount of morality in a relationship by observing its degree of tolerance of imbalance in the reciprocal aspects of the relationship.[2] The greater the degree of tolerance, the more the morality. Secondly, the correlation allows us to rank different relationships in the light of their relative term. Thus we commonly find that relationships classed by the actor as political, neighbourhood, or friendship have shorter term than those classed as kinship and thus are less moral. Thirdly the correlation enables us to see how the effect of the combination of different relationships of different morality explain social life. This will be the subject matter of the second part of this paper.

If it is in following Fortes and stressing the significance of 'moral' relationships and their irreducibility to perceived economic or political reward that this paper will proceed, I am not in such complete agreement with him that there are not certain qualifications which are necessary to make here. First, for Fortes the moral character of kinship is unique and marks off kinship relations from all others. By contrast I am quite prepared to believe that in some societies other types of relationships seem to have equal if not more 'moral' commitment than kinship. When I stress the significance of the morality of kinship for political and economic organisation it is because kinship is, very often, the best type of long-term moral relationship. I would not prejudge the issue whether it is the moral relationship *par excellence* although I am prepared to accept that this might indeed be so. The second point which should be stressed is that even if kinship is the most 'moral' social relationship there are many types of kinship some implying shorter term commitment, some longer term commitment. Fortes' own distinction for the Tallensi between descent ties and ties of affinity is an example. Finally, the third qualification follows from the other two. If the effect of morality is the existence of long term commitments then there is no sharp break between kinship and other commitments but rather we should regard kinship as the end of a continuum consisting of commitments of different terms.

The range of situations in which the significance of the variety of terms of co-existing social relations can be observed, could be drawn from many types of fields. However, by way of example I want to consider the topic of agricultural cooperation which has recently again received attention after the early exemplary studies by Malinowski (1935), Firth (1939) and Richards (1939).

77

Like the Tallensi, the Merina of Madagascar express the obligation between kinsmen as binding, unconditional and without term. They are even more explicit when considering the possibility of people not following the moral dictates implied by kinship: to fail in kinship obligation is to be a witch, *mpamosavy* (Bloch 1971 *b*: 67), in other words to be the opposite of a moral being: a murderer, a bestialist, a lover of death, etc... This is why one must help and assist one's kinsman and one can expect help and assistance from one's kinsman. I assume with Fortes that since informants tell me that this tenet is a powerful force at the back of their actions it is so. This assumption I make because I have no evidence or information that contradicts informants' statements on this subject and it should be a principle of anthropological analysis that people's statements concerning the motive of their actions should be accepted unless reasonable evidence can be produced to justify its being set aside. Furthermore, very many acts of cooperation and help between kinsmen which were to the disadvantage of the helper occur continually, as indeed has been reported for many societies. Because of this mutual obligation kinsmen are the ideal people with whom to cooperate; indeed because the Merina traditionally have no intermediate categories of people between kinsmen and strangers like 'affines' or 'neighbour' they assume that cooperation between non-kinsmen will be of the 'negative reciprocity' type (Sahlins 1965: 148). This notion of kinship was given to me as the explanation why small Merina kinship groups who had moved to areas where the rest of the population were not their kinsmen formed ties of artificial kinship in order to have some reliable cooperators. These ties were created between neighbours who were not genealogical kinsmen (Bloch 1971 *b*: 99) but who ostensibly behaved towards each other as kinsmen. The relationship was however full of ambiguity since these people were felt not to be real kinsmen and although more reliable than strangers not in the end as reliable as real kinsmen. How did this different evaluation between 'real' and 'artificial' kinsmen affect agricultural cooperation? To obtain the answer to this I turned to the analysis of the composition of twenty-four labour teams in a Merina *canton*[3] on which I had sufficient information to know what relationship existed between all the members of the team and the convener. The result of this turned out to be quite unexpected. I had presumed that it followed from what I had been told about the ideal cooperativeness of kinsmen and the lesser reliability of artificial kinsmen that when an individual called a team together he would first call on all suitable real kinsmen and if this was not enough he would make up the number with 'artificial' kinsmen. This was not at all the case. The cooperation teams, although normally containing a few real kinsmen, always included more artificial kinsmen than was necessary, while potential members of the team who were real kinsmen seemed to have been passed over. Two other features were less unexpected but noteworthy. The teams called by an individual in a sequence tended to vary continuously within one agricultural year. In other words there was no question of one individual always calling on the same people again and again. Finally although a clear pattern of exchange of work days existed between people who were artificial kinsmen (although this was denied) the tolerance of imbalance in the work exchange system between real kinsmen was so great that with my very limited data no clear pattern emerged.

On realising the peculiarity of the fact that 'artificial' kinsmen were called upon before 'real' kinsmen I confronted my informants with this fact and pointed out its inconsistency with their complaints about the lack of sufficient kinsmen around them to ensure good agricultural labour teams. Their answer was most revealing. They needed lots of people on whom they could call for agricultural work. 'Real' kinsmen would always come, they said, 'artificial' kinsmen would only come if one kept up the typical kinship behaviour of repeated requests for help. If one did not do so these 'artificial' kinsmen would lapse. In other words the Merina farmer needed agricultural cooperators for two purposes: to help him complete work now but also so that in the future he would have a sufficient pool of potential cooperators to draw on when other perhaps unexpected tasks came up. His concern was to establish this much larger potential pool. The reason why such a pool needed to be much larger than the numbers required in normal cooperative tasks requires little imagination for someone acquainted with peasant life. First of all agriculture itself is a notoriously unpredictable activity requiring different size labour teams from year to year as a result of the ecological variations which affect the crops. Secondly, people, too, are a very uncertain asset, they die, grow old, fall ill, quarrel and so on. The farmer therefore has the problem of all small scale producers. He must have too much in order always to have enough. Artificial kinship gives no guarantee of future cooperation, it cannot be maintained if it is not used and offers a set of social relationships no doubt well adapted to the needs of the particular time but in a sense too well adapted so that it does not provide a store necessary for future times. The value of real kinship by contrast with artificial kinship lies in the fact that the motives of individuals in cooperative activities go beyond the economic uses to which they are put at any particular time and it is this which gives them their economic significance. Such relationships provide potential cooperation continuing through the vicissitudes of time. It is the knowledge of this effect of the morality of kinship which governs the planning of labour teams. For long-term planning, only social relationships which are reliable in the long term can be used and this reliability comes from morality. Furthermore it is this reliability which assures a kind of safety net for the Merina peasant and also gives him the possibility of playing a maximising game in the short term with impunity, transacting for his own interest with artificial kinship. In other words it is the presence of moral cooperators which enables a man to afford to concentrate on manipulating short term links.

It is with the light thrown by this Merina example that we can examine two other well-documented studies of agricultural cooperation, one furnished by P. H. Gulliver for the Ndendeuli of East Africa (Gulliver 1971), the other by E. R. Leach for a Ceylonese village – Pul Eliya (Leach 1960).

The Ndendeuli of Tanzania were studied by Gulliver mainly in 1953. They are shifting cultivators with a cognatic kinship system. Like the Merina, the Ndendeuli associate agricultural cooperation with kinship and express the relationship in moral terms. The Ndendeuli see the statement 'you must help a man because he is your kinsman' as having the same constraining quality as 'you must cultivate because you need food to live' (Gulliver 1971: 217). However, recognition of kinship is not enough to determine who will join together for agricultural work. Gulliver shows how a given local community implies a complex pattern of interpersonal reciprocity, the intimate interconnection of which curtails greatly the timing and composition of actual work parties and hinders the insertion of new people into the network of cooperation. This is most tellingly demonstrated and of course in no way affects the independent existence of a moral commitment. Some aspects are extremely reminiscent of the Merina situation. Although the Ndendeuli kinship system does not produce a sharp break between kinsmen and non-kinsmen, Gulliver distinguishes two categories of potential cooperators: kinsmen, and kinsmen of kinsmen. The former are thought the most reliable cooperators. Although reciprocity is of the essence in both cases, it is openly calculated for kinsmen of kinsmen. This is not so for kinsmen, and temporary imbalance in the exchange relationship is tolerated. This must mean that the exchange relationship is longer term as we would have expected as a result of the moral commitment. Furthermore, Gulliver remarks that the actual composition of the cooperative team seems unexpectedly to show more 'kinsmen of kinsmen' than might have been expected.

Gulliver says that 'this was partly because a man desired to develop relations with other neighbours, relations that would be useful in other situations'. This must imply a pattern like that of the Merina where relationships with kinsmen could continue without being used and so the possibility of increasing the total number of relationships was open by maintaining relationships with kinsmen of kinsmen by continual exchange. The Ndendeuli seem to realise the effect for long-term planning of the long term i.e. moral character of kinship. When faced by request for cooperation from different people on the same day the behaviour of Ndendeuli seems to show the same concern. What the individuals concerned try to achieve in all cases seems to be to fulfil both obligations somehow. Quite clearly if the concern was economic interest here and now it would most often be expedient to use such occasions to break off unwanted ties.

Gulliver himself, however, appears to come close to negating the independence of the morality of kinship and to reduce it to the uses to which it is put. He stresses the selective recognition of who is and who is not a kinsman. If relatives cooperate regularly they will stress their kinship, if not they will ignore or forget it, and when individuals cooperate regularly they will search for and reinforce kinship links. However, as Gulliver admits, this is only true for kinsmen on the periphery of recognition which is anyway always blurred with such a system. More significantly Gulliver concludes that since there is little symbolic elaboration of the concept of kinship the Ndendeuli idea of kinship is really reciprocity. This is clearly right but it is also only one element. Reciprocity, as we have seen, exists with people who do not thereby automatically become kinsmen. It is a special kind of reciprocity whose characteristics derive from the categorical moral nature of the dogma. What the Ndendeuli material shows is how this morality, because it transgresses the reciprocity and exchanges balanced in the short term makes it possible for the farmer continually to adapt to the fluid situation of potential labour requirements and varying available personnel which, although an aspect of all types of agriculture, is particularly marked in shifting agriculture. Here again we find several points which revealingly parallel the Merina situation. First there is a need of a much greater pool of potential cooperators than those who need to be called on at any particular instance. Secondly we have the way in which the Ndendeuli uses the potential of long-term relationships, that is, moral kinship ones, to ensure the existence of this pool by using them to keep up the periphery while the central core can be supplied by more instrumental short-term relationships maintained by short-term balanced exchange.

The organisation of labour in Pul Eliya (Leach 1961) and its relations to kinship is more difficult to interpret as it is not given in the same detail supplied by Gulliver. It is however particularly interesting as the whole book where it is dedicated to the denial of the sociological significance of kinship as a force in itself. The argument concentrates on the ownership of irrigated land as this is clearly the most scarce asset. However, even here production also needs labour and this must be organised. It seems that generally where land and capital is scarce we tend to find kinship systems such as that of the Kandyan Ceylonese well adapted to keeping outsiders out of a strictly defined group, but *within* this group the pattern is more like those agricultural systems where labour is the prime concern such as the Ndendeuli and where kinship minimises strict boundaries and establishes lines of potential linkage in a great many directions.

In Pul Eliya, within the exclusive group, the *variga*, we find an egocentred category, the *pavula*, which forms the basis of cooperation within the village.

Of course, cooperation in Pul Eliya is, as in the two earlier examples, not limited to the formation of labour teams but this is the only documented type of *variga* cooperation described. The *pavula* is ideally defined genealogically but Leach stresses that this does not correspond to the 'effective' *pavula*. It is in keeping with the general argument of the book that Leach should stress the 'reality' of the 'effective' *pavula* as against the 'ideal' *pavula*. Are we to deduce that the genealogical model is a 'way of talking' about cooperation? Leach is much less sanguine on this matter than he is in his analysis concerning land and kinship but the question arises whether, in this context too, kinship has any 'reality' at all. Have the moral obligations also reported for the Ceylonese to be left unexamined? Leach in fact avoids the question by his distinction between the 'ideal' and the 'effective' *pavula* and leaving the matter at that. By contrast the actors use the same word for both and presumably do not distinguish between the two any more than they do between the *variga* and the body of landowners. Is this to hide from visiting anthropologists what is really going on? I would suggest here again that it is because of the morality of kinship that flexibility in the 'effective' *pavula* is able to be maintained or in other words it is because the *pavula* is first of all a kinship grouping that it achieves its economic job not for the convening of one cooperative team but the ranges of economic teams that an individual and perhaps his descendants will need in the future. The 'effective' *pavula* would then be the *pavula* at a particular time and the 'ideal' *pavula* would be the *pavula* over a period of time, 'reality' in this case being the result of the anthropologist's lack of a time perspective.

This, however, is not enough to explain the specific nature of cooperation in Pul Eliya, for one of the most significant points made by Leach is that cooperation is typically between affines, brothers-in-law and cross-cousins rather than between brothers and parents and children. The reasons that Leach gives for this fact are two. First that relationships between brothers are always hierarchical as the system lays great emphasis on seniority. On the other hand relations between cross-cousins and brothers-in-law are relationships of equality and therefore more suited to equal exchange. The second is that rivalry is inherent in the relationship between holder and heir and also between co-heirs. These explanations are however full of difficulties. It seems to me that the relationship between brothers-in-law, in the Ceylonese system, is in no sense one of equality. Indeed much of the evidence given by Leach in the book and also by Yalman (1970) suggests clearly there is inequality of the parties to a marriage. This inequality is rendered worse by the ambiguity of the position of women in relation to land to which in theory they have an equal right but which normally (in the case of *diga* marriages) they will be unable to enjoy. In a way the inequality of age between brothers is replaced by the inequality of sex in the link between brothers-in-law. The fact that women as well as men should inherit means that the household of brothers and sisters are also co-heirs with at least the same reason for competition as the households of brothers. There is however another factor which Leach seems to overlook in his explanation. Most of the book is devoted to showing the close interdependence of co-villagers relying on a system of tank irrigation where each farmer is totally at the mercy of the unselfish use of water by his neighbours. This extra-ordinary but essential forbearance it could be argued is only possible because of the moral character of the relationship between co-villagers and especially neighbours, who are as a result of the inheritance and marriage system liable to be most often classifiable either as brothers or else as father and child. In other words the most extreme form of altruistic co-operation is typical of kinsmen. This seems to negate the contention that it is because brothers are in competition that they cannot cooperate. I would not deny that they have severe conflicts of interests (as have brothers-in-law and cross-cousins) but that the morality of kinship enables them to carry out the necessary agricultural task.

By contrast the much less critical labour cooperation for such tasks as threshing can be left to less moral (that is shorter term) relationships existing between affines as well as between other types of relationship. We see here, as in the other examples, that individuals possess a range of relationships of different terms which they use for different types of social action. The contrast here is between affines and agnates while for the Merina (and to a certain extent for the Ndendeuli) it was between kinsmen and non-kinsmen.

What the above examples show firstly is that peasants relying on others for labour are as much concerned with the bringing together of an agricultural team here and now as to maintain a wide range of relationships for meeting future, but as yet unknown, needs of this nature, and that this can be achieved only because of the existence of moral relationships. Secondly that relationships with different types of cooperators are maintained side by side and these different types of cooperators have relationships to ego of different terms. This is sociologically significant because the long term relationships have a great tolerance of imbalance in the exchanges between individuals, while the shorter term, less moral, relationships only tolerate shorter term imbalance.[4] In order to maintain a larger pool of cooperators than an individual is using here and now, he must both continually be calling upon and be called upon by cooperators with a less moral relationship, because this is the only way these relationships can be maintained. In the three examples we have looked at these were artificial kinsmen, kinsmen of kinsmen and affines, and also rely on morally-charged relationships which can exist while not being used. In other words it is morality which gives the system of labour recruitment continuing adaptability, a task which we may note is partially performed in industrialised society by a labour exchange.[5]

By implication the corollary of the argument about the effects of moral relationships explains the effects of less moral, more instrumental relationships and the use to which they can be put to by the peasant planner. It follows that if the effect of morality is that an individual maintains many relationships which need not be used in the short-term, moral relationships are in the short run expensive. On the other hand because non-moral relationships are shorter term they can be discarded easily when of no use and they enable the individual to choose freely among potential cooperators according to consideration of personal advantage. In this way the less 'moral' relationships are cheaper. Because of this the long-term planning of the peoples in the three examples we have considered displays not only the significance of the use of moral ties but also a concern to balance short-term economy with long-term security, hence the different but parallel use of more moral and less moral relationships.

In the preceding section I have outlined the economic significance of morality for labour recruitment but the same sort of point can be made in relation to other aspects of social life. I want briefly to suggest a few of these here. Firstly we can consider a famous anthropological problem, the relationship of descent and locality among the Nuer. A continual worry to students is why Evans-Pritchard concentrates to such an extent on lineages in his consideration of the Nuer political system while it seems that locality is so much more often the organising factor of local level politics and of the feud. Indeed Evans-Pritchard sometimes leads the reader to consider the lineage system as almost an aesthetic frill to the political situation. The only jarring element is again the fact that total moral commitment, so illuminatingly emphasised by Fortes, is to lineages rather than to locality. It seems to me that another look at the environment and the political process of Nuer society in the middle term supplies the answer to our difficulty. The force which leads to the lack of fit between local structure and lineage structure is clearly shown by Evans-Pritchard as being due to the needs of cattle and the changing seasons. If this was the only consideration for group formation, locality would be governed entirely by non-social factors. The environmental requirements of cattle explain why individuals move away from their home locality to attach themselves to non-lineage kin or affines in other localities. This is the process which results in the state of affairs we see in the localities examined by Evans-Pritchard. There is however another factor. By Nuer standards, the time when Evans-Pritchard did his study was one of extraordinary peace. I would suggest that things would be different in times of hostility and that as feuds develop and intensify the lineages regroup as individuals choose the assurance of stronger, more certain, moral links. Indeed we can imagine Nuer society through time as governed by two opposing forces. One, constant, is the force of the environment leading to population movements which take no account of descent and therefore lead to lineage dispersal. The other force, a fluctuating one, is fighting, and this leads to the regrouping of lineages. In periods of great instability the lineages would therefore regroup; as peace returns and therefore the requirements of the environment become dominant the lineages disperse. Furthermore another point follows from this. The dispersal which enables the Nuer to exploit more efficiently their environment is only possible because of the stronger moral, i.e. long-term content of lineage membership. If we imagine an individual choosing to leave his lineage territory to attach himself to another, that of his brother-in-law, for example, he will be only willing to do this if the link with his lineage members will outlast the break in residence, or in other words will tolerate a longer time to elapse between gift and counter gift than the short term exchanges implied in co-residence. If his lineage relationship could not outlast this break then it would obviously be impossible ever to move in such a warring society since the risk of breaking off existing relationships for the uncertain possibility of establishing new ones would be too great. It is only because one can fall back on moral ties that the risk of trying new ones can be taken. Here again we can say quite categorically that morality is adaptive where maximisation would not be.

Having talked of locality we imperceptibly move to politics and here the significance of morality for understanding the political process seems to me perhaps the most important of all. The recent history of the Merina can serve as an example again. Merina history since the eighteenth century seems almost to consist of two distinct themes. On the one hand there is the history of the Merina kingdoms and the Malagasy state with its administrative structure. The kingdoms appear and disappear, segment and conquer each other at a bewildering rate until the time of the French colonisation in 1895. Ever since then the changes in administrative policy of first the French and then the Malagasy state have meant little more permanence in the political units. On the other hand, there is the history of the Merina descent groups; the demes (Bloch 1971 *b*: 41 ff.). These divide up the descendants of the free Merina and their history is one of very great stability. These groups persisted through the whole period of dramatic political upheaval and still survive today. This apparent contradiction has led writers to write of the two quite separately or to ignore one or the other. However, the building blocks of the kingdoms and to a certain extent of the administrative units were the demes and their territories. Each new kingdom regrouped them, re-ranked them for its own purposes but the demes were only partially transformed because by the time of their integration the political units themselves had changed. It is this dialectic which is the key to Merina history but it is itself the result of the different moral commitment of kinship versus political ties because of their different time commitments. This is also the case from the individual point of view. Although the actor may gain by the manipulation of short-term ties that is playing in the power game of politics, he will only invest a limited amount of his resources in these profitable activities because of moral claims upon him resulting from deme membership. These claims however will assure the ability of the individual to carry on through to the next political state, an essential requirement in such an unstable situation.

The light thrown on the historical process at the local level at least, by the realisation that we are dealing with the effect of concurrently held allegiances of different terms is clearly not unique to the Merina. Abner Cohen's study of Arab border villages in Israel stresses the way in which less specific long-term moral allegiance transcended changing political circumstances and how because they transcend these in time they mould the response of the actors to these circumstances. He describes how after the shallow Arab lineage, the *hamulla*, had lost the functions it had in the period of Turkish rule and during the period of the British protectorate, it gained renewed importance under Israeli rule when put to new ends. The survival of the *hamulla* during British rule is therefore not capable of being understood in terms of the use to which it is put but only in terms of the moral strength of the notion of descent, which, because of the long-term nature of the relationships implied, survived to mould the response to new short term problems. Again it is the coexistence of relationships with different terms which reveals the process of history.

The first conclusion I want to stress here is that Fortes' method which refuses to set aside in any way data from informants whether it be linguistic or otherwise should always be our first guide. If informants stress the morality of kinship then *this* is what we must understand. A method which minimises such data by dismissing it as 'dogma', as 'unreal', or a theory like game theory which has no room for it or like the type of functionalism which assumes that form is a direct epiphenomena of use, these methods or theories will mislead since they are not 'struggling' with what is perceived.

The second conclusion is equally straightforward. I have tried to show that it is only because of the fact that to the actors kinship is moral, that is non-specific and long-term, that it produces an adaptability potential to long term social change. If more rational ties were used, i.e. ties which are the fruit of a process of maximisation, they would be more efficient in the short term but more costly in the middle and long term. This position recalls one of the basic principles of the theory of biological evolution. Perfect adaptation to the environment, although obviously advantageous in the short run, may be disastrous in the long run when the environment changes; which it always does. The adaptation was so specific that it could not handle any change. It is one of the striking features of the adaptation of man that he is in most respects a highly generalised animal. Would it be too much to suggest that the selective value of kinship is precisely the combination of the many functions which it can perform without it being reduced either in character or in time to any single one. In other words it is the generality of kinship and the continuity of kinship which is of prime significance and these features are due to its morality.

Notes

1 There is usually a distinction made between those aspects of social life rules (Barth 1966) which are not explained in this way and ones which are. None the less since we are not told how to distinguish in the social world between 'games' and 'rules' and the analyses only consider the former we may ignore this let-out.
2 It is true that there are non-moral long-term arrangements such as some loans but they are not long-term relationships in the sense that I am using the phrase here, in that they are made once and for all and that they need imply no tolerance of imbalance as is well illustrated by the main plot of *The Merchant of Venice*.
3 Ambatomanoina.
4 Immediately balanced reciprocity of course is the denial of any social relationship.
5 In this respect it is worth noting that the above consideration must be taken into account when we want to understand the willingness or otherwise of peasants to use wage labour, and it also draws our attention to the crucial factor of the peasants' expectation of the future reliability or otherwise of the pool of wage labourers.

The Kith and the Kin

Julian Pitt-Rivers

When Meyer Fortes felt the need to find a term to express the peculiar quality of relationships between kin, that which distinguishes them from other sorts of relationship, it appears to me significant that he should have chosen 'amity'. He suggests this word as the succinct rendering of the 'set of normative premises. . .focused upon a general and fundamental axiom which I call the axiom of prescriptive altruism'. He 'ascribes it to the realm of moral values in contraposition to the realm of jural values ordered to the politico-jural domain' though, he adds, 'the actualities of kinship relations and kinship behaviour are compounded of elements derived from both domains' (Fortes 1969: 251).

The word 'amity' scarcely occurs earlier in his work, but it may be assumed that he did not choose it carelessly, for the concept is implicit in his thinking on the subject of kinship long before it appears in print.[2] I do not recall him using it in his lectures on the subject which I attended between 1948 and 1950 and my lecture notes (unsurprisingly perhaps) do not mention the word, but when I encountered it in 1970 I recognised that it was naming an idea with which I was already acquainted from his work. The axiom of prescriptive altruism is called into existence by the initial assumption that everyman, individually or in solidarity with a collectivity with which he identifies himself, seeks his own interest and advancement, be it directly or through the medium of reciprocity, immediate or deferred, direct or by some system of exchange as complex and circuitous as the *kula* of the Trobriand Islanders and their neighbours. (This initial assumption is indeed a necessary condition for the formulation of the notion of reciprocity.) Where reciprocity is lacking it ceases to be true and an explanation of another order is required. This is provided by the counter-principle of 'altruism', prescribed for behaviour between kin.

But why 'amity'? The word is derived from the French word for friendship and it does not appear to contain any sense which is not covered by its Anglo-Saxon synonym. In view of this the choice looks curious, for friendship, far from being commonly regarded as the essence of kinship is usually opposed to it, as indeed it is in the same work by Fortes himself who refers, not only to the testimony of Goody and Malinowski (p. 63), but of the Tallensi (p. 63) and the Ashanti (p. 192) who both possess, we are told, contrasting words for kinship and friendship. The terms appear to be exclusive to one another, not only in the case of the Tallensi and the Ashanti, but also in the view of many scholars (some of whom have even supposed, despite many examples to the contrary, including the 'bond-friends' of Tikopia (Firth, 1967), that the concept of friendship is an invention of soi-disant 'civilised society' which has abandoned kinship as an organising principle). It appears, then, that Fortes has chosen to define the essence of kinship by appealing to the very concept of what it is not. To some 'kinship scholars' this may look like selling the pass, but I shall argue that it offers the possibility of placing the notion of kinship in a wider framework and of escaping from the polemics concerning its relationship to physical reproduction. Indeed the necessity to do just this is evident when we approach the most perplexing kinship system in the annals of anthropology, that of the Eskimo, who appear to attach scant diacritical importance in their designation of their kinsmen to the facts of birth.[3]

Let me adopt what I believe to be, by implication rather than explicitly, Fortes' standpoint (1969: 239–42), and divide social relations first of all into those of amity or the contrary and then divide these (might one say it?) 'amiable' relations into kin and non-kin; it then becomes apparent that, despite the common opposition of the terms kinship and friendship, there is room for variants partaking in the properties of both, between the pole of kinship, inflexible, involuntary, immutable, established by birth and subject to the pressures of 'the politico-jural domain' (in Fortes' words) and the pole of friendship, pure and simple, which is its contrary in each of these ways. All these 'amiable' relations imply a moral obligation to feel – or at least to feign – sentiments which commit the individual to actions of altruism, to generosity. The moral obligation is to forego self-interest in favour of another, to sacrifice oneself *for the sake* of someone else.

A system of thought that takes the individual as its starting-point and assumes that he is motivated by self-interest, faces a difficulty in confronting the examples of behaviour that is not so motivated and this difficulty has given rise in western literature to theories of altruism, moral, religious and psychological. We need not here go into them, for the majority of the world's cultures do *not* share the individualism of the modern West and have no need to explain what appears to them evident: that the self is not the individual self alone, but includes, according to circumstances, those with whom the self is conceived as solidary, in the first place, his kin. *Alter* then means not 'all other individuals' but 'all who are opposed to self, the non-amiable'. We have been told that in many simple societies relations with all who are not kin are necessarily hostile. Whether we are right to believe this or not, there is no lack of examples, from equally simple societies, or institutions which create 'artificial' ties of kinship on the basis of mutual agreement rather than of birth.[4] Thus, if Fortes would make kinship a category of amity, we must also observe, with him, that non-kin amity loves to masquerade as kinship. This leads us to the question: when is kinship artificial and when is it 'true kinship'? The criterion of birth is hardly adequate everywhere, even for defining the relationship between mother and child as Smith's study of Carriacou[5] or the Eskimo, cited above, showed. From this also stems the difficulty of distinguishing analytically between the various forms of ritualised friendship and even non-ritualised friendship. The distinction between blood-brotherhood and spiritual kinship or bond-friendship depends, if not simply on the whim of the ethnographer in his choice of terms, on the particular substance or technique employed in the rite initiating a pseudo-kin relationship. But given the various connotations of blood in different cultures this criterion is clearly inappropriate for setting up a general category of institutions. How many forms of what has been called 'blood-brotherhood' employ *both* the concepts of 'blood' and 'brotherhood'?

Though kinship, the extension of self, cannot be reduced simply to the ties established through birth and marriage, nevertheless physical reproduction furnishes everywhere the model of such extensions, for if birth is not a sufficient criterion of filial status in all societies, at least there are none in which it is not the primordial mode of ascribing it. It is also the mode of linkage between kinsmen whichever links may be recognised. This is equally so in the case of affinity which looks to relations of co-filiation in the future, even where they do not yet exist, and even where this hope is not in fact rewarded, it is nonetheless by virtue of the hypothetical child of the marriage that affinal relationships *are* what they *are* within the structure of kinship. Moreover even though affines are by definition allied through marriage, if the marriage is sterile their relationship does not become fully effective, for their mutual roles hinge upon their relations to the offspring. My brother-in-law is above all my child's mother's brother or my sister's child's father in any society. For this reason a sterile marriage, though it may figure in genealogies, is never considered in a kinship diagram. 'The full significance of marriage alliance lies in the kinship it creates.' This remains true even though the act of sexual union is in itself a means of establishing ritual alliance, as we can see in the customs of sexual hospitality, wife exchange, or temple prostitution. Brothers-in-law who do not stand as father and mother's brother to the same child, the two families who have married their children but have no grandchildren, are allied, but one is tempted to say ritually rather than structurally, for they will never become consanguineal kin of the same person. Their relationship remains frozen at the point of departure, unproductive and immobile like the ties of ritual kinship.

The distinction between natural systems conceived by the scientist and systems of thought devised in different cultures to explain the world of experience must always be made from the start and the latter, not the former, is where the principles of kinship are to be found, but if our explanation of them is to have general validity they must be common to all cultures. Children are everywhere thought to be *of the same substance* as their parents because they are produced by them; 'like breeds like' in every system of thought. How it does so varies greatly, for the necessary conditions for physical reproduction may be interpreted in many ways. Sometimes the blood is thought to be transmitted from parents to children as in our own culture. Elsewhere other bodily substances may be passed on. In lineally organised societies one may find that a different substance is thought to be acquired from either father or mother. Nonetheless this principle of the likeness of those connected biologically provides always the most impelling manifestations of what I should like to call *consubstantiality*, the prime nexus between individuals for the extension of self. This is what kinship is 'made of' however the selective principles of the kinship system in question may order the classification of those who are connected in this way.

Louis Dumont (1971: 37) has opposed 'a logic of substance' to 'a structural logic for which each relationship is what it *is* by virtue of its place in an *ensemble*'. The stress laid on the notion of substance in the concept I have devised to account for amity should not mislead the reader into thinking that my argument belongs to the former rather than the latter. The 'substance' on which consubstantiality is founded is the *notion* of substance only, a notion as far divorced from the physical scientist's concept as that of Christian consubstantiality. Indeed the consubstantial in religious thought is but one manifestation of the universal notion that possession of a common substance is the basis of a mystical bond. The very different doctrine of consubstantiation is another demonstration of the same principle.

Amity derives in the first place then from consubstantiality either through birth or through fostering: the ingestion of the mother's milk. The strongest emphasis is given to fostermotherhood in the thought of the Eskimos where it is equated with birth as the pretext for the maternal bond, but the same notion is surely present, if in a weaker form, in those societies where fostering, though not equated with full motherhood, nevertheless creates between foster children a prohibition of incest. The Koran provides the best known example[6] but we can also point to the pervasiveness of the idea in the custom of sanctuary by which an enemy can render himself immune by touching the breast of his aggressor's mother.[7]

Consubstantiality can also be established by the act of love. The idea is most explicit in Christian marriage which makes the spouses 'of one flesh'. Conversely an unconsummated marriage is not a marriage in the eyes of the Catholic Church and the Albigensian heretics who maintained the contrary gave their supposed founders, the Bulgarians, a bad name which is with us to this day. Moreover not only the mother's husband but in many kinship systems her illicit lover is consubstantial with her and the child is recognised as the product of their consubstantiality. Thus the status of genitor may be recognised by people who entertain quite different notions of begetting (cf. Fortes, 1970: 96–7). By this principle a Trobriand father is con-substantial with his progeny via his union with its mother regardless of whatever theory of generation the anthropologists manage to attribute to that much-glossed people. Consubstantiality within the nuclear family is thus seen to be in no way dependent upon a 'correct' theory of procreation. A curious example from our own culture might be cited to demonstrate the profound roots of the idea: it is often believed in the sporting world that a thoroughbred mare will be spoilt for ever for breeding purposes if she is first mounted by an ill-bred stallion. Her subsequent foals will all bear the mark of this first unworthy consubstantiality. In the same spirit I am told that the Kennel Club used to refuse to register litters of a pure-bred bitch subsequent to a mongrel litter. A more mystical idea could scarcely enter the heads of persons concerned practically with breeding. Is it exaggerated to suggest that they have projected on to those animals which they so eagerly assimilate to the human kind the basic premise of all kinship systems? The same principle of consubstantiality through sexual union can also be in-voked to explain the prohibition of incest in relation to a woman with whom a man's brother has had sexual relations in certain North American tribes, or, vice versa, the establishment of ritual kinship through wife exchange among the Eskimos, as also among the Chamars; among the Plains Indians, the use of the term 'brother' between two men who have had intercourse with the same woman bears the same sense. In the first case the man's paramour has become kin (and therefore inaccessible) to his brother; in the second, two men who were not previously related become pseudo-brothers through the same channel.

The initial tie of kinship can be modified[8] or reproduced by acts of individual will. Consubstantiality can be established by other ways than by breeding as the example of blood brotherhood shows. The tie of amity can be formalised even without any demonstration of consubstantiality, but by a mystical analogy with parenthood, as in the *compadrazgo*. In brief, the reproduction of the tie of kinship appears to follow either the principle of consubstantiality or that of simulation. In the first instance the principle of consubstantiality can be invoked to explain all those forms of blood-brotherhood, using the term in a loose sense, which are established through a rite involving direct exchange, as it were: the ingestion of a bodily sub-stance of the future brother. The rite commonly involves mixing the blood of the two participants before swallowing it and often mixing it with another liquid. But this is not the only way in which such rites can function, for we also find the same bond established, indirectly as it were, through the ingestion together of a sacramental substance, solid or liquid, without any *exchange* of bodily substance. Thus blood, saliva, semen, milk, meat, fruit, vegetables or beer can make consubstantial those who are related through no womb, vagina or breast. Moreover this same principle is to be found in relationships in which the ritual aspects is not explicit; the exchange of food through commensality is a means of sealing friendship in many more societies than our own and I have pointed elsewhere to its importance as a rite in the integration of strangers throughout the world.[9] The first social criterion of a common humanity is to be able to eat the same food, but this is no more than the weakest form of a principle which leads, via the rituals of blood-brotherhood, to the commensality involved in sacrifice and to the fellowship of the Holy Ghost. It is the multiplicity of contexts in which the notion of consubstantiality is effective that validates it in preference to more restricted explanations.

The principle of simulation can account for all the other forms of ritual kinship of which the best known is undoubtedly the *compadrazgo* of the Mediterranean and Latin America. Here ritual ties of kinship are established on an *analogy* with the nuclear family, not through consubstantiality but through a spiritual emanation, called in the case of the *compadrazgo*, 'grace' – this concept is fundamental to the institution of baptism from which compadrazgo derives and it is seen in the popular usage of the phrase 'padres de gracia' (grace parents) to refer to the god-parents.

The simulation of the Holy Nuclear Family in the institution of god-parenthood has been very well brought out by Stephen Gudeman (1972). Simulation is also the principle which establishes ritual siblingship in some of the forms of bond-friendship, but the two principles of consubstantiality and simulation are anything but exclusive to one another. Indeed it is significant that the forms of *fictive compadrazgo* often utilise the principle of consubstantiality: in northern coastal Peru it may be established through broaching together a barrel of *chicha* and in Spain there exists a fictive form initiated by the ritual ingestion of a peach with two kernels which is halved between the would-be compadres. Something similar is done in Mexico with a double corncob. The twinship represented by the double fruit is absorbed by the participants. The bond of brotherhood established through delivery by the same midwife – in the case of the Eskimos such a bond even establishes an incest taboo – might be interpreted in accordance with either principle: the midwife can be viewed as surrogate mother or as the person through whose hands the act of birth was accomplished.[10]

Let us examine, then within the realm of amity the analytical distinctions to be made.[11] The people themselves commonly distinguish between 'real' kin and adopted kin; and the distinction is significant, since only the 'real' kin are fully part of the kinship system. It must always be shown whether the adopted kin (and this is never in any way the case with ritual kin) accede through adoption to a status identical with a born kinsman. There are in fact few examples where this *is* the case. More usually the adopted child does *not* sever his kin-ties with his born kin and adopts those of his adopter to a limited degree in supplement to his own. Moreover he does not necessarily become subject to the incest prohibition in relation to his adoptive siblings (though this is sometimes the case with ritual kinsmen). One of the forms of adoption in Japan is practised precisely with the intention of marrying the adopted son to a born daughter. The Eskimo, on the other hand, appear to equate their adoptive kin to real kin in all ways and if this is so one might put it better by saying that, unlike the rest of the world (except perhaps certain corners of New Guinea), they recognise the possibility of changing 'real' kin relations, rather as we, like them, recognise today the possibility of changing marital relations. Elsewhere kin status is established by birth and kin role is expected to be performed by those who have kin status. The Eskimo appear to attach less importance to birth than others and to attach much more to the fact of residence. One can understand that those who spend the winter in a warm womb made of snow, far separated spatially from their less close kinsmen, should be inclined to give priority in their evaluation of kin relationships to the facts of residence in the present over the record of origins in the past, but I would not press an ecological explanation. The evidence appears to me not yet conclusive that genuine kin-status can be acquired other than by birth or by adoption in infancy, though this has been asserted. Nonetheless we can say that in Eskimo society kin-role tends to establish kin-status rather than the contrary. In addition to transposing upon non-kin, through various forms of pseudo-kinship the attitudes idealised in the image of kinship, the Eskimo also make them in certain relationships kin.

Such marginal cases may be difficult to decide, for the extent of the fiction involved in adoption varies greatly. But this does not obliterate the necessity to recognise the distinction between adoptive kin and 'real' kin insofar as it is distinguishable in terms of status and insofar as it is in fact distinguished by the people themselves. Adoption involves a jural fiction which is accompanied by a social fiction to a greater or lesser extent: the rights and obligations of filial status may be acquired by persons not born to the parent in default of a child to fulfil them (or in addition to the children born). The adoption is jural in the first place rather than moral and it involves no special demonstration of consubstantiality nor of mystical bonds. The adopted kinsman is a surrogate, a make-shift kinsman, born not of flesh and blood but of necessity. In all these ways he can be contrasted with the ritual kinsman whose position does not aspire to assimilate him to the literal kin. The ritual kinsman is not a *fictive* kinsman at all but a *figurative* one whose role, far from being identical with the literal kin is, rather, complementary. Thus, once the distinction between kin and pseudo-kin has been made we face a much more significant distinction between jural and non-jural kin. It would be misleading to name them moral kin for this would imply that literal and adoptive kinship have no moral domain and this would expel them from that of 'amiable relations'. Yet it is the

95

very essence of ritual kinship that it is excluded from the jural domain. In this it partakes of the nature of friendship, a relationship founded upon sentiment not upon rights and duties.

To express it in the form of a diagram:

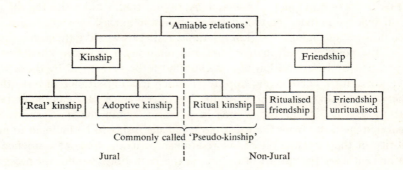

It has not perhaps been sufficiently realised that there is a theoretical antithesis between the notions of jural and moral relations (though Fortes has done much to emphasise it).[12] They have frequently been confused and for good reasons: all those who exercise power claim that they do so in accordance with moral values and even arrogate to themselves the right to dictate what these are. No legislator can afford to admit that he does not speak for the society as a whole and represent its moral consensus, if not the will of its deities, for to do so would expose his authority to question and authority questioned is authority lost. Therefore the tyrant's crowning glory is legitimacy and he uses all his power to attain it, for without the moral charter that it represents he cannot 'sleep o' nights'. Yet the moment one concerns oneself with ethnographic fact rather than political theory the different natures of law and morality become evident. Moral values are seated in the sentiments and conscience of the individual and they cannot be induced by coercion, for free will is their very essence; jural values are derived from institutions which govern relations *between* individuals. Where all are in agreement there is no need for sanctions (without which law is said not to be able to exist). Hence jural sanctions fulfil the function of transposing moral conflicts into the jural domain where they find their resolution at the level of action; they cease to be *moral* once sentiments become subjected to jural concepts of right and obligation, and the moral autonomy of the individual to the judgments of society.

The notion of friendship is founded upon sentiment, but at the same time, the sentiments of the participants must be mutual, for it is a particular-istic relationship, not a general attitude. For this reason, it is said that the friend of everybody has no friend. There must be reciprocity in friendship, for failure to reciprocate in action is a denial of the reciprocity of sentiment, yet this cannot be admitted for fear of the relationship becoming jural. The only sanction in friendship is the withdrawal of sentiment, for to a friend one can have only moral commitments. If friendship is placed upon a jural basis it denies its nature: the altruism which is its foundation is revealed to be false. Lacking the sentiment of amity it is nothing but the exploitation of an implicit right to reciprocity. The paradox of friendship lies in this: though the favours of friends must be free, they must still be reciprocated if the moral status quo is to be maintained. Hence the typology of friendship suggested by Eric Wolf (1966: 10 ff.) which would divide the institution into instrumental and expressive or emotional friendship invites confusion, for it is founded upon the unverifiable motives of the participants, who remain ever in potential doubt as to the exact nature of the sentiments which they inspire.[13] By definition all friendship must be both sentimental in inspiration and instrumental in effects, since there is no other way to demonstrate one's sentiments than through those actions which speak plainer than words. The instrumental aspect validates the affect. This much is true anywhere, though the degree to which the utility of friendship is overtly recognised or its emotional expression is thought proper varies from one culture to another and according to social circumstances; the age and sex of the participants, the number of their friends, the extent of their recognised commitment, their relative status and so forth can all be invoked in explanation of the characteristics of friendship in a given situation, but once a tally of favours is kept the amity has gone out of it and we are left with a tacit contract; the relationship is no longer simply moral but implicitly jural. The injured party can declare what is due to him and can take steps towards its recovery, exercising the sanctions which relate to reputation. But these cannot be used while the moral nature of the relationship is still accepted, for the disillusioned friend who complains that his favours have not been reciprocated destroys his own reputation by implying that he expected they should be, that he gave them only out of calculation in expectation of a return. Friendship often totters on the brink of this admission, but once it is made it cannot be retrieved and the relationship collapses, for it has been revealed that the sentiment is not mutual. For this reason it is precisely in those situations where economic cooperation is effectuated under the guise of friendship that the loudest claims to disinterestedness are heard. In the system of cooperation between neighbouring farmers in the south-west of France great stress is always laid on the absence of any accounting – 'je ne suis pas regardant' – but the helping hand (coup de main) of the neighbour is nonetheless a vital element in the economic system. It is operative above all in times of crisis, hence everyman would like to be in a position of credit with regards his neighbours in that system of dyadic ties that admits no accounting. It can be viewed as an insurance system and it is this which makes reckoning impossible and lays a premium on the value of goodwill. One might even say, pursuing the analogy, that the 'premium' is the reputation for goodwill without which a man is unlikely to receive his neighbours' help. Such a system depends upon an approximate equivalence in economic terms of what each neighbour can put into it and it therefore breaks down with the introduction of new expensive machinery whose economic viability has to be exactly calculated.

There is a second paradox in friendship: moral equality is essential even between unequals, for the only admissible reciprocity is in sentiments. It must be accepted that *my* sentiments are of the same value as *yours* even though I cannot demonstrate them by material equivalence – 'it's the thought that counts'. For this reason economic equivalence must be denied. Yet for this reason also it becomes possible to find a structure of patronage erected upon the ties of friendship between unequals: protection and influence are given in return for service and prestige, and the greater the value of protection the greater the counter-prestation that can be expected in return. Thus the moral basis of the relationship frees it from economic equivalence to the advantage of the patron who gives in return for the labour which he receives only the assurance that his clients will not be victimised by others as powerful as himself. Nor is there anything surprising in the fact that ruling classes, once their position is secure, should attempt to juralise their ties with their clients and invoke legal sanctions to ensure their fidelity. Amity can be dispensed with at that point.

The difficulty inherent in moral relationships is that they depend on the state of the heart which cannot be known for sure, since sentiments can be feigned. How can the fidelity of friends be secured if they cannot be subjected to jural provisions for the reasons given above? Ritual comes into its own at this point, for it confirms social relations in their legitimacy and permanence. Appeals to divine witness, manifest in the oath, seek to shore up by supernatural sanctions that which cannot be entrusted to human justice and the analogy with literal kinship invokes the immutability attaching to consubstantiality by birth. The simulation of kinship in ritual kinship is inspired by this concern: to borrow the qualities attached to 'real' kinship in order to cement a relationship initiated by nothing more than mutual agreement. It is only this which distinguishes the blood-*brother* from the bond *friend*.

There is another point: the permanence of a relationship cannot be assured by contract, for jural reciprocity is terminated by the counter-prestation. Once the material account is wound up each party regains his freedom and if actions speak plainer than words in the present they say nothing about the future. The assurance that cooperation will be maintained in the unforseeable situations to come can only be secured by the permanence of sentiments, the attachments of the heart. Hence if moral contracts are sometimes guaranteed (at the cost of their moral nature) by jural stipulations, we also find that the participants in jural reciprocity are tempted to secure the permanence of their ties by instigating a relationship of amity; once tried the business associates become kith; trading partners ritualise their relationship and go so far in the emulation of kinship as to grant a preferential right to each other's daughters in marriage, even, going further, in another example, to recognise an incest prohibition between their children. Thus the moral and jural domains each look to the other over their antinomy for the security they lack.

Let us look more closely at the notion of reciprocity. I have shown that it is essential to the *practice* of friendship, but at the same time I have accepted Fortes' definition of amity as the axiom of prescriptive altruism, 'sharing without reckoning' (Fortes, 1969: 238). Since autruism might be taken to exclude reciprocity we appear to be headed for a logical contradiction. First of all the reciprocity of amity is of the heart and instrumental reciprocities can be accepted only as manifestations of sentiment and only as long as their potential interpretation as economic transactions is disallowed.[14] But prescriptive altruism implies something more than that material equivalence cannot be admitted. It implies that there must be a genuine desire to give without wanting a return. To resolve the contradiction we must go back to the notion of the gift.

Altruism is founded upon the concept of the unreciprocated gift, the 'free gift'. Gifts may be thought to be free, but they must nevertheless be repaid, for they are transactions which establish a moral relationship between donor and recipient. If they are not returned they change the nature of the relationship, hence Mauss subtitled his essay on that subject 'on the necessity to return presents'. We may well ask then, what is the 'free gift' free of? It would appear that it is free of any jural obligation. It is an act of homage, a demonstration of the state of the heart. Something of the person of the donor accompanies the gift so that all gifts are, over and above their economic value, gifts of self, for they remain morally attached to the giver. Therefore though they are, and must be, conceived as free of obligation they create a relationship of amity which must receive recognition – (the cognate word is used in French for gratitude). The unacknowledged gift, far from honouring the recipient, humiliates the donor. The slang expression 'brush off' puts graphically the refusal to accept the tie of proffered amity.

The gift might be defined then as an act of dispossession of self in favour of a person with whom a relation of amity is desired, i.e. through whom the donor wishes to extend his self. As a moral act it is first of all dispossession on the part of the donor rather than an accretion to the recipient. The use of flowers as gifts in our society makes the point tellingly: the giver may be poorer – he certainly is, these days, if he has to buy them – but the recipient is no richer. But since, excluding this example, this is likely to be the same thing in material terms, an ambiguity creeps in which renders such transactions always liable to misinterpretation. To give to someone in need (because his need is recognised) is not to honour him but to humiliate him because it is implied that he cannot reciprocate. Thus the same gesture can bear two contradictory interpretations as to its moral significance. Gifts of alms to beggars are truly free, but beggars have a special status which places them outside the network of dyadic ties, at the same time execrable and divinely sanctioned (Pitt-Rivers, 1968).

Gifts, then, can either honour or humiliate; the beggar seals his inferior status by accepting on the basis of non-reciprocity, the honoured recipient gives acknowledgement and recognises the moral bond established in this way. But on account of this ambiguity they can also be given as a challenge to reciprocate, for failure to do so entails humiliation, as in the *potlach*, where the interpretation of the initial feast as either an expression of honour or contempt is left to be decided by the response.

The act of dispossession, as Gusdorf (1948) saw, aspires to convert having into being, a material possession into a moral state, and this is the basic mechanism of the gift, as it is of sacrifice. Both aim at the establishment of a moral relationship. The recipient of a gift commits himself by accepting it to proceed to an equivalent act. The reciprocal gifts of friendship therefore pass through a moral converter, as it were, which renders their material aspect contingent. In jural reciprocity the material aspect is primary, the moral relationship is contingent. Accepting this distinction we can see that moral reciprocity is unspecific as to equivalence, time and even in the extreme case the person from whom it is due, while jural reciprocity is the opposite and we can construct a scale ranging from systems of purely jural to purely moral reciprocity. The immediate and direct exchanges of commerce are purely jural; the self is in no way extended through them. They require no more moral input than agreement as to the equivalence of the articles exchanged and the undertaking to abide by the rules. Systems of indirect exchange are necessarily less specific and require a greater degree of trust; social sanctions replace legal sanctions. The time lag between prestation and counter-prestation recedes into the unforeseen future.[15] When we reach undifferentiated exchange even the person who should furnish the reciprocity is unspecified. Trust is no longer a question of confidence in a specific known individual but in the rest of humanity; 'do ut des' becomes 'do as you would be done by', the first moral principle a child learns. It depends on nothing more than the collective acceptance of the same values. The end of the scale is reached when no return gift in any form is envisaged – at any rate this side of Paradise. A good deed is its own reward. Such abstract generosity finds little place in the simple bounded societies studied by most anthropologists but corresponds rather to universalistic religions which proclaim the *brotherhood* of all mankind. Self aspires to a universal extension. With this we find the conception of dispossession of self for its own sake, the renunciation of the world, the annihilation of personal ambition, the end of all jural engagements.

Before we reach this extreme we encounter the principle of kinship amity. The reciprocity is undifferentiated in that it requires that a member of the group shall sacrifice himself for another, that kinsmen shall respect preferential rules of conduct towards one another regardless of their individual interests. Such reciprocity as there is comes from the fact that other kinsmen do likewise. Parents are expected to sacrifice themselves for their children but they also expect that their children will do the same for theirs. The reciprocity alternates down the chain of generations, assuring that the grandparental generation will be repaid in the persons of the grandchildren to whom they are linked by that principle that Radcliffe-Brown first made clear. The system of reciprocity is not closed as in the Kula system, but open towards the future. It is not longer consciously conceived but implicit only, in the operation of a code of behaviour.

If kinship's nature can be defined by the principle of amity it is not free of jural considerations. Rights and duties are distributed differentially to kinsmen because kinship is a system not a network of dyadic ties like friendship. Status within it is ascribed by birth. Siblings occupy an equivalent position within it until they marry, but their children will not have the same consanguineal kin as they or as each other. The progress from generation to generation implies continual differentiation. Rules of succession and inheritance are required to order that which cannot be left to the manifestations of brotherly love. Those who have identical interests at birth have opposed interests by the time they are grandfathers. A revealing assertion echoes through the literature on ritual kinship: 'Blood-brothers are like brothers', it is said, then comes, 'in fact they are closer than real brothers.' The implication is troubling for it would appear that true fraternity is found only between those who are not real brothers. Amity does not everywhere enjoin the same open-ended generosity least of all between kinsmen, who quarrel only too often in contrast to ritual kinsmen who are bound by sacred duty not to do so. But kinsmen quarrel along predictable lines. Amity, the basis of their solidarity in the face of the non-amiable, is laid in abeyance when the non-kin are forgotten and the demands of the social structure reassert themselves. Society imposes its rules, but imposes them, not on individuals as such, but on relationships. The individual is the same person throughout his life but in the course of the developmental cycle his status changes. Rites of passage mark these changes and set the seal of recognition on his changed relationship to others. But individuals are finite in contrast to the continuity of the social unit within which they live and which requires them to replace each other as they grow up, grow old and vanish. Hence one can distinguish between the person in himself, the self as individual, the seat of the sentiments, and the person in society, the 'right-and duty-bearing person', the *social* self. The distinction is clearly marked in the naming system of our own culture: the Christian name identifies the person in himself and distinguishes him from his siblings, the surname identifies him as a member of a social group (family or lineage). Now it is significant that while he gets his surname automatically from his parents, his Christian name is given to him in the ritual of baptism not by his parents but by his godparents. This is the occasion for initiating the ties of ritual kinship which are known as the compadrazgo.[16] Ritual kinship is, in every context here, opposed to real kinship. In its conceptualisation it is sacred rather than profane and in the roles which it creates it is complementary not supplementary to real kinship. Moreover the amity which it imposes is recognised as purer than that which links real kin precisely because it is not prescriptive. 'You can refuse your compadre nothing', it is said, 'all that is yours is his', a statement that is certainly never made about brothers in the Andalusia from which this statement comes. Despite the political uses to which it is put the relationship remains ideally, that is to say, conceptually, a *purely* moral one, untrammelled by the jural domain which regulates the affairs of the social family. It is subject only to individual will and the values of the heart.

It is significant also that it is invoked at the rites of passage of the god-child who is sponsored at each step in his progress towards adulthood by a godparent (in place of a parent) and whose individual destiny is pursued under this patronage. The godparent can be viewed then as the guardian of the individual self in opposition to the social self which is under the protection of the parents. In the Mediterranean, excluding the tribal areas, the nuclear family is the effective unit of kinship and the individual destiny of the child is to found his own nuclear family replacing that of his parents. Hence the godparents are chosen only from outside the nuclear family and are in fact frequently kinsmen. The conflict of interest between parents and children is assuaged by the role of the godparent who is *compadre* (co-parent) to the parents. Thus he is a kind of spiritual affine bound to the parent like a terrestrial affine in common interest and in conflict. Indeed, it is said that *consuegros* (co-parents-in-law) are compadres. But whereas consuegros are bound in earthly rivalry in relation to their common grand-children, the parent and godparent are concerned in different aspects of the same child and differentiated by their responsiblity either material or spiritual: that is to say by their activity or inactivity within the jural domain. For this reason, though consuegros are said to be compadres, the tenor of their relationship is very different. In the tribal society of Serbia studied by Hammel the opposition to the social self must come from outside the range of kinship altogether (Pitt-Rivers, in press) and we therefore find that god-parenthood is vested in a lineage which is unrelated to the parents.

The example might be taken as no more than a peculiarity of traditional Mediterranean culture were it not in so many ways reminiscent of the institutions of ritual kinship in other parts of the world. In all the contexts in which the individual destiny of the person is at stake one is liable to find the ritual kinsman in a leading role: birth, initiation and death. This is not to deny the importance of kin on such occasions but the sense of their participation is different. We have seen that the midwife is often considered as a kind of ritual kinswoman and in mortuary ceremonies the blood-brother, like the godparent, comes to the fore in a complementary role. The lineal kin are concerned with the future ancestor, while the corpse, all that remains of the person in himself, is handled by the blood-brother. (In Spain the child's coffin is commonly paid for by the godfather, rather than the father.) Now this is not always the case, but it is significant that where it is not, a similar role is frequently accorded to the non-lineal kin or to the affines. This leads me to suggest that for the purpose of examining the notion of amity, we should perhaps revise the distinction represented in the diagram on page 96 and distinguish the jural and the non-jural kin, not simply on the basis of real versus ritual kin, but of structurally stressed versus unstressed kin. The former would still include adoptive kin of whom we saw that they owe their status to the acquisition of rights and obligations within the nuclear family, while the latter would be comprised not only of the ritual kin *always* but, according to the particular social structure certain of the non-lineal kin, commonly the mother's brother in a patrilineal system, or the father in a matrilineal – and also normally the affines, the non-lineal kin of the next generation. These are the people whose amity is free of jural pressures and who are found in consequence in the role of sponsor of the individual self; at initiation ceremonies,[17] as gift-givers at the stages of advancement in a child's development, at marriages, as undertakers in mortuary rites, as peace-makers in tribal disputes. Their concern is not with the solidarity of the group but with individuals through personal attachments.

The complementarity which Fortes perceived between filiation through lineal descent and complementary filiation which comes from descent in the unstressed line (as I would put it) and gives rise to membership of no social group corresponds to the distinction between extensions of self along the lines of primary grouping, i.e. jural corporation, and extensions across these lines to persons whose amity does not derive from common membership of a social unit, from shared identity.

The complementarity is therefore not *only* between lines of filiation but, at the level of the person, between two aspects of his social relations, two *personae* of the same individual: the baby and the heir, the affine and the sibling, the bond-friend and the clansman, the blood-brother and the age-mate, the lover and the spouse, the corpse and the ancestor, the kith and the kin.

103

Notes

1 The Shorter O.E.D. glosses the phrase *Kith and Kin* as follows: '*orig*. Country and kinsfolk; in later use, acquaintance and kinsfolk; now often taken as pleonastic for kinsfolk, relatives'. The word 'kith' we are told is obsolete or archaic except in this phrase, and we are also told that it is derived from a root that means 'to know' and in later times it was occasionally confused with kin. How this confusion should have been able to occur is a matter on which it is hoped this essay will throw light. It will also be seen that Radcliffe-Brown's gloss as 'neighbour' is an over-simplification.

2 He states that the concept was brought to his notice a dozen years earlier in the work of Peter Lawrence and he refers to the usage of the word 'amity' by Burridge (1960), Fortes 1970: 240. In fact he had already referred to sacrifice as 'both an expression and a pledge of mutual amity and dependence', Fortes 1945: 98.

3 'When a child was adopted at birth or soon afterwards it became, socially, a true child of its adoptive parents. The kinship terms used in this case were exactly the same as those of a consanguinal relationship.' Saladin d'Anglure (1967). As the author makes clear, to give a child in adoption was an alternative to infanticide.

4 This was part of Robertson Smith's argument regarding blood-brotherhood which he believed demonstrated that kinship was originally the only effective form of social tie. See also Fortes 1969: 241.

5 Smith 1962: 196, 234, 270. The difficulty of distinguishing is not confined to the criteria adopted for filiation. For example, in the highlands of Chiapas the term 'kermano' (my brother) is often found in use between fellow-members of the same township (sometimes also called 'tribe'). The word is a Spanish loan from 'hermano' (brother) and this has led a number of anthropologists to argue that this usage of a kin term demonstrates the recognition of kinship to all members of the tribe. In fact kermano is not a kinship term but a pseudo-kinship term introduced by the monks who used it between themselves and no doubt thought it appropriate for use between members of the religious sodalities which are the backbone of the political government of the Indian communities. This becomes plain when we observe that the term kermano is applied without regard for relative seniority and that the first rule of Tzeltal and Tzotzil kinship distinguishes between elder brother and younger brother; there is no 'true' kin category of brother undifferentiated as to age. Kermano is not merely a Spanish loan in contrast to the other terms of kinship which are maya, it is not part of the kinship system at all.

6 Ch. IV (Sales' translation).

7 Pitt-Rivers (1970).

8 From my field notes I am able to provide an example of modification in a family of small tenant-farmers in Andalusia: a dominant mother married her son to the girl who came to work for them. The child born of this marriage was taught to call her grandmother 'mama' and to call her mother by her Christian name (a practice totally unknown otherwise). In effect the grandmother usurped the status of parent and turned mother and child into siblings. This case was unique in my experience in Andalusia, but the adoption of the status of parent to a grandchild appears to be very frequent among the Eskimos.

9 Pitt-Rivers, 1967.

10 The analogy with Frazer's principles of magic will not have escaped the reader,

and Frazer himself viewed blood-brotherhood as an example of homoeopathic magic. It is worth also pointing out that both magic and ritual kinship involve associations effectuated through the two principles of which Lévi-Strauss has made such striking use: metonym and metaphor. Consubstantiality involves association through a direct line ($x = y$), simulation through a link between two relationships (x is to a as y is to b). Two blood-brothers are consubstantial, but a godfather is to a godchild spiritually as a father is to a child terrestrially.

11 Cf. Pitt-Rivers, 1968. It must be noted that the expressions 'ritual kinship' and 'pseudo-kinship' are in fact misnomers, for the relationship reproduced is not one of kinship but of the nuclear family. They are always blood-*brothers*, god-*parents*, or -*children*, but there are no blood-*cousins* or god-*uncles*, (a point which is not without significance for the theory of kinship). I shall continue to use the words ritual and pseudo-*kinship* nonetheless for the sake of convenience.

12 I use the term 'jural' as Fortes in the phrase 'the jural domain' where the actor is the 'right-and-duty-bearing person' in contrast to the moral domain in which he is the sentient being.

13 'A man, sir, should keep his friendship in good repair' said Samuel Johnson (quoted by Jean La Fontaine, Munro Lectures, 1971) yet he did not succeed in doing so himself well enough to save Mrs Thrale from wondering whether he came to dine with her only out of gluttony.

14 On this point see Bourdieu (1972) who refers (p. 228) to 'la méconnaissance institutionnellement organisée et garantie qui est au principe de l'échange de dons'. The whole chapter is of the greatest importance for an understanding of the notion of reciprocity.

15 The temporal dimension of reciprocity is examined in this volume by Maurice Bloch.

16 I have made a more detailed study of this institution and its relations to the naming systems of Europe in Pitt-Rivers, in press.

17 Examples abound in the literature on Africa. Let me mention only two. The role of the father in the initiation ceremonies of the matrilineal Ndembu (see Turner 1969) is essentially similar to that of the mother's brother in those of the patrilineal Gisu. In this connection La Fontaine (1971) speaks of the mother's brother as a patron.

The Nature of the Family

Kinship, Attachment Behaviour and the Primary Bond

Derek Freeman

Kinship, despite a recent blunt assertion that there is 'no such thing' is certain to remain one of the central concerns of anthropology, and, in *Kinship and the Social Order*, Meyer Fortes has given us a masterly discourse which transcends the quirks of anthropological fashion to focus attention on what are fundamental issues.

It is one of Fortes' prime objectives (1969: 250) to 'establish the thesis that the domain of familial and kinship relations, institutions and values, is structurally discrete'. He does this by analysing a range of 'ethnographical specimens', and, on the basis of this evidence, reaches the conclusion: 'that the realm of custom, belief and social organization, which we descriptively identify by the overall rubric of kinship, is both analytically distinguishable and empirically specifiable as a relatively discrete domain of social structure founded upon principles and processes that are irreducible'. There is, Fortes concludes, something elemental and immutable about kinship relations: a kind of *a priori* and automatic character that defies further analysis. 'Kinship', he observes (*ibid*: 242), 'is binding: it creates inescapable claims and obligations'. There is, however, no source apparent, other than kinship itself, to which these claims and obligations can be referred. They exist between kinsfolk, so it would seem (*ibid*: 238), 'simply by reasons of the fact that they are kin'.

Here, Fortes is giving recognition to an undoubted characteristic of all close kinship bonds – a characteristic the phenomenology of which may be studied in any human society. In my judgment, this recognition is of crucial importance for it puts the investigator in the position of having to try to account for the special character of kinship bonds and behaviour.

Meyer Fortes' approach to this problem, as a social anthropologist, is to consider kinship in relation to what he calls 'the axiom of amity'. Amity here refers to the 'mutual support' that kinsfolk habitually offer to one another, this being an expression of a 'rule of prescriptive altruism'. This kind of behaviour, according to Fortes, is intrinsic to the relations of close kin: 'kinship predicates the axiom of amity'.

With 'the axiom of amity' established Fortes continues with his discerning analysis of filiation, descent and related issues in the theory of kinship. No solution is offered to the problem of why it is kinship bonds should have the special characteristics that they do, this being marginal to the theme of his Morgan Lectures. It is made clear, however, that the problem is a real one when Fortes comments (*ibid*: 251): 'It is conceivable – and I for one would accept – that the axiom of amity reflects biological and psychological parameters of human social existence. Maybe there is sucked in with the mother's milk, as Montaigne opined, the orientation on which it ultimately rests'.[1] In this brief paper I wish to point to one of the 'biological and psychological parameters of human social existence' which does, I think, deserve the attention of students of kinship behaviour.

Since the mid-1930s when Konrad Lorenz published his revealing paper 'Der Kumpan in der Umvelt des Vogels', the processes whereby the young of an animal species become attached to older con-specifics, and, in particular, to their mothers or mother-surrogates, has been the subject of much research. Lorenz's pioneer enquiries on imprinting in birds was followed by comparable work on attachment behaviour in quadrupeds, especially notable being the researches of Scott and his associates (Scott and Fuller, 1965) on the dog, and these investigations have been supplemented by studies of the behaviour of infants and their mothers in several species of infra-human primates (e.g.: Harlow, 1958, and 1961; Jay, 1963; DeVore, 1963; and Lawick-Goodall, 1971 *b*).

All of these studies have demonstrated the profound significance of attachment behaviour, revealing it as one of the principal means by which social continuity is achieved in populations of birds and mammals. Attachment behaviour, contributing as it does to species survival, thus emerges as one of the most fundamental forms of social adaptation to be found in the higher vertebrates. During the last two decades a body of evidence has been accumulating which indicates that the attachment of an infant to his mother is also of decisive importance in the development of human social life.

Although the behavioural repertoire of a human baby at birth is of a very simple description he possesses nonetheless a series of fully-formed behaviour patterns (Prechtl, 1969 *b*), prominent among them being crying, rooting and sucking, which facilitate the establishing of infant-mother interaction. In other words, there exists at birth 'an inherent co-ordination between organism and environment' (Wolff, 1969 *b*: 355), which, as Prechtl (1969 *a*: 3) has phrased it, 'is the product of a long evolutionary process of selection and mutual adaptation to the specific ecological conditions of rearing and nursing'.[2]

At first the crying behaviour of the infant, of which Wolff (1969 *a*) has recently made an illuminating study, is of prime importance. As Formby (1967: 297) has shown, a human mother, within two or three days of having given birth, learns to recognize her own infant's cry, and, once having attained this discriminatory power, she will awake during the night, even in crowded conditions (like a multi-bedded ward), at the sound of the cry of her own infant, to whom she is at once drawn and to whom she will, if she can, go. Crying is thus a care-eliciting behaviour, and, once the infant is in close proximity to one of his mother's breasts his rooting and sucking reflexes ensure that he gets the nourishment he needs.

At this initial stage, the neonate's genetically programmed response repertoire while adequate (given the presence of his mother) to ensure the nutrition and care on which his survival depends is still of a quite rudimentary kind. Moreover, the fact that this repertoire is so limited means that at first an infant experiences his mother as a composite of care-giving objects rather than as a social partner. The beginnings of more developed social interaction (which is characterized by mutual recognition) have to await the maturation of his central nervous system.

A principal index of this maturational process is to be found in the visual development of the neonate. Studies of the brain of the new born (Ellingson, 1964), using the electro-encephalogram, have shown that at birth there is an absence of alpha waves – an indication (which is supported by other evidence) that the neonate's visual capacity is, at first, quite limited. This condition persists for approximately six weeks (Bronson, 1969: 208), at which time the average infant will smile at the presentation of a human face, so demonstrating the presence of some measure of pattern recognition.[3] The emergence of this capacity at about six weeks of age, the evidence suggests, is dependent on the attainment of a specific level of neocortical maturation. Dittrichová (1969: 165) has reported that premature infants, despite having had as much as ten additional weeks of visual experience, do not smile any earlier than full-term infants. The theory that the emergence of smiling and related behaviours is dependent on neocortical maturation is also consistent with the conclusions of Conel's researches (1939, 1941 and 1947) on the postnatal development of the human cerebral cortex from birth until the third month of life.

At about the age of three months, when the alpha rhythm appears as a persistent phenomenon (Lindsley, 1963: 4), the infant enters fully upon a decisively important period of development which ordinarily culminates in the formation of his first and most lasting social relationship.

Among the behaviours especially characteristic of this period is smiling, which, since the publication of Spitz and Wolf's pioneer monograph in 1946, has been much studied. As a result of these researches smiling as it occurs in neonates is now viewed as a genetically-programmed physiological mechanism. Humphrey (1969: 81), in the course of her remarkable researches on prenatal behaviour, has demonstrated the neuro-anatomical basis of smiling in the 14 week foetus, while Wolff (1963: 116) has recorded spontaneous smiling in a number of premature infants of 28 to 34 weeks gestation. Again, the researchers of Eibl-Eibesfeldt (1970: 403 *seq.*) on the smiling of infants born both blind and deaf have provided further conclusive evidence that smiling is, in its first manifestations in the human infant, an unlearnt behaviour.

In infants, as Ainsworth (1967: 432) has phrased it, smiling 'serves the biological function of inviting or sustaining tender attention', and, by helping to secure this kind of attention, it tends to promote survival. Smiling may thus be viewed as an evolved mechanism,[4] and one of the principal behavioural adaptations of infants of the human species.

Here smiling is seen as originating within the organism and there is good reason for viewing much of the rest of an infant's behaviour, during the early months of life, in the same way. In a revealing (if rather inhuman) experiment carried out at the University of Virginia in the 1930s, an experimental psychologist and his wife adopted two female non-identical twins of north European stock at 36 days of age, and systematically studied their behavioural development during the ensuing 14 months under conditions of greatly reduced social stimulation.

The rudimentary bodily needs of the two infants were formally attended to, but the experimenters 'did not reward or punish the subjects for any response nor instruct them in any way'. The aim of the experiment (Dennis, 1941: 147) was 'to determine what behavioural development would occur when the care of infants was reduced to the minimum attention which would ensure their comfort and well-being'.

The principal conclusion of this experiment was (*ibid*: 180) that 'practically all of the behaviour of the first year of life is autogenous' – that is, it has the characteristic of originating within the organism. In other words, a healthy infant possesses an evolved range of behaviours which emerge in the course of maturation during the first year of life to permit the growth of the social relationships on which his future welfare depends.

Prominent among the autogenous behaviours listed by Dennis is that of smiling. 'We wished...' he reports (*ibid*: 152), 'to know whether positive responses towards us would develop if we refrained from smiling at the twins and from petting, cuddling and fondling them. In order to determine the answer to this question we avoided these expressions during the first 26 weeks.' Despite these conditions both twins smiled at six weeks (*ibid*: 174), and from the 15th week onwards almost invariably greeted their straight-faced care-takers with a beaming smile.

The peak of non-selective smiling, as the researches of Ambrose (1961) and others have established, occurs at about 13 weeks of age in home-reared infants. At this stage anyone who approaches and looks at a baby is likely to be smiled at by him.[5] Such a baby is entering upon a phase of behavioural development during which his responses are of a kind particularly conducive to the formation of a social relationship,[6] and, by about seven months of age, or soon thereafter, he will, in the ordinary course of events, have become attached to the individual who has been caring for him. It is this attachment which brings into being what may properly be called the primary bond, for, in developmental terms, it is the first and most fundamental of all forms of human mutuality.[7]

In the great majority of instances the other individual in this basic bond is the infant's own mother; but that he becomes attached to her results, of course, not from their genetic relationship, but from the circumstance that it is she who interacts with him during the crucial period of care-taking that precedes attachment. Attachment, the evidence indicates, stems very largely from evolved behaviours and propensities, and is, therefore, a biologically-based phenomenon. The biology, however, lies in the very process of behavioural interaction, and, having participated in this vital interaction an infant will become attached to his care-taker, whoever she (or he) may be.

Lady Violet Bonham Carter has written of the aristocracy of Victorian England (1967: 25): 'The task of bringing up their children was. . .delegated to a Nannie – an essentially English institution of great permanence and power. . . A Nannie must enter into her kingdom when the baby is a month old, not a day sooner or later. "I had him from the month" is for her equivalent to saying "He is my own child" – and from that day on he is.'

Winston Churchill (born in 1874) was brought up in this way by an illustrious Nannie called Mrs Everest (or Woom) with consequences that are better understood now than they were a century ago. Of his mother Churchill has written (1959: 13): 'She shone for me like the Evening Star. I loved her dearly – but at a distance. My nurse was my confidante. Mrs Everest it was who looked after me and tended all my wants.' When Woom died (in July, 1895) her 'darling Precious Boy' (as she used to call him) was at her bedside. 'She had been', wrote Churchill afterwards (*ibid*: 80), 'my dearest and most intimate friend during the whole of the 20 years I had lived'; and, to the end of his life her photograph hung in his room.

In other words, Winston Churchill's primary bond was to Mrs Everest, a Kentish woman (of a social class very different from his own) to whom he was entirely unrelated genealogically.[8] Furthermore, in the light of our present knowledge, it can be said that this bond, with its deeply emotional character, had come into being because Mrs Everest it was who had contact with and cared for the young Winston Churchill during the crucial period from about three months of age onwards when a human infant is in a high state of sensitivity for developing attachment behaviour.

During my investigation of attachment behaviour in Samoa I located a number of comparable cases, one of which I shall here mention. Aperila, having been born on 19 April 1955, was abandoned by her mother, Lei, some five months or so later, when Lei eloped and went off to live in a distant part of the island of Upolu. In this situation the care of Aperila was taken over by Uiese (the elder sister of Lei's mother), who was then aged 59 years. It was thus to Uiese that Aperila became attached. In 1966, when

I was able to make a close study of Aperila's behaviour, her genetic mother, Lei, was once again living in the same *'āiga*, or extended family, but it was Uiese her care-taker in infancy (or, behavioural mother) to whom Aperila was strongly bonded, sleeping and eating with her, and going to her for all her needs. Lei she ignored. The people of the *'āiga* concerned were well aware of what had happened. 'Aperila knows that Lei is her mother', they would say, 'but has no love for her; the heart of Aperila adheres to Uiese'. (*''Ua iloa Aperila 'o Lei 'o lona tinā, ae peitai'i 'ua lē alofa ia te ia; 'ua pipi'i le loto 'o Aperila ia Uiese'*).

Cases such as these in which a child is cared for in infancy by someone other than his (or her) genetic mother demonstrate something that some anthropologists have, I believe, insufficiently recognized: that kinship in addition to having to do with genealogical linkages, and with jural and moral principles, has a behavioural basis. Moreover, in the light of the illuminating researches of Bowlby and the many others who have worked in this field in recent years, anthropologists are now in a position to begin extending their theories to take into account the behavioural basis of kinship in early infancy.

As Schaffer (1963), Stevens (1971) and others have shown, specific attachments tend to occur during the third quarter of the first year of life, that is, some three months or so after the peak of non-selective smiling which marks the onset of the period of special sensitivity for the development of attachment behaviour. Then, approximately one month after he has formed an attachment to his principal care-taker, an infant begins to display a discernible fear of strangers, and non-selective smiling is at an end.[9] The mode for this change (which helps to ensure that the attachment already formed will not be interfered with) lies at about eight and a half months (Stevens, 1971: 142), and is thus often coincident with early developments in locomotor ability. However, even with the attainment of full mobility the attachment of an infant to his mother continues to be highly characteristic of his behaviour during his second and third years of life (Anderson, 1972). Although variations do occur under some conditions (Schaffer, 1963: 187), there is a marked tendency for the attachment of an infant to be monotropic, that is, to one care-taker, in particular.[10]

I cannot within the confines of this brief paper present any kind of adequate summary of the seminal contributions of Bowlby to the understanding of attachment behaviour.[11] Perhaps his principal achievement has been to devise a theory (stemming mainly from comparative ethology) which views attachment behaviour as a phenomenon which occurs when certain behavioural systems (crying, smiling, clinging, following and sucking, being examples) are activated in an infant within his environment of adaptedness. This makes attachment behaviour intelligible in evolutionary terms, and it is seen (Bowlby, 1969: 179) as 'a class of social behaviour of an importance equivalent to that of mating behaviour and parental behaviour' with 'a biological function specific to itself'.[12] The biological function of such a basic behaviour pattern must be sought in its significance for species survival and it is Bowlby's theory that attachment behaviour evolved in the prehistoric environment to which the hominids had to adapt, its prime function being the protection of the young of the species from predators. While this theory, given its historical nature, cannot be directly tested, it is consistent with what is known of predation in infra-human primates, and does account for the emotional intensity of the attachment of human infants to their mothers – real or surrogate.

'No form of behaviour', as Bowlby (*ibid*: 209) has noted, 'is accompanied by stronger feeling than is attachment behaviour.' In the presence of the individual on whose sustaining care he depends for his existence the infant feels secure, and towards her he directs his loving gaze. The bond that results from attachment behaviour is thus both intimate and profound; an infant, as Paracelsus long ago remarked, 'needs neither stars or planets; his mother is his planet and his star'. Further, it is a bond which provides the behavioural basis for the formation of all subsequent relationships. Ethnographers, as Fortes records (1969: 255), have 'never failed to find the mother and child couple', and it is to attachment behaviour and the primary bond, I would suggest, that we can trace both 'the axiom of amity' and the fact that kinship is inescapably binding.

But is this all, to revert to Montaigne's metaphor, that is 'sucked in with the mother's milk'? In *Kinship and the Social Order*, having recognized 'the axiom of amity' as the 'central value premise' associated with 'the notion of kinship', Meyer Fortes goes on to observe (1969: 237) that 'many ties of close kinship. . .subsume rivalries and latent hostilities that are as intrinsically built into the relationships as are the externally oriented amity and solidarity they present'. And, in illustration, he quotes from a Lozi song (Gluckman, 1955: 154) the lines:

He who kills me, who will it be but my kinsman,[13]
He who succours me, who will it be but my kinsman

We are here, it seems to me, confronted with an issue of some importance in the study of kinship behaviour. Why is it that bonds of close kinship are so often characterized by feelings and behaviour of a kind inimical to the rule of amity? Has research on attachment behaviour any contribution to make to the solution of the apparent paradox of the co-existence within the same relationship of varying degrees of love and hate? I would like to suggest that perhaps it has.

As we have seen the attachment of an infant to his mother results in the formation of a bond of a most intense kind, having as it does the biological function of securing species survival. It is thus an adaptation which helps

115

to ensure that an infant receives the loving care which his mother is disposed to give, but beyond this it also provides a biologically decreed setting for the vicissitudes of the behavioural and emotional interaction of mother and child, whatever these may be. Given the sub-cortical behaviour mechanisms of both mother and child, these vicissitudes are always, to some extent, stormy. Indeed, long before individual recognition of the mother has been established the average infant has been swept by irate feelings in her presence, when, for whatever reason, his appetites have not been gratified. As Bertrand Russell's mother reported of her son three days after his birth in 1872 (Russell, 1967, I: 17): 'I have lots of milk now, but if he does not get it at once or has wind or anything he gets into such a rage and screams and kicks and trembles till he is soothed off. . .'

Irate reactions of this kind commonly continue intermittently throughout the entire period of an infant's attachment to his mother, and, once recognition has been established, are directed against the mother as an individual. In the case of one of the infants whose behaviour I had under observation in 1966, individual recognition of his mother was clearly present at 98 days, when, if he were in a well-fed and quiescent mood, he would greet her advent with a radiant smile.[14] When he became hungry, however, as when his mother had been away weeding taro, he would respond to her approach in a most irate manner. At 112 days when his mother, having returned from her labours, sat cross-legged and placed him across her lap, he flexed his body and flailed his arms in an incipient tantrum, as he cried aloud in rage.[15] On subsequent occasions when in the same situation he would sometimes angrily reject his mother's breast when it was offered to him. And later still, after his attachment to his mother had become fully established, he would, on occasion, lash out at her violently when the sustenance he expected was delayed or refused.[16]

In this and other kinds of ways attachment inevitably leads to contention situations in which an infant becomes irritated, angered or enraged with his care-taker. Attachment, however, triumphs over all such vicissitudes and persists even in the face of a punitive regime. In Samoa it is not uncommon for an infant to be frequently punished during the second year of life. Yet this treatment seems only to intensify attachment. After a beating an infant will still seek contact with his mother and even when enraged to the point of tantrum will stumble passionately after her should she begin to move away.

It is one of the most important outcomes of attachment behaviour then that alternating moods of love and anger eventually lead to the co-existence of contradictory impulses and emotions towards the same individual. The primary bond, in other words, is always characterized by ambivalence. This ambivalence, moreover, once established, tends to continue throughout life.

My investigation of the attitudes of Samoan children towards their mothers (using the methods of play analysis and the analysis of drawings) showed that beneath their avowals of love there were feelings of fear and antagonism. These ambivalent states were also detectable in the behaviour of adolescents and adults, and, indeed, persist long after the death of the mother when they are directed towards her ghost (*aitu*).[17]

Let us now return to kinship at large, and to the puzzling fact that 'latent hostilities' are often 'as intrinsically built into' the bonds of kinship as is 'amity'. If one proceeds from the assumption that kinship bonds are the expression of a moral and jural order the circumstance that they are so often characterized by both enmity and amity remains a paradox. The problem dissolves, however, as soon as kinship bonds are, in addition, approached in behavioural terms and analysed ontogenetically. It is then seen that the ambivalence which is so integral to the primary bond between child and mother tends to be transferred, in some degree, to all of the subsequent relationships into which an individual enters, and that, on this basis, each new relationship comes to develop, in the course of further interaction, its own ambivalent character.

When such a behavioural approach is made it becomes possible to comprehend the simultaneous presence in kinship bonds of love and hate, and to discern that one of the functions of 'the rule of amity' among kinsfolk is the containing of ambivalence within manageable bounds. Or, to put it in more direct terms: 'hatreds never cease by hatreds in this world',[18] and only by actively valuing amity are we humans able to live together like good kinsmen.

Notes

1 Meyer Fortes, in contradistinction to those who have sought to exclude biological and psychological variables from the purview of social anthropology, has always advocated a naturalistic approach to the study of man. As he expressed it in his inaugural lecture as William Wyse, Professor of Social Anthropology at Cambridge (1953*b*: 33): 'It is accepted that language, culture and organized society place man on a higher evolutionary level than any other species has reached; but this does not put these unique possessions outside nature. Whatever the schoolmen might say, anthropology cannot ignore the fact that social systems come into being only through the medium of living people.'

2 This interpretation also applies to maternal behaviour. In this present paper I am accepting the fact of maternal behaviour and directing attention to the way in which attachment behaviour contributes to the formation of the bond between an infant and his mother. For a discussion of maternal behaviour in infra-human mammals, see Rheingold, 1963.

3 Historical information on the onset of smiling in infants is limited. We do, however, have Charles Darwin's report (1877: 288) that his eldest son (b. 27 December, 1839), of whose behaviour he made a detailed study, 'smiled when 45 days old'; and that another of his children smiled when 46 days old. 'These smiles arose',

commented Darwin, 'chiefly when looking at their mother, and were therefore probably of mental origin. . .'

4 I am using the term 'evolved' in the same sense as Freedman (1967: 484) to refer to behaviour which while plainly having an important phylogenetic basis has become 'completely interdependent with learning'.

5 Investigations which I was able to carry out in Samoa, in Western Polynesia, in 1966–7 confirmed this now widely reported phenomenon. A home-reared Samoan infant during his fourth month of life, when non-selective smiling was at its peak, would smile at complete strangers, and respond with a marked smile even when approached by someone wearing a mask with a highly threatening expression.

6 The smiling of an infant tends to release a joyful and contact-seeking response in his care-taker. A Samoan mother (of 28 years) when asked how she felt when her infant son (aged 98 days) smiled at her, replied: 'My heart is happy and I want to play with him' (' *'Ua fiafia lo'u loto ma 'ua fia ta'alo ma ia*'). The 'play' consisted of dandling and fondling the infant and so making contact with him.

7 Scott (1963: 2) has used the term 'primary socialization' to refer to this same phenomenon.

8 This is an occurrence, obviously, that would have to be taken very much into account in any thorough-going study of the development of Winston Churchill's personality.

9 The Samoan infant (mentioned in Note 5) who, during his fourth month, had smiled at any human face and even a threatening mask, when tested again at the end of the third quarter of his first year did not respond when smiled at, and when confronted with the same mask he had beamed at some five months previously, turned away in alarm and clung closely to his care-taker.

10 Mead (1962: 56) has asserted that in Samoan society, which is composed of extended families, or *'āiga*, the mother-child tie is 'diffused'. When, in 1966–7, in the course of my study of attachment behaviour among Samoans, I conducted the experiment of having the women of an *'āiga* walk away one at a time (or be driven away in a motor vehicle) from a particular infant, it was demonstrated by the agitated reaction of this infant to the departure of his own mother (and her alone) that attachment in Samoa, as elsewhere, is monotropic. Furthermore the study of mourning behaviour in Samoa confirms this conclusion.

11 See Bowlby (1969), and the publication, listed therein, for an account of his researches over the last twenty years.

12 This conclusion that attachment behaviour is dependent on the maturation of species-specific response patterns has supplanted the interpretation of Freud (1964, **23**: 188; orig. 1940) and others which attributed attachment to 'the satisfied need for nourishment' and so classed it as a learned response.

13 The poignant hyperbole of this line does spring from an indubitable statistical reality. As Morris and Blom-Cooper (1964: 276) have noted, murder is disinguished from other crimes by 'the extent to which the killer and the victim are related or known to each other'. In England, as they report, 'murder is overwhelmingly a domestic crime in which men kill their wives, mistresses, and children, and women kill their children. Of the murder victims over the age of 16, 70 per cent are female, and of these females nearly half are killed by their legal husbands and a quarter by other relatives or lovers. When considering victims under 16, again, about three-quarters are killed by their parents or other relatives.'

14 Individual recognition was tested for by having a number of women (including the mother) present themselves serially to the same infant, and then inferring recognition from the intensity and duration of the smile with which the mother alone was greeted.

15 See Wolff (1969: 82) for an account of the angry cry of the human infant; inc. Plate 12 for a spectogram of this cry.

16 Lawick-Goodall (1971*a*: 211) has described how an infant chimpanzee when refused the breast of his mother would hit and bite her. I am grateful to Dr John Bowlby (personal communication) for the following comment: 'I regard some measure of anger as serving an adaptive function through its coercive effects on the mother, e.g., discouraging her from leaving the child. Only when excessively aroused may such anger become maladaptive.'

17 For a discussion of the bereavement reaction and its relation to attachment behaviour, see Krupp (1962).

18 These words are from the fifth pair of verses of the Yamakavagga in *The Dhammapada* (Nārada, 1954: 15), and date from the fourth century B.C., or earlier.

The Matrifocal Family

Raymond T. Smith

I regard it as now established that the elementary components of patri-filiation and matrifiliation, and hence of agnatic, enatic, and cognatic modes of reckoning kinship are, like genes in the individual organism invariably present in all familial systems (Fortes 1969: 309).

...I regard the succession of generations in the process of physical and social reproduction focused in the relationships of filiation and descent as the keystone of kinship structure. For this process to go on, institutional-ised forms of alliance are not essential. What is indispensable is parent-hood, and for this any form of permitted procreative cohabitation is sufficient (Fortes 1969: 308).

Throughout his writings on kinship Meyer Fortes has been concerned to isolate the 'elementary components' of kinship and family structure. Despite careful qualification and meticulous attention to ethnographic exceptions, consistently he has found those components within the elementary family of parents and children, which more often than not constitute a domestic group, which is 'In all human societies the workshop, so to speak, of social reproduction' (Fortes 1958 b: 2). While he recognises evidence which shows that social placement does not always depend upon legitimate paternity, he continues to believe that patrifiliation is a universally required social attribute.

This brings us back to the proposition that no one can become a complete social person if he is not presentable as legitimately fathered as well as mothered. He must have a demonstrable *pater*, ideally one who is indi-vidually specified as his responsible upbringer, for he must be equipped to relate himself to other persons and to society at large bilaterally, by both matri-kinship and patri-kinship. Lacking either side, he will be handicapped, either in respect of the ritual statuses and moral capacities that every complete person must have (as in Australia) or in the politico-jural and economic capacities and attributes that are indispensable for conducting himself as a normal right-and-duty bearing person (Fortes 1969: 261–2).

This insistence upon the importance of bilateral affiliation as a moral principle of universal significance serves to re-establish the nuclear family (or something very like it) as the universally necessary matrix for the reproduction of social beings. It also forges a strong link in the theoretical chain between domesticity and kinship, and comes dangerously close to reintroducing the confusion between biology and kinship.

These ideas seem to run counter to the understanding of kinship which Fortes has been developing over the past decade. For example, he identifies the 'axiom of amity' as the irreducible principle of morality on which all kinship rests, and he rejects the 'genealogical fallacy' that kinship derives from some actual network of biological ties. But he then qualifies these conclusions by saying 'It is conceivable – and I for one would accept – that the axiom of amity reflects biological and psychological parameters of human social existence' (1969: 251). It is difficult to see why biological and psychological parameters should be introduced into what is presented as a purely analytical distinction unless there is a lingering feeling that the kinship domain grows out of the domestic domain, which is *par excellence* the domain of child-rearing and social reproduction.

In this paper I wish to explore the implications of Fortes' arguments through a reconsideration of the concept of 'matrifocality' which I first used in the early 1950s as a means of characterising certain features of the domestic organisation of Guyanese coastal villagers (Smith 1956). Meyer Fortes has drawn on some aspects of that work to support his view of the importance of patrifiliation (Fortes 1969: 259–69, fn. 17), and so the re-examination of these data and their analysis may feed directly into his ongoing theoretical concerns.

II. Derivation of the term 'matrifocal'

During the summer of 1952 I made a preliminary analysis of material collected in the course of a field study of the social structure of a community of Guyanese descendants of African immigrants whose ancestors had established a free village in the early 1840s, soon after the abolition of slavery. I decided to concentrate upon the analysis of household composition, marriage and child rearing, because of the increasing theoretical interest in West Indian family structure as well as the supposed practical problems of illegitimacy and family stability. The subject was hardly new since it had been treated extensively by North American sociologists (Frazier 1939; Herskovits 1941; Drake and Cayton 1945), and Professor and Mrs Herskovits had devoted attention to it in their work on Surinam, Haiti and Trinidad (1934; 1937; 1947).

The model for my own analysis was Fortes' pioneering use of quantitative data in 'Time and social structure: An Ashanti case study' (1949 *b*). My data showed that these Guyanese villagers lived in households with a high proportion of female heads, a situation curiously similar to that in the two villages studied by Fortes in the Ashanti area of Ghana.[1] In both areas the ideal form of household appeared to be that established by a man upon marriage, consisting of himself, his wife and their children. Another striking similarity was in the strength of the mother–child relationship, and in the tendency for the unit of a woman, her children and her daughters' children to emerge as a particularly solidary unit, often constituting the core of a domestic group. Fortes reports that an Ashanti man of means would always be expected to set up a house of his own, but interestingly enough this could be done not to provide shelter for himself, his wife and their children but because 'One of the strongest motives is the desire, among both men and women, for domestic independence of the effective minimal lineage consisting of the children and daughters' children of one woman' (Fortes 1949 *b*: 68).

With all these similarities there were notable differences, the major one being the absence in Guyana of unilineal descent groups. Fortes' analysis stressed the complex consequences for domestic group composition of the contrary pulls of marriage and lineage ties and he suggests 'that the type of domestic unit found in any particular case is a result of the balance struck between the obligations of marriage and parenthood on the one hand and those due to matrilineal kin on the other' (1949 *b*: 70). The situation in Guyana was quite different because race and social class, not lineage ties, were of major importance in defining social position in systems 'external' to the domestic domain.

The key to understanding the Guyanese system seemed to lie in the recognition that male occupational and class roles constitute the point of intersection of domestic and politico-jural domains, while female roles are primarily confined within the domestic domain. Those male occupational and class roles are relatively independent of familial or kinship roles, so that the two domains do not articulate in the same way as they would in the Ashanti case.

The aspect of Fortes' work which proved most relevant was his emphasis upon family structure and domestic organisation as a process in time with a cyclical development through the genesis, maturation and decay of domestic groups parallel to the physiological processes of the individual's life-cycle. My problem was to determine the 'normal' developmental cycle for the groups with which I was concerned. In retrospect it is easy to see that much room for error lay in the choice of procedures for establishing this normal pattern, and even though Fortes' essay had been written as a solution to the problem of establishing 'norms', it left a number of issues unresolved.

The central question is whether one can derive the 'norms' which govern behaviour and give 'structural form' to a particular aspect of social life from the examination of tables showing the frequency of particular items of behaviour. Fortes leaves unclear the nature of the relationship between cultural principles, which are to be grasped 'qualitatively', and structure, which is 'meaningful in terms of magnitude' (1949 *b*: 57). One possible interpretation of his argument is that in stable and homogeneous societies there is no difference between culture and structure: principles are expressed directly in action so that one may 'arrive at the "norms" by comparison of and induction from repeated instances' (1949 *b*: 58). In more complex societies norms have to be established by the application of statistics because the comparison of, and induction from, repeated instances is too difficult to achieve directly. Here again 'structure' and 'culture' become different ways of arriving at the same thing, and therefore 'norms' and 'behaviour' are ultimately the same thing. However, Fortes is not consistent for he contrasts a '"paradigm" or cultural "norm" sanctioned by law, religion and moral values' (60) with structure 'governed by internal changes as well as by changing relations, from year to year, with society at large' (1949 *b*: 60). Then to make everything more complex he states that because modern Ashanti is neither stable nor homogeneous 'there *appears* to be no fixed norm of domestic grouping' but it can be discovered by 'rigorous methods of a statistical kind' (1949 *b*: 61).

Fortes has raised a crucial theoretical problem, but he has not resolved the question of the relationship between the normative elements and the frequency of actual behaviour; certainly he has not derived or discovered normative principles by rigorously statistical methods. At best he has demonstrated the effects of certain moral norms, such as matrilineage loyalty or conjugal attachment, upon the patterns of household composition.[2]

A similar problem surrounds the analysis of the Guyanese materials. In order to construct a model of the developmental cycle one must first settle upon the generative principles which are assumed to produce the variations seen in the frequency tables. The dominating assumption in my original discussion of Guyanese lower-class household composition was that child-rearing is the central function of domestic organisation and that the 'nuclear family' is both an ideal form and one which is approached as a part of the 'normal' developmental cycle. Variations from the normal pattern are produced by the failure of male domestic roles to be supported by male performance in the occupational and status systems (Smith 1956: 112).

The developmental sequence was presented as follows (1956: Chaps. v & vi). Households come into being when a man and a woman set up house together and this is the normal starting point of the developmental cycle. Either or both partners may have had children already and some of them may be brought into the new household. During the period of early co-habitation (which may or may not be based on legal marriage), the woman is fully occupied with child-rearing and maximally dependent upon her spouse, but while men contribute to the support of the household they do not participate very much in child-care or spend much time at home. As the children grow older, they gradually begin to drop out of school to help with household tasks or with jobs on the farm and running errands. The woman is gradually freed from the constant work of child-care and when the children begin to earn, they contribute to the daily expenses of the household. It is at this stage that one begins to see more clearly the underlying pattern of relationship within the domestic group; whereas the woman had previously been the focus of affective ties she now becomes the centre of an economic and decision-making coalition with her children. This increasing 'matrifocal' quality is seen whether the husband-father is present or not, and although the proportion of women who are household heads increases with age – principally because of widowhood – matrifocality is a property of the internal relations of male, as well as female, headed households.

In choosing the term 'matrifocal' in preference to such descriptive terms as 'matri-central', 'matriarchal', 'female-dominated', 'grandmother family' and so on, I specifically intended to convey that it is women *in their role as mothers* who come to be the *focus* of relationships, rather than head of the household as such. In fact it was central to my argument that the nuclear family is both ideally normal, *and* a real stage in the development of practically all domestic groups.

The 'normal' developmental sequence of household groups is rounded out by noting that young men and women begin to engage in love affairs while they are still in their parents' homes. If children result they may be assimilated to a filial relationship to the maternal grandmother, and in this way household groups are often extended to three generations. Upon the death or desertion of the male household head, his spouse simply assumes headship, and the cycle comes to an end with her death. Sometimes a widower will manage to keep a household together with the aid of a mature daughter, or a group of siblings may hold together for a year or two, but household groups normally dissolve upon the death of the focal female.

The argument which I then developed to account for the configuration of this developmental cycle was that both late entry to co-residential unions and early decline in effective male domestic authority are due to the discrepancy between ideal and possible performance of male domestic roles. Men's low status and power in the economic and class systems reacts back upon their roles in the domestic system, making it impossible for them to live up to the norms. The obvious next step was to see whether similar cases existed in other societies. Although the material I examined in *The Negro Family in British Guiana* – on Latin America and Scotland – was very sketchy, the fact that I chose cases where there was neither high illegitimacy rates, female-headed households nor marital instability shows clearly that my definition of matrifocality included none of these things (Smith 1956: 240–54).

III. Development of the concept of matrifocality

It would be neither easy nor profitable to review every version of the concept of matrifocality. I have already reviewed some of the developments in the study of Caribbean kinship (Smith 1963), and will confine myself here to some of the theoretically more important issues.

Among the earliest comments on *The Negro Family in British Guiana* was the criticism that it had confused household composition with family structure and, through lack of rigorous definition, had obscured the import-ance of familial relations between those who lived in separate households.[3] There is some merit to this criticism; unfortunately Solien and M. G. Smith, whose comments were the most carefully considered, each introduced other problems instead of clarifying the issues. Solien's arguments are particularly diffuse and although she raised an important issue, she rushed into a collec-tion of errors from which she did not manage to extricate herself through a series of articles and the belated publication of her Ph.D. thesis (Solien 1959 *a*; 1959 *b*; 1959*c*; 1960: Solien de González 1961; 1965; 1969). In dis-cussing her own fieldwork she argues that Black Carib society exhibits a 'type' of household organisation which includes a series of 'forms', the most important of which are (1) consanguineal (the members related by consanguineal ties and 'no two members bound together in an affinal relationship'), and (2) affinal (where there is an affinal tie between any two (members) (1969:4). Solien de Gonzálaz jumps to the mistaken conclusion that I had used the term 'matrifocal' to identify her 'consanguineal' family form, and that matrifocal families in Guyana are always female-headed.[4] I cite this only because it represents a more general tendency in the litera-ture to use the term 'matrifocal' to refer to either female-headed house-holds or households composed exclusively of blood-kin. All such usages can be summarily dismissed as being pointless since there is nothing to be gained by coining a new term for these easily designated types. The classic statement of this misguided point of view is a paper by Kunstadter (1963). Although the shortcomings of the paper were pointed out by Randolph (1964), this has not prevented it from being the most cited source on the matrifocal family, and therefore a constant source of confusion.[5]

Gonzalez, in the rest of her analysis, sets up the consanguineal household as a special type and then tries to relate its frequency of occurrence to migrant wage labour and demographic factors in what she calls 'neoteric' societies (1969: 10). This seems to be merely a lower level and more rigid specification of the general principles set out in my original association of matrifocal family structure with colour/class factors in Guyana.[6]

M. G. Smith also draws attention to the relationships existing across household boundaries, and particularly those which have come to be desig-nated Visiting Unions (M. G. Smith 1962). He argues that it is variations in mating relations which produce different types of parental roles and give rise to variations in the composition of domestic groups. Despite the com-plexity of his presentation the argument is quite simple; it is predicated on the assumption that the nuclear family based on legal marriage is a normal form providing adequate 'parenthood'. In the West Indies, 'The persistence of high illegitimacy rates, unstable unions, and anomalous forms of domestic groups. . .are all due to the same conditions' (1962: 260). The conditions are the past existence of slavery and the failure of the church to do anything more than introduce legal marriage as an *alternative* form of mating. M. G. Smith does not depart very far from the ideas and the methods of investigation set out in *The Negro Family in British Guiana*; he distinguishes between family relations and domestic structure and argues that family relations are prior to, and determinate of, domestic organisation, but the principles of family structure are derived from 'the analysis of domestic groups [and] we can use the data on household composition to verify or illustrate them' (M. G. Smith 1962: 9). Furthermore, he sees the different configurations of family and domestic relations which are revealed by his analysis as being substitute forms of parental care. The focus is thus shifted from a developmental model of a normal type of household composition, to an array of alternative forms which emerge to supplement, or substitute for, 'marginal parenthood' (1962: 219). And where 'marginal parenthood' exists, it is as a result of the persistence into the present of forms of mating which originated in slave society. Matrifocality is not an issue for Professor Smith; he is concerned only with household headship and where a situation exists of male headship co-existing with the complex of authority and organisational elements I called matrifocal, he assumes that a condition of instability has arisen which will soon lead to disintegration. The appearance of complexity in M. G. Smith's work is produced by an empty formalism which insists upon multiplying categories, a procedure well expressed in the statement

> Given a mating system which contains three equally valid alternative forms, there will be six divergent forms of parenthood, one for each sex in each type of union (1962: 219).

Elizabeth Bott's well-known study of urban family structure in England (Bott 1957) is more relevant to the issues being considered here than is most of the work on the Caribbean. The question with which she was concerned is the effect upon domestic family relations of role performance in external systems; in order to determine this she chose to make a detailed examination of the family life of twenty couples. Her book *Family and Social Network* has been widely discussed and I shall deal with only a small part of it.

She points out that the literature on American and English working class family life often characterises the husband-father as 'authoritarian' while at the same time the family structure is 'mother-centred'. These apparently contradictory statements can be reconciled if it is recognised that such couples generally exhibit 'segregated conjugal roles' – a concept which she develops at some length. In short it means that they have separate spheres

127

of activity within the family and interact separately with friends and kin outside the family. Discussing one of her case families she shows that while the husband has a network of friends with whom he spends time at the pub, in cycle racing or playing cricket, the wife's close contact is with neighbours and above all with her mother, her mother's sisters and her maternal grandmother.

> These women and their children formed an important group, helping one another in household tasks and child care, and providing aid in crises. . . Within the network of relatives, there was thus a nucleus composed of the grandmother, her daughters, and her daughters' daughters; the relationships of these women were sufficiently intense and distinctive to warrant the term 'organized group' (Bott 1957: 69).

The emergence of these groups of female kin depends most immediately upon the pattern of segregation of conjugal roles, which is a special case of marked sex-role differentiation. Despite their greater prevalence in the working class they may appear anywhere in the status scale. Close emotional ties between mothers and children are to be expected but are not sufficient to account for the emergence of these clusters of female relatives.

> To phrase the discussion in general terms: whenever there are no particular economic advantages to be gained by affiliation with paternal relatives, and whenever two or preferably three generations of mothers and daughters are living in the same place at the same time, a bilateral kinship system is likely to develop a matrilateral stress, and groups composed of sets of mothers and daughters may form within networks of kin. . . .these groups of mothers and daughters have no structural continuity. They do not last for several generations; they are not named; they tend to break up when the grandmother dies, and they are readily dissolved if their members are separated from one another (Bott 1957: 137–8).

If Bott's analysis is correct then we should expect to find this matrilateral stress in kinship ties occurring in many different societies. The reason for the lack of 'structural continuity' is that the ties originate and have meaning within the domestic domain; they are rooted in the identity of interests and activities of women whose principle role is that of mothers. This is very close to the assumption which underlay my own analysis of the Guyana materials; the difference there is that the surrounding complex of male roles produced significant differences in domestic group structure.

The real question then, is whether the emergence of this 'matrilateral stress' is in itself sufficient to warrant the application of the special term 'matrifocal', and whether that term should be applied to the system of familial relations or to domestic organisation.

A number of other studies have identified matrifocal family structure in societies as widely separated as Java, Mescalero Apache, and the poorer sections of the population of Naples (Geertz 1961; Boyer 1964; Parsons 1969). In all these cases we find the same combination of an expectation of strong male dominance in the marital relationship and as head of the household, coupled with a reality in which mother–child relations are strongly solidary and groups of women, daughters and daughters' children emerge to provide a basis of continuity and security. The writers offer various explanations and hypotheses to account for this state of affairs, but essentially the issues raised are as I have set them out above.

IV. Cultural principles, norms and social behaviour

In all the reports of matrifocal family structure that I have cited there is the suggestion that it is somehow anomalous. It is rarely made clear whether the anomaly exists for the people being studied or for the investigator, and while all the investigators tend to stress the positive or adaptive value of matrifocal tendencies only Bott treats them as being 'normal'. In this section I shall reconsider some of my earlier conclusions about Caribbean kinship in the light of further work carried out in Guyana and Jamaica between 1967 and 1969.[7]

This more recent study was designed to explore in greater depth, and more directly, cultural values and norms in their relation to behaviour. The method used involved repeated interviews with a small number of informants rather than wide-ranging surveys using pre-determined questions. This method is statistically limited but it elicits material from which one may better arrive at those basic axioms, cultural paradigms and accepted principles which are fundamental to an understanding of 'norms'. The first task I set myself was the accurate determination of informants' cultural conceptions in the domain we refer to as 'kinship'.[8]

I have already touched upon some of the difficulties of Fortes' discussion of norms, and before going further I should make clear some of the analytical distinctions made in this study.[9] Schneider, following Talcott Parsons, has argued that it is important to analyse cultural systems in their own right as systems of symbols and meanings, distinct from, but empirically related to social systems. The cultural system is 'abstracted' from norms which are the rules and regulations for proper behaviour. The cultural system

> . . .consists in the system of symbols and meanings embedded in the normative system but which is a quite distinct aspect of it and can easily be abstracted from it. By symbols and meanings I mean the basic premises which a culture posits for life: what its units consist in; how those units are defined and differentiated; how they form an integrated order or classification; how the world is structured; in what parts it consists and

on what premises it is conceived to exist, the categories and classifications of the various domains of the world of man and how they relate one with another, and the world that man sees himself living in (Schneider 1972: 38).

But the cultural system is held to be separable into two parts – a 'pure' level and a 'conglomerate' level. The conglomerate level brings together elements from different 'pure' domains into models for the action of 'persons'; thus the person 'father' will be a conglomerate of elements from the kinship domain, the sex-role domain, the status and age role domains, etc.

> The conglomerate system is oriented toward action, toward telling people how to behave, toward telling people how-to-do-it under ideal circumstances. It is thus much closer to the normative system. The pure system, however, is oriented toward the state-of-being, toward How Things Are. It is in the transition from How Things Are and How Things Ought To Be to the domain of If That Is So, How Then Should One Act that the pure systems come together to form the conglomerate systems for action (Schneider 1972: 42).

I have quoted Schneider at some length since I have employed his distinction between analytically separable cultural and social system levels. However, Schneider nowhere explains the difference between the conglomerate and the normative system except to say that the former elements are found in a normative matrix which also contains social system elements (Schneider 1972: 44). While it is analytically convenient to separate 'basic assumptions' from 'normative rules', and to recognise a measure of continuity in the array of symbols which are transmitted from one generation to the next, one must recognise that those symbols acquire their meaning from the experience of social life and not from some inherent property of the timeless principles and axioms. It is precisely the device of separating the 'is' from the 'ought' as in the quotation from Schneider above, that lies at the root of the sterile philosophical dispute between idealism and positivism. The issue was dealt with by Marx in his extensive notes on Hegel's *Philosophy of Right*, and by Feuerbach who summed up the issue in his contention that 'space and time are modes of existence... Timeless feeling, timeless volition, timeless thought are no-thing, monsters' (Feuerbach 1843: quoted in Avineri 1970: 11).

I shall assume that norms, by their very nature, are subject to variation; they are developed in the process of understanding particular situations in terms of cultural assumptions and prescriptions, knowledge of system requirements, and calculation of individual and group interests. They are ideas-in-action and have to be treated as such. Useful though it may be for us as anthropologists to construct an intermediate 'conglomerate' level which indicates to us the manner in which social actors combine cultural elements from different domains in the processes of social interaction, we should not assume that they constitute unvarying 'models for action'.

Let us now examine our data and the concept of matrifocality in the light of these considerations.

(*i*) *Cultural Principles*

There are persistent reports in the literature on Caribbean kinship of a belief that 'blood' is transmitted exclusively through one or the other parent. Writing of land tenure in Jamaica, Edith Clarke states that rights to family land may be inherited 'through the blood' or 'by the name', which suggests a conceptual distinction between inheritance of 'blood' through females and 'name' through males (Clarke 1957: 44, 48). In fact Miss Clarke footnotes an extensive quote from Rattray on the Ashanti distinction between blood, inherited matrilineally, and spirit or semen, inherited patrilineally (1957: 71). Although she does not say so directly the point of the quote would seem to be to suggest that there is some continuity of African concepts. African concepts do survive in the New World of course, but the question is – how widespread are they and to what extent do they constitute a set of beliefs which dominate thinking about kinship at the present time?[10]

The evidence from our studies shows unequivocally that all our informants, irrespective of class or race, and whether Guyanese or Jamaicans, share the assumption that 'blood' is transmitted to the child from both parents and that conception follows a single act of sexual intercourse during which the male seed is implanted in the female womb there to fertilise an egg which grows into a baby. There is considerable variation and confusion about the precise anatomical and physiological details of this process, but the general idea is clear.[11] It is believed that both father and mother contribute physical material to the formation of the child and transmit to it such intangible features as gestures, manner of walking, speech patterns and temperament. This is amply confirmed by informants' discussions of the transmission of racial characteristics which is a topic of central interest in the Caribbean.

Within this general framework one may find differential stress upon the matrifilial and patrifilial ties, as when Jamaicans assert that 'mother-blood is stronger than father-blood'. But all these distinctions are made within the framework of a general ideology of bilateral affiliation. It is interesting that when Miss Clarke reports the distinction between inheritance through the blood or by the name, she does so in the context of a discussion of the *equivalence* of these two methods of inheritance. Blood relationship is believed to flow from the natural act of conception and each individual has one 'real' father and one 'real' mother. Many children grow up apart from

131

Table 1. *Affinal composition of kin-type chain by union type*

Kin-type chain	Kingston Jamaica middle-class		Kingston Jamaica lower-class		Jamaica rural areas		Guyana East Indians		Guyana all others		All cases	
	No.	%	No.	%	No.	%	No.	%	No.	%	No.	%
CA (Legal)	400	90.0	308	57.7	305	60.1	99	88.4	411	67.5	1523	69.0
CA (Common-law)	14	3.1	108	20.2	105	20.7	10	8.9	115	18.8	352	15.9
CA (Visiting)	24	5.4	110	20.6	88	17.4	3	2.7	76	12.5	301	13.6
CA (Unspecified)	6	1.4	8	1.5	9	1.8	0	0	7	1.2	30	1.3
Total CA	444	100.0	534	100.0	507	100.0	112	100.0	609	100.0	2206	100.0
CA (Legal) C	699	96.5	239	44.7	388	56.7	35	100.0	226	87.5	1587	71.0
CA (Common-law) C	2	0.3	142	26.5	193	28.2	0	0	13	5.0	350	15.6
CA (Visiting) C	22	3.0	153	28.6	103	15.0	0	0	19	7.4	297	13.2
CA (Unspecified) C	1	0.2	0	0	0	0	0	0	0	0	1	0.2
Total CAC	724	100.0	534	100.0	684	100.0	35	100.0	258	100.0	2235	100.0
CA (Legal) CA+	512	99.4	73	51.7	136	44.6	9	100.0	88	83.8	818	76.0
CA (Common-Law) CA+	0	0	33	23.4	133	43.6	0	0	10	9.5	176	16.3
CA (Visiting) CA+	2	0.4	35	24.8	36	11.8	0	0	7	6.7	80	7.4
CA (Unspecified) CA+	1	0.2	0	0	0	0	0	0	0	0	1	0.2
Total CACA+	515	100.0	141	100.0	305	100.0	9	100.0	105	100.0	1075	100.0

Note: The analytical technique of tracing kin-type chains is adapted from the unpublished manuscript by Schneider and Cottrell, *American Genealogies*.

one, or even both, 'real' parents, but the believed-in *physical* bond cannot be destroyed entirely.

Relatives 'by law' constitute the second important component of the culturally defined kin-universe of West Indians, but the meaning of 'law' is extremely complex. Although legal marriage creates the model 'in-law' relationship, in fact relatives by law are simply those who have 'come into the family' through the establishment of any kind of conjugal union. The term 'bye-family' is used (though rarely by members of the middle class) as a general category for all those who have 'come into the family' either through the establishment of conjugal unions or through the adoption of behaviour appropriate to kinsmen.[12]

It is well-known that in the Caribbean non-legal unions are common, though it is often suggested that these unions are quite different from legal marriage in terms of the relationships they generate (as we saw M. G. Smith suggesting in the quotation on page 127), and that they are institutionalised only among 'the folk' or the lower class. Neither contention is correct; one finds unions of all types among all classes and racial groups (though the incidence of occurrence certainly varies) and our data show that legal marriages do not generate proportionately more kinship links than other forms of union. This can be illustrated by reference to Table 1 which compares the proportions of affines of consanguineals, and their kin, which are generated by various kinds of union.

The 'kin type chain' is arrived at by tracing the links on the genealogy from Ego to each person on the genealogy, and noting each time a change is made from a consanguineal to an affinal tie. For example, if one is tracing the relationship from Ego to his mother's brother's wife's sister's daughter's husband's brother's child, then the first consanguineal chain (C) runs from ego to mother's brother where an affinal tie intervenes, (A) and then another consanguineal chain runs from the wife to her sister's daughter (CAC), another affinal link and a final consanguineal chain from the husband's brother's child. Thus the total kin type chain in this case is CACAC. By noting the type of union involved in these chains we can compare the propensity to recognise consanguineal relatives of spouses of different types – legal, common-law or visiting. In order to make the comparison meaningful we must know the proportions of each union type occurring in the sample as a whole, and this information is provided in Table 2.

Taking all cases it would appear that relatives by common-law and visiting unions are somewhat *more* likely to be recognised than relatives through legal marriages, but this varies by class and race, as a close examination of the tables will show. The general point to be made is that non-legal unions certainly do generate recognised kinship ties, especially among lower class informants.

Both legal and non-legal unions create blood ties through the birth of

Table 2. *Union types*

Union type	Kingston Jamaica middle-class		Kingston Jamaica lower-class		Jamaica rural areas		Guyana East Indians		Guyana all others		All cases	
	No.	%	No.	%	No.	%	No.	%	No.	%	No.	%
1. Extant Unions												
Legal	1701	98.3	923	73.7	1133	83.6	269	93.0	1110	84.9	5136	86.6
Common-law	17	1.0	241	19.2	196	14.4	18	6.2	144	11.0	616	10.4
Visiting	11	0.7	88	7.0	26	2.0	2	0.8	53	4.0	180	3.0
Total	1729	100.0	1252	100.0	1355	100.0	289	100.0	1307	100.0	5932	100.0
2. Extant and Terminated												
Legal	2005	97.5	1062	71.4	1284	78.4	306	93.1	1261	81.7	5918	83.9
Common-law and Visiting	50	2.5	425	28.5	353	21.6	23	6.9	283	18.3	1134	16.1
Total	2055	100.0	1487	100.0	1637	100.0	329	100.0	1544	100.0	7052	100.0

children, but there is also another principle at work. Despite the primary distinction between blood kin and relatives 'by law', informants consistently tend to reduce the distinction between consanguines and affines by stressing the assimilation of affines to 'the family'. This seems to be part of a more general cultural process among the lower class in which there is an emphasis upon creating and keeping open as many relationships of diffuse enduring solidarity as possible (see Schneider and Smith 1972).

One crude measure of the shape and extent of the area of social relationships embraced by 'kinship' is a simple count of the persons recognised by informants as being in some way connected to them by ties of consanguinity and affinity. Table 3 presents the gross figures for those cases which were considered to be complete enough for this kind of analysis.

The very method of collecting genealogies tends to filter out relationships which, while lacking a basis either in consanguinity or by virtue of a sexual union, nonetheless share the general code for conduct of diffuse enduring solidarity, and are regarded by informants as being 'like family'. In some cases such relationships were included on the genealogies because the informant asserted that a kinship tie existed even though they could not say just how, but we must assume that many 'kin-like' relationships are in fact excluded.

The range of variation in the size of kin universe between informants raises some interesting questions. For example, the largest case in the Guyana group, containing 1,106 individuals, was collected from a 41-year-old woman from a large, predominantly Black, coastal village in which intra-village conjugal unions have been common for over a century. Therefore many of the people she knows *as fellow villagers* she also knows to be connected to her by some kinship tie. For the inhabitants of this village it is axiomatic that village territorial ties are kinship ties at a certain level – an axiom summarised in such statements as 'All August Town is one family' (see R. T. Smith, 1956: 203–20). Whether one regards village ties as kinship ties, or genealogical ties as being recognised because of territorial ties, is of little significance at this level. Both are characterised by ideal relations of diffuse, enduring solidarity. One of the reasons, then, for the variation in genealogy size is the differential experience of individuals in growing up in local communities of varying size and kinship composition.

Another interesting aspect of Table 3 is that while the ratio of males to females among recognised living relatives is close to normal for this population, informants consistently recognise slightly more dead males than females. This might partially be accounted for by an actual preponderance of dead males available to be recognised within the shallow generation depth of these genealogies, but the fact is significant as a counter to the idea that females are somehow more important across the total social field.

Table 4 reinforces some of the impressions gained from Table 3. The

Table 3. *Kin living and dead by sex*

Vital status	Kingston Jamaica middle-class		Kingston Jamaica lower-class		Jamaica rural areas		Guyana East Indians		Guyana all others		All cases	
	No.	%	No.	%	No.	%	No.	%	No.	%	No.	%
Living												
Male	1171	46.4	1336	45.3	1171	43.4	259	42.9	1172	41.5	5109	44.1
Female	1210	48.0	1256	42.6	1176	43.5	234	38.8	1202	42.6	5078	43.8
Unknown	138	5.4	354	12.0	352	13.0	110	18.2	444	15.7	1398	12.1
Total	2519	100.0	2946	100.0	2699	100.0	603	100.0	2818	100.0	11585	100.0
Dead												
Male	469	46.2	285	50.6	406	50.3	41	60.2	236	55.6	1437	50.0
Female	368	36.2	208	36.9	324	40.1	21	30.8	175	41.2	1096	38.2
Unknown	177	17.4	70	12.4	76	9.4	6	8.8	13	3.0	342	11.8
Total	1014	100.0	563	100.0	806	100.0	68	100.0	424	100.0	2875	100.0
Total living	2519	71.2	2946	83.9	2699	77.0	603	89.8	2818	86.9	11585	80.1
Total dead	1014	28.6	563	16.0	806	22.9	68	10.1	424	13.0	2875	19.9
Grand total	3536	100.0	3510	100.0	3506	100.0	671	100.0	3242	100.0	14460	100.0
Number of cases	12		14		11		2		12		51	
Mean size	295		251		319		335		270		284	
Largest case	733		606		661		465		1106		1106	
Smallest case	41		52		121		206		80		41	

proportion of blood kin on the father's side is consistently higher than on the mother's side. Again it is possible that there were more patrilateral than matrilateral consanguines actually available to be recognised, but the finding is suggestive in dispelling the notion that West Indians do not recognise patrilateral kin ties as much as those through the mother.

ii. Norms and behaviour

So far it would appear that these Caribbean data support Fortes' contention that bilateral filiation is a universal aspect of kinship; at least they do not contradict it. However, it is vital to distinguish between the conceptual dogma of bilateral filiation, which is a cultural assumption of a particular kind, and the structure of the norms which mediate behaviour in the process of social interaction; it is here that the distinction between cultural conceptions and norms comes into play. These norms do not require bilateral filiation in the sense implied by Fortes' assertion that a person 'lacking either side. . .will be handicapped, either in respect of the ritual statuses and moral capacities that every complete person must have. . .or in the politico-jural and economic capacities and attributes that are indispensable for conducting himself as a normal right-and-duty bearing person' (Fortes 1969: 262). Fortes' own presentation of material on Ashanti kinship and marriage leads me to doubt the generality of this statement. He has stated unequivocally that 'an Ashanti woman need not be married in order to have legitimate children. Once sexually liberated [by performance of the nubility ceremony], she is free, as we have already seen, to produce offspring for her lineage, provided she does not violate the incest prohibitions, which is one reason why she must be able to cite a licit genitor' (Fortes 1969: 209). We are somewhat handicapped by the absence of detailed case material, but it would appear that the important consideration is not the establishment of a pater for the child, but rather the avoidance of the suspicion that the woman has engaged in an incestuous relationship.

Even if we take Ashanti as exemplifying the generalisation that both patrifiliation and matrifiliation are invariably present in all kinship systems, Fortes' work makes it clear that it is quite unjustifiable to move from the cultural dogma that every child must have two parents (which, incidentally, I do not believe to be universal), to the assumption that it is normatively prescribed that children should be brought up in two-parent households, or that the nuclear family is a normal configuration based upon the functional requirements of child-rearing. The early studies of household composition and the developmental cycle in household groups in Ashanti made it clear that the contrary pulls of marriage and lineage attachment could result in a wide range of outcomes which renders the idea of the empirical universality of nuclear families as co-residential child-rearing units quite erroneous.

Table 4. *Composition of consanguineal kin*

Kin type	Kingston Jamaica middle-class		Kingston Jamaica lower-class		Jamaica rural areas		Guyana East Indians		Guyana all others		All cases	
	No.	%	No.	%	No.	%	No.	%	No.	%	No.	%
Blood Kin – Father's side	569	48.3	639	47.4	522	38.8	143	42.8	886	57.3	2759	48.0
Blood Kin – Mother's side	445	37.7	439	32.5	487	36.2	92	27.5	402	26.0	1865	32.4
Siblings and direct descendants of self and siblings	164	13.9	269	19.9	334	24.8	99	29.6	257	16.6	1123	19.5
Total consanguines	1178	100.0	1347	100.0	1343	100.0	334	100.0	1545	100.0	5747	100.0

Here our data from the Caribbean are clear: they show that there is nothing anomalous in the apparent complexity of household composition, the shifting of children between households, or the changing patterns of mating relations. The lower class West Indian family is not based on marriage or on the nuclear family, and our informants show no concern about implementing some abstract norm, or value, of nuclear family solidarity. This is true even though marriage is a statistically 'normal' pattern of mating and the nuclear family is the most frequently occurring form of domestic group. The documentation of this by means of extensive case material will have to be left for future publication, but once we abandon the *a priori* assumption that the complex household and mating patterns are distorted forms of a basic nuclear family system, then many of the supposed problems of interpretation disappear. Child-rearing is doubtless an important task, as is the provision of support for women and children, but these things do not require a nuclear family unit for their accomplishment. The evidence for this is super-abundant, and one need only examine the average lower-class genealogy to appreciate the impossibility of arranging the individuals on it into co-residential nuclear families.

In view of the foregoing discussion is there any point in retaining the designation 'matrifocal' for this family system, and if so, what should we mean by it?

In 1956 I stated that the mother–child relationship is the basic unit of all kinship systems, and that we should examine the way in which males' roles are structured in relation to it. This Radcliffe-Brownian view of kinship now seems less useful, since I believe that the question of what constitutes the elementary units of all kinship systems should be left open for further investigation. The elements which have been included in the matrifocal complex can be more adequately understood as follows.

(a) Domestic relations: in any system of marked sex-role differentiation where men are excluded from participation in child-rearing, cooking, washing and other domestic activities, women will be 'dominant' within this sphere. Such a statement does not presuppose any particular kin ties between the women, or between the women and the children; it merely asserts the segregation of adult males from the major activities of the domestic domain. Adult males are likely to relate to female-focussed domestic groups as consumers of services, providers of support, and as linking elements between the domestic group and the 'external' systems of social, economic, political and ritual activity.

These are all functional, or social system, considerations which arise in a situation of marked sex-role differentiation where men are marginal to domestic activities. Such marginality may be expressed in the physical absence of men from the physical environs of the house for most of the time, or it may be expressed in the form of spatial segregation within the house or compound. To the extent that sex-role differentiation excludes women from participation in 'external' systems they will be correspondingly dependent upon males to relate them to such systems. It will be clear that I am using the concept of domestic domain here in a way similar to Fortes who sees it as the setting for the performance of familial roles as opposed to the jural roles of the external kinship system.

Thus we can find 'matrifocality' in domestic relations in a wide range of situations, from those where males virtually monopolise political, economic and ritual life – as in China and India – to those where women are active in all or some of those spheres – as in the Caribbean, Java or West Africa – and there will be a range of variation within this continuum. The reason that the domestic relations are mother-focussed rather than simply female-focussed is that 'mothering', or child-rearing, is the central activity of the domestic domain and is productive of the intense affective relations which pervade it.

There can be considerable variation in the manner in which particular women relate to particular men within the system of reciprocal dependencies of the division of labour by sex. Women may be under the authority and protection of the men of a group defined as being a consanguineal entity, as in the case of the Ashanti *abusua*, while having sexual relations with 'lovers' or husbands from other groups; they may develop exclusive attachment to a husband; or they may be related to a number of men, simultaneously or serially, in a number of different ways. There is no inherent or systematic limitation on this.

The 'Bott effect' – the development of solidary but non-permanent groups of mothers and daughters – is a subsidiary effect of the system of sex-role differentiation when it is combined with geographical propinquity and the absence of countervailing pressures such as status or property considerations. It does not appear in India for example, because the ideal is to make a sharp break between a woman and her kin at marriage.

(b) Familial relations: by far the most important element producing a matrifocal quality in lower-class West Indian kinship is the low priority of solidary emphasis placed upon the conjugal relationship within the area of 'close family' ties.[13] There has been a tendency in the literature on the Afroamerican family to attribute this to the residual effects of slavery, or to the effects of 'poverty' in rendering males ineffective as the sole support of wife and children. As a kind of functional compensation, it is suggested, women are inclined to spread the risk of failure among a number of different men. This is not a particularly convincing explanation, even though it is certainly true that in the practice of social life under conditions of economic deprivation and insecurity, the failure of men to meet the responsibility of supporting their wives and children could lead to marital break-up, or conflict. But quite apart from this functional consideration, what we find is priority of emphasis placed upon the mother-child and sibling relationship, while the conjugal relationship is expected to be less solidary, and less affectively intense. It is this aspect of familial relations which is crucial in producing matrifocal family structure.

In this paper I have paid relatively little attention to the controversial topic of marriage which has so dominated the discussion of Caribbean kinship, so it may be well to conclude with some observations on it.

Most writers on Caribbean kinship make a sharp distinction between legal, religiously-sanctioned marriage and non-legal unions. I have already referred to M. G. Smith's elaborate typology distinguishing various types of parenthood according to the sex of the parent and the status of the union. Few writers adopt such formalistic rigidity, but many share the same basic idea which mis-represents the situation in important ways. There is no essential difference in the nature and quality of the relationship between those in various types of union where both partners are lower class. The distinction between legal and non-legal unions is entirely in terms of their status and legal significance, and this latter may be of minor importance to the majority of lower-class people. Marriage is an act in the status system and not in the kinship system.[14]

It is frequently assumed that visiting unions and common-law unions are distinctively 'lower class' or 'folk' institutions, and insofar as lower-class people marry, this is an indication of their internalisation of middle-class values and culture. Again this is untrue. Marriage, common-law unions and visiting unions form a coherent series in which each one is defined by contrasting it with the others. All forms of mating are practised at all class levels (though with different frequencies), but higher status males marry status equals, or superiors, and mate extra-legally with status inferiors. Among the lower class where status differences are constricted, this rule becomes transformed into the idea that marriage is an act conferring prestige to be entered into when the partners can afford it. Marriage as a public act of status affirmation is quite distinct from the process of contracting and entering conjugal unions, which is almost casual. The situation is in some ways reminiscent of that reported by Yalman for the poorer inhabitants of Terutenne in Ceylon, who often dispense with marriage altogether (Yalman 1967: 133–4; 150–88). Such informality in the making and breaking of unions is associated with status group endogamy, absolute bilaterality in inheritance, and a marked segregation of conjugal roles with relatively little concern over sexual fidelity.

All these conditions hold for the West Indian lower class; the conjugal relationship, ideally, is one of mutual respect and consideration rather than intense effect, but the most important fact is that conjugal ties rank below other primary kinship ties in the hierarchy of solidarity. If we consider this fact in conjunction with the segregation of males from the activities of the domestic domain, it is easy to see why conjugal unions can be unstable without markedly affecting family structure, and why visiting unions are a perfectly viable form. Visiting unions embody the same core relationship as that in marriage or common-law unions, but here the union is separated from the domestic domain. The relationship which remains strong throughout life is that between mother and child, or between the child and the woman who 'mothered' or 'grew' him.

(c) Stratification and economic factors: poverty, racism and marked status distinctions are a palpable fact of life in the West Indies, as in many other parts of the world, and all these factors affect the day-to-day relationships in which people are involved. However, I do not think that they are the sole reason for the development of matrifocal family relations. Theoretically, such a system should be capable of maintenance in a variety of economic settings. The absence of property and status considerations is particularly conducive to the development of a matrifocal system, but this need not imply poverty. It is possible that groups of unequivocally high status and ample property are so secure and so tolerant of unstable marriage that they develop a system very similar to that described for the West Indian lower class. In such groups women may hold and manage property equally with men, and be quite capable of holding together a diverse household group, or providing the focus for a complex familial network.

Traditional Ashanti, with a very different economic system, came very close to having a matrifocal family system. However, despite the frequency of occurrence of female-headed household groups, the close linkage between the familial system and the wider politico-jural system – a linkage effected solely by men in the status of brother, or mother's brother, to the women of the household – shifts the focus of the kinship system away from mothers, to mothers' brothers, despite the structural prominence of the mother role. Similarly, once the maintenance or demonstration of status, or the transmission of crucial property, is effected through marriage, then the focus of the familial systems tends to swing back onto the marital tie and paternal authority, despite the intensity of affectual relations between mother and children.

V. Conclusion

The coining of terms does not solve problems, and may in fact obscure more than clarify. The concept of matrifocal family and domestic relations is a difficult one because of the complexity of the factors involved. In this paper I have tried to set out the major dimensions of the problem as I see them, rather than attempting a 'definition' of matrifocality. A subsidiary purpose was to demonstrate the existence of a family system in which legitimate paternity is not a pre-requisite for the development of full social personality (or psychological health), and in which the central relationships can tolerate an attenuation or elimination of the conjugal bond without becoming pathological. In doing so I was led to question some of Meyer Fortes' generalisations about the elementary structures of kinship, and particularly his idea that the bilaterality of kinship systems universally arises out of the experience of parenthood and procreative cohabitation.

The West Indian kinship system is clearly bilateral; children are believed to share common substance, 'blood', with both parents and their respective consanguineal kin, and all kinship relations are believed to be properly imbued with prescriptive amity. These beliefs, assumptions, general concepts, or cultural principles, remain the same no matter what the particular circumstances of individuals' particular lives may be. They are not a projection of domestic experience on to other levels. Furthermore they do not transform simply and directly into 'norms' which then 'govern' behaviour, any more than behavioural regularities are crystallised into norms, which are then rationalised into concepts or mythical charters. The process is much more complex and can only be understood by focussing attention upon that point at which cultural assumptions and moral axioms are brought into conjunction with other aspects of reality in the process of social life. This above all is the lesson one learns from the richness of Fortes' field material, and from his example in pursuing the analysis of data even into their inconsistencies.

Notes

1 For example, Fortes reports that 40% of household heads at Asokore and 47% at Agogo are women; for the three Guyanese villages the percentages are 35.5%, 17% and 34.5%. The proportion for the contemporary United States is roughly 20% if one includes females living alone; the proportion among those who are classified as non-white is much higher and comparable to that for Guyana – 33.4% in 1969.

2 Barnes (1971*b*: 194–226) has noted the same difficulty over Fortes' varying definition of 'norms'.

3 While I can accept the criticism that the analysis placed too little emphasis upon the distinction between familial and domestic relations, I cannot accept the idea that this was due to some failure to distinguish between them at a definitional level. A careful reading of the book will show that the decision to treat the household as the most important locus of family relations was deliberate and not due to mistaken identity.

4 She says for example 'R. T. Smith... has used the term "matrifocal" to identify the type, thereby emphasising the role played by the female.' To dispel any uncertainty as to whether she equates my use of the term 'matrifocal' with her 'consanguineal form' she specifically states that 'the report [Smith's] lacks detail on the actual relationships existing between various members of the family, which makes it difficult to ascertain the nature of the consanguineal household (called "matrifocal family" by Smith)'. '...we are never certain from his description just what

the matrifocal family *is*, other than that it is "woman-headed" ' (Gonzalez 1969: 128).

5 Thus in a recent book by Farber (1972) we find an extended discussion of matrifocality based on Kunstadter's article.

6 It is gratifying to see that in her most recent article (Gonzalez 1970), she has extricated herself from some of these difficulties and returned to a point of view remarkably similar to that set out in my earlier work (Smith, R. T. 1956 and 1957). For example she rejects the simple identification of matrifocal with either female-headed households or consanguineal families, and she recognises that the matrifocal quality of relationship patterns only appears because of the peculiarity of male roles.

7 The study was supported by a grant from the National Science Foundation (NSF-GS-1709) for which grateful acknowledgement is made. I am also indebted to David M. Schneider for many of the ideas used in this study both at the stage of data collection and analysis.

8 That there may be a problem in deciding just what to include or exclude from that domain will be evident if one reads Schneider's paper 'What is kinship all about?' (Schneider 1972).

9 See R. T. Smith 1970 for a fuller discussion of the distinction between cultural, normative and behavioural aspects of kinship.

10 Since there is considerable, and growing, interest in the whole issue of continuities in culture from Africa to the New World, I should make it clear that my argument in this paper does not preclude the importance of such continuities. I have myself reported knowledge of Ashanti day-names and survivals of totemic beliefs, witchcraft concepts and ritual activities clearly of African origin, among Guyanese villagers of African descent (Smith, R. T. 1956: 131, 158, 164–7). However, it is also crucial to recognise the manner in which these items of cultural material are incorporated in contemporary conceptual systems and the way in which they are used in the process of social life in the modern West Indian context.

11 Spiro's letter to the editor of *Man* (Spiro 1972), correcting Montague's misconceptions about the ideology of 'virgin birth', explains very clearly the issues involved here and sets straight the question of what degree of understanding of reproductive processes is involved.

12 The use of the expression 'bye-family' among the West Indian lower class may be an example of the survival of old English terms, or the creation of terms out of English words. The term 'bye' in English means secondary, or subsidiary, which is precisely the meaning it has when combined with 'family' in the West Indies. The term is also used in cricket (which is the West Indies national sport) to mean a run scored without actually hitting the ball; again a suitable parallel. However, there is also a possibility that it derives from a Hindi word such as *Bhai* (brother).

13 The idea of a hierarchy of solidary emphasis within the close family relationship complex is dealt with in a preliminary way in Schneider & Smith: 1973.

14 Freilich and Coser in a recent paper comment on the similarity between different types of union in Trinidad, and suggest that the terms Legal marriage, Common-law marriage, etc. 'are all structurally and functionally the same' so far as Trinidadian peasants are concerned (1972: 6). I think that this is true, except for the prestige factor.

Furies, Witches and Mothers

Grace Harris

Some years ago, in the Taita District of Kenya, I overheard two men discussing proposed changes in the bridewealth laws. One said, 'Why should I pay bridewealth at all? Why should I pay for my own children, for my own blood?' The other answered scathingly, 'What are you saying? Do you think that your children are not also of their mother's blood?' Hearing their exchange I thought of the scene in Aeschylus' *Oresteia* when the Furies and Apollo argue the case of Orestes' murder of his mother Clytemnestra. Is he guilty of shedding kindred blood (as the Furies claim) or is the mother not really a parent (as Apollo asserts)? The East African scene might appear to have only a superficial resemblance to a great drama of ancient Greece. Yet I believe that a social anthropological examination of the *Oresteia* can shed some new light on it. Perhaps, also, that examination can pose some further questions for social anthropologists.

Being no classicist, I could not (if I would) refer to the vast literature on the *Oresteia*. Reference will instead be to only two articles. One is R. P. Winnington-Ingram's 'Clytemnestra and the Vote of Athena'. That essay points to the subtle ways in which Aeschylus treats the relations between male and female characters. I make use of some of the author's suggestions and I try to build on his interpretation in terms of 'the sexual antithesis' (1948: 132). In 'Zeus in Aeschylus', Hugh Lloyd-Jones rejects interpretations that see a refined and ethically 'advanced' Zeus-religion in Aeschylus. The Furies do not really undergo a 'change of heart'. The *Oresteia*, he says, does not move from the 'primitive' ethics of retribution to an 'advanced' ethics of wisdom-through-suffering. The ethical motif is still that the doer must suffer (1956: 64–6). According to him, the third drama of the trilogy, the *Eumenides*, exhibits 'naive dramaturgy' in the tie-breaking vote of Athena 'for the male' (p. 64). With Lloyd-Jones' rejection of 'progressionist' interpretations I completely agree. But I argue that the Furies do undergo an important transition, albeit not a transformation. The charge of 'naive dramaturgy' is questioned.

There are two major movements in the trilogy as a whole. One leads from the complexities of human interaction through the distinguishing of social relations from one another, to the formulation of ritual relations. The other movement brings, out of vaguely-personified Fury or Furies, the Furies-Eumenides as specifically *maternal* figures. Both movements receive attention. I ignore the euphemistic aspect of the title *Eumenides*.

145

Those familiar with the work of Meyer Fortes will recognize an attempt to make use of a number of his concepts and working methods:

1. The concept of domains (particularly jural-political, familial or kinship and ritual) (1969: 95–100).
2. The view of unilineal descent groups as having two aspects: one jural-political and the other familial (Chap. V).
3. Correspondingly, recognition of the fact that in societies with unilineal descent groups (whether matrilineal or patrilineal), the jural-political and familial or kinship domains are interconnected through the descent system (1970 *a*: 48–9).
4. Discrimination of the elements from various domains which, interwoven, give coherence to complex situations of interaction (1969: 96).

Needless to say, any inappropriate uses of 'Fortesian' thought are my own and not Meyer Fortes' responsibility.

I. The Agamemnon: interwoven elements

Although full-scale patrilineages are not portrayed in the *Oresteia*, the social setting shows use of a principle of patrilineal descent. Orestes is not merely Agamemnon's legitimate son, but a descendant of Agamemnon's father Atreus and Atreus' father Pelops (Grene and Lattimore 1959: 35–171). The ghastly events which have occurred before the play's opening show two competing lines within a four-generation patriline, the sort so familiar to ethnologists of Africa (Forde 1947: 213–24). First and most cataclysmic was the rivalry between the full brothers Atreus and Thyestes, sons of Pelops. In the next generation Agamemnon and Menelaus, full brothers and sons of Atreus, oppose their patrilineal first cousin Aegisthus, son of Thyestes. By becoming the consort of Clytemnestra, wife of Agamemnon, in the latter's absence, Aegisthus achieves indirectly what his father Thyestes sought: transfer of the kingship to Thyestes and his descendants. Hence Agamemnon's son Orestes must be viewed as an enemy of Aegisthus. That is so apart from any plan of Orestes to avenge the death of Agamemnon at the hands of Clytemnestra and Aegisthus. It is dramatically convenient that, when Orestes has completed his vengeance, there are no other male descendants of Pelops to contend with.[1] He has no brothers and no patrilineal first or second cousins to carry on the rivalry. When Orestes wins out over Aegisthus he alone carries on the House of Atreus and, with it, the line of the shadowy great-grandfather Pelops. Matters are truly settled.

Agamemnon is 'king' and Orestes his heir-apparent in the House of Atreus. Thus the relationships among the patrilineal descendants of Atreus (and Pelops) are both kinship and jural-political. In narrowing the action of the first play to focus largely on Clytemnestra and Agamemnon, Aeschylus makes use of the interweaving of familial statuses with political ones. (To the complexity of the interactions portrayed he has added individual personalities that do not always fit well their social roles.) As a device for displaying the interweaving of elements, I list the ways in which the main characters are addressed and referred to.

Agamemnon:

1. The watchman calls him his *lord* (31) and his *king* (33). The Chorus also call him *lord* when they reproach Clytemnestra for murdering him (1400).

2. The Herald of course announces the return of Agamemnon as *king* (521). But he sees the palace as 'hall of kings and house beloved' (518). Hall and house are one building with two aspects, political and familial.

3. Agamemnon and Menelaus are Atreus' sons. The Chorus murmurs that their quarrel as members of the House of Atreus has caused sorrow to the citizens (458). The brothers are spoken of as wrongly involving the *politeía* in affairs of their own lineage by warring with Troy over Helen, Menelaus' errant wife. The Chorus thereby makes a distinction between the patriline as a descent group and its royal position in the jural-political domain.

4. Later the Chorus cries to Agamemnon, 'Behold my king: sacker of Troy's citadel, own issue of Atreus' (783–5). He has returned with a military victory. Then he can be referred to as Atreus' son because this is his legitimization as king!

5. Clytemnestra speaks of Agamemnon both as *husband* and as *king*. But until her last long speech to him, she emphasizes his marital relationship to her and his political relationship to others.

6. Agamemnon's reference to himself echoes the Herald: 'So to the *king's*[2] house and the home about the hearth I take my way' (851–2): he is both *king* and *husband*, returning to a woman who is both *queen* and *wife*.

7. Clytemnestra's first speech to Agamemnon is a masterpiece of cunning in which she repeatedly calls attention to the interweaving of their statuses as *husband* and *wife*, *king* and *queen*. He is her 'beloved one', her 'lord', 'sacker of Ilium'. She presents herself as having been a typical war-wife, worrying about her husband, but also as a wary queen. She has guarded their son, but for reasons of political danger has sent him away in another's care (for the son is Agamemnon's heir-apparent). The complexity of address and reference in her speech makes Agamemnon's return anything but a simple homecoming.

8. The next and last time Clytemnestra speaks of Agamemnon he is dead, murdered by her in his bath. First she calls him 'Agamemnon, my husband', but soon he is merely 'this corpse', neither husband nor king.

Clytemnestra:

1. The Chorus' first speech to Clytemnestra recognizes her complex social personality: she is 'lady, daughter of Tyndareus, Clytemnestra, our queen' (83–4). Seeking her counsel they do not remind her that her authority depends on being married to Agamemnon. At the end of the speech they sum up their political relationship with her by calling her 'our Apian land's singlehearted protectress' (257).

2. Clytemnestra refers to herself as Agamemnon's wife, 'watchdog of the house' (607) in a hypocritically boastful speech before the Herald. She is a *wife* welcoming her *husband* home from war.

3. A number of speeches identify her as a woman who exercises political authority or power by virtue of being the *wife* of a *king* and therefore a *queen*.

   a. The Watchman must cry the news of the beacons to 'Agamemnon's queen' (25) that she 'may rise up from her bed of state' (26).

   b. The Chorus, seeking information, give grounds for their homage in calling her the 'prince's lady' whose authority is legitimate when her husband is away. They say they come in reverence, but they take care to mark her as a person whose authority is not exercised in her own right (257–60).

   c. In her climactic speech after the murder of Agamemnon, Clytemnestra tells the people never again to call her Agamemnon's wife: she is now 'this corpse's queen' (1500). She has exchanged derived authority for dynastic power seized by violence.

4. Clytemnestra as a *woman* is also treated in a complex way:

   a. To the watchman she is a woman with 'male strength of heart' (11).

   b. The Chorus give her a backhanded compliment when they tell her that 'no man could speak with better grace' (351).

   c. Clytemnestra refers to herself as 'a woman merely' (347), but the Chorus misses her sarcasm. Later she denies that she can be bullied as 'a woman and vain' (1401).

   d. Agamemnon at his return (and after her fantastic 'welcoming' speech) addresses her as 'Daughter of Leda, you who kept my house for me' (914). From him she receives no honorifics or even any suggestion that the house is also hers. She is a woman born of woman.

   e. Finally the Chorus, horrified by the murder, call her *woman* and suggest that she has acted under the influence of drugs (1407–9). No longer the complex personage of the Chorus' first address to her, she is threatened with banishment.

As seen by others, Clytemnestra's violence has reduced her from being a high-born lady, daughter of Tyndareus, queen, protectress of the Apian land to: woman. As seen by herself, Clytemnestra has emerged from the deceptions of being *Agamemnon's wife* to being *queen*. To her Agamemnon, dead, is a non-person. But to others he is still lord and king, though fallen.

As the modes of address and reference change, there is an ever-shifting emphasis in the play from one set of statuses and relations to another. Aeschylus has subtly presented complex interactions in which familial and political (as well as ritual) elements are interwoven. Surely the skilful use of social complexities accounts for much of the play's depth and tension.

Potential and actual conflict between familial and political statuses appears most poignantly in the Chorus' account of how Agamemnon came to slay Iphegenia. Committed to war against Troy, should he disband the becalmed fleet out of unwillingness to sacrifice his daughter? Or should he invite another kind of disaster by killing her? The Chorus says, 'Her supplications and her cries of *father* were nothing, nor the *child's* lamentation to *kings* passioned for battle' (228–30). This was 'the second sacrifice unholy, untasted, working bitterness in the blood and faith lost' (151–2). It has worked bitterness and lost faith within Clytemnestra. In order to set right this *familial* wrong, Clytemnestra murders Agamemnon *as her husband*. But in this and in ruling together with Aegisthus she herself commits both political and familial wrong.

The last speeches of Clytemnestra and Aegisthus show how two differently placed persons involved in the 'same' event see it differently. To Clytemnestra, Agamemnon's death is 'last blood' for Atreus' slaughter of his brother's children: she concentrates on the wrongs done against kin as kin. But though Aegisthus retells the same story of the House of Atreus, he gives it a wholly political flavour. He, the last survivor of Thyestes' offspring, has come home to the house as king's palace. That the palace is henceforth his domestic home is almost incidental. Suitably he treats Clytemnestra's part in the murder as trivial, for he sees himself as the successful dynastic rival who will beat down opposition. The final howl of the Chorus calls Aegisthus a cockerel strutting by his hen: a political upstart profiting from an illicit domestic attachment. The scene is set for the return of Orestes to deal with Aegisthus as a political rival and with Clytemnestra as a woman who has wronged him as her son, and as her husband's son and successor.

II. The Libation Bearers: the jural-political choice

The second play of the trilogy strikingly emphasizes the jural-political aspects of Orestes' relationship with Agamemnon. True, Orestes wants vengeance for the death of his father-as-kinsman, but that aspect appears subsidiary. With the emphasis on the jural-political tie between father and son goes a stress on Agamemnon's own position in the jural-political domain. The shape which the lines give to Orestes' action link his status as heir and successor to Agamemnon's status as a warrior-king and head of an office-bearing patriline.

Orestes:

1. Orestes calls on his 'fathers' to 'be my savior and *stand by my claim*' (2).

2. Electra tells her brother to 'win back your father's house again' (237).

3. Orestes, explaining the evils that will befall him if he fails to avenge Agamemnon's death says, 'Here numerous desires converge to drive me on: the god's urging and my father's passion, and with these *the loss of my estates wears hard on me*' (299–301). The threat of mystical sanctions joins the resentment of a cheated heir.

4. Orestes' prayer to Zeus asks for retribution 'for the right of our fathers' (385).

5. He calls himself the 'last of the sons of Atreus' (407), 'cast from house and right' (409). Not as Agamemnon's offspring only, but as the last of a patriline does he act.

6. After killing Aegisthus and Clytemnestra, Orestes displays their bodies as 'these two who killed my father and who sacked *my house*' (974).

Agamemnon:

1. Orestes and the Chorus mourn Agamemnon's death as a war leader and king. They would rather have had him die at Ilium with 'a *lord's* majesty' that would have given renown to his children (345–2).

2. Orestes will kill Agamemnon's murderers 'as they by treachery killed *a man of high degree*' (556–7).

3. The Chorus' last lament recites again the history of the House of Atreus. After the eating of the children and the curse of Thyestes, 'Next came the *royal* death, when a man and *lord of the Achaean armies* went down killed in the bath' (1070–2).

Orestes and Agamemnon:

1. Orestes addresses the dead Agamemnon, saying, 'Father, O king who died no kingly death, I ask the gift of lordship at your hands to rule your house' (479–80).

2. Seeking Aegisthus, Orestes suggests that he might find him 'seated on my father's throne' (571–2).

3. The anxious Chorus hope that Orestes will 'win the domain and huge treasure again of his fathers' (864–5).

4. In their last speech the Chorus say, 'Here on this house of the kings

the third storm has broken, with wind from the inward race, and gone its course' (1065–7). 'Inwardly' there has been another domestic murder. But in a house of kings such murder is also 'outward', political.

Of course audiences, past or present, have been aware that the *Oresteia's* characters were, by the conventions of Greek drama, royal personages, heroes and deities as well as kin. I nonetheless assert that Aeschylus here uses the conventions in a special way. If his special uses are noticed more carefully, I maintain, they shed light on climactic scenes and on the final denouement.

Significantly, then, neither Electra nor Orestes dwells either on the loss of a fond parent or on any personal characteristics of the dead father. Electra does mention her 'love for a pitilessly slaughtered sister', love which, like the love she cannot give Clytemnestra, must go to Orestes. Agamemnon receives no blame for Iphegenia's death, but no pardon either. Agamemnon as an individual and father-as-kinsman receives no mournful word or even any mention. His social personality undergoes idealization by impoverishment, its other aspects swallowed up by his jural-political status.

In order for Orestes and Electra to carry out and to countenance the murder of Clytemnestra, she also must be 'impoverished'. She must not be allowed the claims of that closest of all kinship ties nor must she, as an individual woman, draw any sympathy. The solution stresses Clytemnestra's wrongdoing as a *wife*, their *father's wife*, and treats her failure as a mother and woman as derived from that wrongdoing. Aeschylus makes the linkage in two ways. One refers to her erotic misdeeds and the other to her murderous cruelty. So Electra says that Clytemnestra has exchanged her children for Aegisthus: 'our mother bought herself, for us, a man' (133). Her murderousness serves to make Electra and Orestes steel themselves to kill her: they will be like wolves born of a wolf, from 'a savage mother' (420–1). All the complexities condense in Electra's cry, 'O cruel, cruel all daring mother' who 'dared bury your unbewept lord' (429–33).

In confronting Clytemnestra, Orestes repeats the same lists of wrongs, then momentarily loses his resolution when she, exposing her breasts, reminds him that nothing can change the fact that she bore and nurtured him. He again fends off her maternal claim by recourse to her wrongdoing as father's wife: 'Come here. My purpose is to kill you over his [Aegisthus'] body. You thought him bigger than my father while he lived. Die and sleep beside him, since he is the man you love, and he you should have loved got only your hate' (903–7). Those words, 'you thought him bigger than my father' concisely join her wifely infidelity, the first of her wrongs against the great man, to wrongs against the great man's son. Even here, or perhaps especially here, Orestes speaks as his father's heir and successor.

In a brief skirmish over the relative hardships of men and women and the associated temptations, Orestes plays the part of the father-like male who dominates in the jural-political order: 'The man's hard work supports the women who sit at home' (921).[3] Clytemnestra brings him to the real issue: 'I think, *child*, that you mean to kill your *mother*' (921). And now she can threaten him with, 'Take care. Your mother's curse, like dogs, will drag you down' (925). Soon she takes the final, fatal step by calling him the snake that 'she gave birth to, and gave the breast' (928). Identified with the terror of her dreams, Orestes seems no longer her dependant or threatened child and he can kill her.[4]

When Orestes finally displays the dead bodies of Aegisthus and Clytemnestra he distinguishes between their deaths.[5] The killing of Aegisthus he counts as nothing: 'he has his seducer's punishment, no more than law' (989). But to justify murdering Clytemnestra he must yet again recite her misdeeds, displaying the robe in which she trapped Agamemnon. Once again he speaks as his father's heir and successor, taking vengeance on his father's wife.

His satisfaction lasts briefly. For father's wife was also mother. His wits begin to leave him and when the Furies appear he has already spoken of himself as seeking 'to escape the blood that is my own' (1038). He recognizes the Furies as the bloodhounds of his mother's hate (1053). The heir and successor in the jural-political order cannot escape from the ultimate kinship bond.

Compare the action of the Furies with that of Aegisthus' men-at-arms. Aegisthus' follower has cried sorrow for his 'stricken lord' (875). But he will not 'fight for one who is dead and done for. What use is there?' (880). Orestes has no more trouble with Aegisthus' followers. In short, they calculate as men attached to a leader without dynastic, familial claims on them. However Aeschylus may have intended their swift desertion to contrast with Orestes' determination, they stand out as the only actors in a purely political relationship. They choose retreat as a practical action. Clytemnestra has, for her tenacious avengers, mystical figures who will assert an absolute moral claim. The Furies rush forward to punish the ultimate in familial wrongs. Clytemnestra, high-born lady, daughter of Tyndareus, Agamemnon's queen and protectress of the Apian land, has become a wronged and vengeful mother. The Furies take shape as *maternal* figures.

III. The Eumenides: action in the ritual domain

The usual emphasis on the court of the Areopagus as the scene of critical action directs attention to Aeschylus' supposed interest in social institutions. I suggest that such concern is evident in the play and that it is best understood by attending to what takes place in the ritual domain. The first scene, at the Delphic shrine of the Pythian Apollo, almost completes the movement to that domain.

Orestes has not destroyed his kinship with his mother. But the struggle between Clytemnestra and Orestes is at first transformed into one between the Furies and Apollo:

1. Clytemnestra becomes more closely identified with the Furies in their loathsome aspects. The fearsome and noisome Furies having been described by Pythia, Clytemnestra speaks like a self-confessed witch. She reminds the Furies of her secret, night-time sacrifices to them and her speech becomes an evil spell commanding the Furies to hunt down Orestes, 'the beast' (131–139).

2. Apollo has vowed that he will not desert Orestes. He directs Orestes to flee to the shrine of Pallas Athene where *we* shall find those who will judge this case' (81).

3. The Furies and Apollo have their first argument about what crime is more heinous: the killing of a mother or the murder of a husband by his wife. Finally, the Furies claim that the Olympian gods are opposed to the chthonic powers driven on by the 'motherblood' to hunt down a matricide (229–31).

The last scene of the play and of the trilogy takes place at the shrine of Pallas Athene. It achieves (a) the final freeing of Orestes from the Furies' pursuit and (b) the establishment of the Furies as the Eumenides. Although the two dramatic movements are intertwined, Orestes' pardon can be treated separately. It finds accomplishment by means of the emphasis *in a ritual setting* of masculine superiority in the jural-political domain. To the Furies' cries for vengeance on a shedder of kindred blood, Orestes again cites the justice of killing his mother to avenge his father. Athene's establishment of the court of the Areopagus follows when she calls the matter 'too big for any mortal man who thinks he can judge it' (470–1), too big even for her alone. She respects Orestes' rights but she cannot ignore the Furies for fear that 'the venom of their resolution will return to infect the soil' (478–9) of her city.

When the Athenian citizens convene, the Furies charge Orestes again with the greater wrong: he offended against his 'mother's intimate blood' (608). Apollo first tries to dispose of the relative wrongs of the two killings by referring to the status of the murdered persons. Agamemnon was a *man* killed by a *woman*. (A man might die honourably by a woman's hand had an Amazon's arrow struck him down in battle, but he was killed treacherously in his own house, in his bath.) Agamemnon, moreover, was a man of blood (625), 'honoured with the king's staff' (626), 'a great man solemn in all men's sight' (636–7). Clytemnestra merits only one appellation, 'the woman'. Apollo has 'called the woman what she was, so that the people whose duty it is to try this case may be inflamed' (638–9). The life of the daughter of Tyndareus, high-born lady and Agamemnon's queen must not be valued as much as the life of Agamemnon, man, king and warrior. Apollo's argument is couched wholly in the evaluations of the jural-political domain.

But the Furies, returning to the killing of Clytemnestra as a *mother*, take up the ritual aspect of kinship relations. If Orestes goes home to Argos, they say, how can he participate in the rituals of kinship: 'Is there a brotherhood's lustration that will let him in' (655–6). Apollo tries again to escape to the safety of jural-political distinctions *by denying that the mother is a kinsman at all.* 'She is only the nurse of the new-planted seed that grows. The parent is he who mounts. A stranger she preserves a stranger's seed, if no god interfere' (659–61). If the mother were not kindred at all, then it would be possible to avoid an issue which is central to the play: how are jural-political ties and kin ties to be weighed against each other? Not men and women, but the two domains with which they are especially associated, compete for the goddess's favour.

After she charges the jury (in a crucial speech to which I return below), Athene announces that if the jury's votes are even hers will set Orestes free. 'There is no mother anywhere who gave me birth and, but for marriage, I am always for the male with all my heart, and strongly on my father's side. So in a case where the wife has killed her husband, lord of the house, her death shall not mean most to me' (735–40). The human judges do indeed cast a tie vote which is broken by Athene's preference for the father-husband-lord-of-the-house. 'Lordship' over the house, the superordinate position of husband-father, issues from the jural-political domain as its rules shape familial relations. Since Athene operates in the jural-political domain she uses its standards. Orestes, as the exemplification of those standards, finds her favour and he goes free.[6]

I must now say why I disagree with Lloyd-Jones' disparagement of the scene's alleged 'naive dramaturgy'. Not only Orestes and Clytemnestra; not only women and men; but the familial and jural-political domains, with their respective principles, are at odds. Since the beginning of the play, the Furies (and, briefly, Clytemnestra's ghost) on one side, Apollo and Orestes on the other, have been arguing about *two different kinds of claims*, issuing from two different domains. On one side, the claims of the familial domain have an absolutist moral quality well represented by the Furies' unyielding anger. That the Furies should have emerged as *maternal* figures reflects the nature of the mother-child bond as both the foundation and the paradigm of all kinship ties. On the other side, jural-political claims are the claims of 'law and order' represented by Apollo's 'rational' arguments from and for male superordination. These favour Orestes as the royal male's heir and successor and also the conjugal tie as the proper regulator of male-female relations.

How is a merely human jury to make a decision between the two *kinds* of claims? Every human has a mother and a father, true. But also, every human is involved in the 'mother-like' familial domain and in the 'father-like' jural-political domain. That Aeschylus has Athene make the decision is sociologically (and psychologically) faultless. In choosing 'for the male' she chooses in favour of the jural-political domain and its rules, rules which give dominance to males such as Orestes. Athene's lack of a mother leaves her untrammelled by the absolutist claims of kinship morality and free to make the choice she does make. If this part of the *Oresteia* reads today like 'naive dramaturgy', then so also must the second chapter of Genesis and, indeed, most myth. For in this scene we are in the ritual domain where the greatest problems of human life, being exhibited, are settled in ways that often seem arbitrary, perplexing and even funny.

Athene's decision sets Orestes free of the kinship claims upon him. Appropriately, his last speech presents him yet again as Agamemnon's heir and successor. Offering to Athens the friendship of his state, he suits his thanksgiving to his position as a man of political consequence.

Athene has given the Court of the Areopagus a rule for deciding between kinds of claims: but only in the context of the Court itself. She has not disposed of the Furies' claims and, indeed, she does not want to do so. Far from tricking the Furies into becoming the Eumenides, she finds a place for their ineluctable standards of right and wrong. Her speech charging the jury provides the clue to her intentions and action. She declares the founding of Athens' court on the Hill of Ares and says, 'Here the reverence of citizens. their *fear* and kindred do-no-wrong shall hold by day and in the blessing of night alike all while people do not muddy their own laws with foul infusions' (689–94). She continues: 'No anarchy, no rule of a single master. Thus I advise my citizens to govern and to grace, and *not to cast fear utterly from your city*. What man who fears nothing at all is ever righteous?' (696–9). Apollo and the Furies counsel the jury to beware of the consequence of a wrong decision. But Athene has told them to *bring fear within the city*. She herself does so when she persuades the Furies to stay and accept ritual honours.

The Furies accept Athene's offer, not simply because they are bribed to bless rather than curse, but because they are allowed to remain essentially unchanged. They will still bring retribution 'against the man who has fallen horribly in love with high renown' (864–5). No household will prosper without their will (895). They will help to 'straighten the lives' of all who worship them (897), working for generations of 'upright men' (912). In her speeches establishing 'spirits who are large, difficult to soften', (929) Athene in fact has echoed the Furies' own earlier arguments: 'There are times when fear is good. It must keep its watchful place at the heart's controls. There is advantage in the wisdom won from pain. Should the city, should the man rear a heart that nowhere goes in fear, how shall such a one any more respect the right?' (517–25). Under Athene's guidance, the citizens of Athens will refuse to be ruled by a single master, they will refuse the rule of one.

With the Furies-Eumenides watching over their lives they will also refuse anarchy, the rule of none. The absolutist moral claims of the familial domain are to be harnessed to the jural-political order. How? By bringing into the city's ritual life the powerful mystical representations of the mother-child tie. The fear of retribution remains an instrument of Zeus' judgment as it always has been. But that instrument now has a mother's face engraved upon it.

If Aeschylus was interested in social and political matters, as I think he was, he was not wholly enthusiastic about Athenian democracy. The public, 'above-ground' jural-political order, he seems to say, can only deal with acts after they are committed. It does not prevent wrongs. Humankind being what it is, people will set a limit to their actions only if there are also 'subterranean' powers guiding their lives. Men must be taught to *fear*. The Furies-Eumenides, derived dramatically from Clytemnestra's maternal vengefulness, become protectors of the city and sources of its continuity.

IV. Some problems for Anthropological study

The ending of the *Oresteia* is fully in the realm of symbolic representations where Aeschylus has linked maternal figures with salutary fear. The Taita people of Kenya, mentioned at the beginning of this essay, would find the association quite reasonable.[7] They extol the mother as the one person from whom 'care and indulgence'[8] can be expected. At the same time, they attribute to her the most fearful mystical sanctions. A mother's curse carries more power than any other. Yet the mystical sanctions associated with motherhood operate in the familial domain alone. There is no point in seeking there for a genuine ethnographic parallel to Aeschylus' remarkable idea.[9]

One feature of the *Oresteia*'s resolution will stand out to anyone familiar with the work of Meyer Fortes: the drama's social setting is a society observing a rule of patrilineal descent, yet the ritually powerful Furies-Eumenides are maternal figures. In writing of the Tallensi of Ghana, Fortes has demonstrated the importance in a living society with large-scale corporate patrilineal descent groups, of maternal origin and of the 'uterine line'. The separate maternal origins among sons of a polygynist lay down the lines of lineage segmentation and fission (1945: 32). Female forbears receive ritual attentions in the ancestor cult (1959 *b*: Chap. IV). Most important for my purpose here, mystical powers travel by way of descent through women. Although uterine descent brings people together in good fellowship, it also transmits the potentiality for witchcraft. That tie also carries the mystical blood-guilt falling on someone who has instigated (perhaps unwittingly) a fight in which someone has been killed (1949 *a*: 32–37). Two mystical evils, then, travel by way of the mother-child tie.

In another Ghanaian society, Ashanti, women rather than men pass on membership in corporate unilineal descent groups: descent is matrilineal. Besides belonging to a matrilineage and to a matrilineal clan, every free-born Ashanti is a member of a ritual grouping determined by paternity. A person's destiny is fixed by the transmission to him of his father's spirit, and a person cannot thrive if he is for some reason deprived of the spiritual attributes coming from the father (Fortes 1950: 266–7).

The two cases resemble each other only partly. In each, one parent trans-mits membership in a corporate descent group while the other parent transmits mystical potentialities, powers or attributes. The patrilineal Tallensi assign special mystical proclivities to uterine descent, while the matrilineal Ashanti do the same for the paternal link. Beyond the pattern of complementarity stand both an important difference and an important similarity. As to the difference: the mystical attributes travelling in the Tallensi matriline are evil whereas in Ashanti the patriline carries necessary and beneficial mystical elements. But the two societies are similar in that Ashanti, like Tallensi, assigns the transmission of witchcraft to the matri-line. In sum, the two societies differ as to rule of descent, but both allot the passage of *evil* mystical attributes to the uterine tie. Clearly, Fortes' principle of complementary filiation will not cover this aspect of the situation (1969: 200; 1970 *a*: 58–63). It appears more useful to remember that in Ashanti and Tallensi, as in all societies, men are the superordinates in the jural-political domain while women are identified primarily with the domestic domain.

The double association of women-as-mothers with life and nurturance on the one hand and with death and destructiveness on the other is certainly widespread and may be well-nigh universal. The vast anthropological literature on witchcraft and sorcery certainly provides evidence of the frequency with which women or ties through women figure in the systems of belief and in accusations. Although the puzzle has not caught the attention of social anthropologists generally, an article by Dr Esther Goody makes a significant contribution.

In her article, Dr Goody starts with the question: '...why do the Gonja [of Ghana] make a dichotomy between male witches, whose standing in the community is enhanced rather than injured by suspicions of witchcraft, and female witches, who are feared and abhorred, and not infrequently severely punished?' (1970: 207). She has found that among the Gonja males are expected to use aggressive mystical powers. But women are forbidden to be aggressive at all except when defending themselves and their children from violent attack. Consequently, 'Gonja women who are thought to have witchcraft powers are always condemned as evil' (p. 242),[10] while male witches are not so condemned and are rarely punished.

Dr Goody believes that the ban on female aggression arises from their almost total involvement in domestic life where they are mothers as well as wives who must be subordinate to their husbands. She concludes, 'It seems highly likely that because of their basic identification with domestic and kinship roles, women will usually be denied the legitimate expression of aggressive impulses. But in whatever roles aggression is not legitimate, it is in these that we can expect to find that imputations of covert mystical aggression are made, and, further, that they evoke publicly sanctioned counteraction; that they are considered evil (p. 243).

I suggest that Dr Goody's conclusion might be usefully reformulated as follows: whatever are the statuses in which aggression is not legitimate, occupants of those statuses will be singled out for imputation of covert mystical aggression, or transmission to others close to them of evil mystical proclivities or both. Since in their primary association with the domestic domain women are denied the legitimate expression of aggressive impulses, women will commonly be singled out for such imputations. Occupants of the specified statuses, including women, lend themselves to ritual and mythic treatment in which they are used to create symbolic representations of aggression, including retributive aggression.

The above formulation might not be satisfactory just because it will serve to cover such a wide range of cases, from Tallensi mothers to the Clytemnestra of Aeschylus. But it can also serve as an invitation to social anthropologists to study the articulation in various societies of familial and jural-political domains in relation to the sexes as they are represented in myth and ritual.

This is not quite sufficient. In an article on Tallensi divination, Meyer Fortes points to what he calls 'the irreducible factors in social relations (e.g. the mother–child nexus at one end of the scale, the authority of society at the other) (1966: 413). It seems that the mother-child nexus and other ties through women always and everywhere appear both bad and good precisely because they *are* 'at the opposite end of the scale' from the 'authority of society'. The mother-child nexus is not wholly intractable before the demands of the jural-political order. But it is, as Fortes might say, 'rooted' in a so-far unchanged biology standing often in opposition to jural-political rights and obligations.

Whether or not the affective claims of the mother-child nexus really are 'natural', people generally believe (and perhaps wish) them so. Treated as the source of inescapable axiomatic claims, the mother-child nexus can appear threatening to the jural-political order. The latter requires members of a society to enter statuses with demands that may conflict with the axioms of kinship. From the point of view of individual development also, the private delights and sorrows of the mother–child nexus must be drastically modified. (Here, as Meyer Fortes might note, the boundary is reached which separates social anthropology from psychology.) Women, as the actual or potential carriers of the paradigmatic kinship bond lying at the heart of the familial domain, always and everywhere appear to have two aspects: as Furies-witches and as Eumenides.[11]

The final dramatic triumph of the *Oresteia* lies in Aeschylus' device for uniting the 'two irreducible factors' in his imagined Athenian world. But to call his solution a dramatic triumph does not make it humane or ideal. Perhaps the time has come for social anthropologists to study intensively the solutions and non-solutions offered by various societies, including their own.

Notes

1 At this point in the drama it is not known for certain whether Menelaus is dead, but it is known that he has no son.

2 My emphasis here and elsewhere.

3 Winnington-Ingram says that '...the contest between mother and son...resumes the contest between husband and wife...' (*op. cit.*, p. 139), but he is referring, apparently, only to the 'sexual antithesis'.

4 Of all scenes in the *Oresteia*, this one perhaps offers the most temptation to dabble in psychoanalytic interpretation. I desist, at the same time believing that the reading I offer is not at variance with a psychoanalytic approach.

5 *After* he has first linked them.

6 It will not do to be too much misled by Athene's being called Zeus' daughter. She is not so much daughter as emanation, his brain-child, having issued from his head, not his loins. That a 'kinship term' is used accords with the counter-influence that the familial domain exerts on the jural-political domain, when relationships are phrased in a kinship idiom.

7 Field-work among the Taita was carried out jointly with Alfred Harris, 1950–2, under grants from the Colonial Social Science Research Council.

8 The phrase is from Radcliffe-Brown, who brought the mother–child bond into serious social anthropological study. A. R. Radcliffe-Brown 1925: 25.

9 But see final paragraph.

10 It is not possible for me to do justice here to Dr Goody's subtle discussion of what it means for aggression to be 'illegitimate'.

11 It might be asked why barren women and old women are so often and in so many societies prime suspects for witchcraft. They appear to be connected with mother-hood, but without the caring and nurturant association. That leaves only the Furies-witch aspect.

Marriage and Affinal Roles

Some Aspects of Levirate

R. G. Abrahams

'Siblingship does not cancel out the uniqueness of the individual' (Fortes, 1949 *a* p. 243).

The levirate has long been a popular ingredient in the anthropological stockpot of exotic kinship institutions. For Frazer and others it provided evidence of ancient forms of group marriage which they, paradoxically, did not live long enough to see, and for some its main interest lay, apparently, in the discovery of Old Testament custom in the more remote parts of the modern world.[1] Others, more recently, have noted how the institution illustrates such diverse features of kinship systems as the equivalence of siblings, the non-equivalence of *genitor* and *pater*, and the interconnectedness of forms of marriage and descent rules.[2]

As with many such anthropological chestnuts, however, the move beyond description and *ad hoc* illustration to more systematic analysis and comparison has proved rather difficult. Thus Gluckman, who has made some of the most significant contributions to our understanding of the institution, has described how he suspended full-scale study of it when he discovered 'how unclear were reports on whether a widow remained married under the true levirate to her dead husband, or was married by his kinsman in a new marital union'.[3] Here, of course, Gluckman is referring to the now well-known distinction between ordinary widow-inheritance and 'true' levirate, which Evans-Pritchard, Radcliffe-Brown and he himself have forcefully drawn, and he has in mind the failure of many writers to clarify such matters as whether in a particular society the dead husband or his kinsman living with his widow is counted as the father of the children whom she subsequently bears.

But even where fieldworkers have been clearly conscious of the definitions and distinctions underlying Gluckman's comment, it has been by no means always simple to decide how the raw data they encounter in the field ought to be labelled. Of course, the situation has been relatively clear cut in some cases, for example among the Nuer, Zulu and Tswana.[4] Cunnison, however, writing of succession to the role of spouse among the Luapula peoples, reports that in the case of men it seems to constitute neither true levirate nor simple widow inheritance; and Gulliver seems to have faced a comparable problem in his study of the Turkana where it becomes clear that children born to a widow and her husband's kinsman are, in various respects, the socially recognised offspring of both the dead man and his successor.[5]

Some case material from my own research work in Labwor, in northern Uganda, reveals some of the complications to be found in such data.[6] One old man, named Omara Opepel, responded to questions about the identity of his father with the information that he had more than one father. Nor was this a simple reference to the classificatory kinship terminology. Firstly, I was told, there was the father, Omara, who paid bridewealth for his mother, Akelo. When this man died, the mother was inherited without payment of further bridewealth by a relatively distant clansman called Akorio, who was 'the father who begot me'. But before Omara Opepel was born, a quarrel arose in Akorio's household when his first wife became jealous of help he was giving to the pregnant widow in her work. The two full brothers of the dead man, Oboke and Onyer, became angry at this quarrel over their dead brother's wife and insisted that she be returned, whereupon they gave her to the son, Omino, of one of their paternal half-brothers (Fig. 1). At his birth, my informant was named Omara in customary remembrance of his mother's original husband, Opepel being a cattle-name which was acquired later. It should be added that a child is never named after the father who begot him.

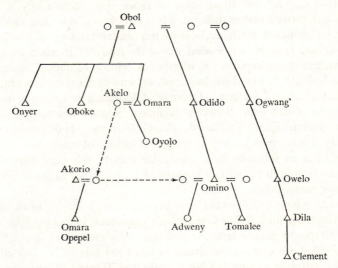

Fig. 1. Genealogy of Obol's descendants.

At the time when he inherited Akelo, Omino – 'the father who reared me' – was living in one homestead with Oboke and Onyer who had themselves inherited other wives of Omara. Omino had come there after the death of both his parents and had neither wife nor property of his own. Later, Oboke and Akelo gave him bridewealth from the marriages of Opepel's sisters, Oyolo and Adweny, so that he could marry another wife, the mother of Tomalee. When Opepel was ready for marriage, Omino paid the bridewealth for him, and when Omino died Opepel was senior heir to his estate. Later he paid the bridewealth for Tomalee's first marriage. He calls Tomalee 'brother' and he called Omino 'father'. However, he calls Clement son of Dila 'grandchild', and says this is because 'Omara and Ogwang' were brothers'. Over the years the clan has divided into two main segments and Opepel belongs firmly to the group descended from Obol rather than to that which now contains the children of his genitor Akorio's own bridewealth marriages. On the other hand, his generation group affiliation, in the age and generation group system, is reckoned from Akorio, rather than from Omara as would be the case among the Karimojong and Turkana.[7]

A full discussion of this and other, complementary Labwor material is not possible in this context.[8] The main point I wish to establish at this stage is that the sorts of definition of the levirate offered by Radcliffe-Brown and others, and the binary contrast between levirate and widow-inheritance which these definitions entail, are not wholly adequate for the interpretation and analysis of such data. Radcliffe-Brown's statements that in the levirate it is the duty of a dead man's brother 'to cohabit with the widow in order to raise children which will be counted, not as his, but as children of the deceased' and that 'the widow remains the wife of the dead man' hold partially but by no means completely for the Labwor and other material to which I have referred.[9] The relevant features of the statuses of husband and father in the societies concerned appear to be too complex to fall readily and exclusively into one or other half of such a relatively simple dual formulation. Moreover, the capacity of these, and of the linked statuses of sibling, mother, wife and child, for fine variation between cultures is likely to blur any sharp boundaries which we might be tempted to construct between whole structural sub-systems at this level of analysis. As a result, attempts to solve the problem merely by intensification of the classificatory process and the multiplication of categories seem to be doomed to failure. Similarly, Gray's brief suggestion of a taxonomic hierarchy, initially based on differences between patterns of property transmission, seems at first sight promising, but it ultimately begs more questions than it answers.[10] Gray proposes a new main distinction between 'husband succession', in which the husband's estate remains intact after his death, and 'widow inheritance' in which the estate is merged with that of the successor. True levirate he classes as that form of 'husband succession' in which children born to the successor and the widow are counted as belonging to the dead man. Even granting the debatable pre-eminence of property considerations in such contexts, however, it is by no means clear that ethnographic data will fit easily into such a system of progressive sub-division. Among the Jie, for example, we find that most property is typically held by a group of full brothers, though it is mainly administered by the senior of these, and it is not easy to talk of an individual's estate at all in these circumstances, let alone of one that remains intact after death. On the other hand, we are told that a widow remains the wife of her dead husband and any children she bears to his successor are reckoned as members of their mother's yard within her husband's 'house'. In addition, the sorts of problem we encountered earlier concerning dual or multiple paternity are not so much resolved as simply pushed one stage further back in Gray's formulation.

This type of problem is of course not new in social anthropology, and its solution, like that of analogous linguistic problems, ultimately lies in the recognition of a range of structural levels. It becomes necessary to abandon the search for a simple typology whose subdivisions will correspond exactly with the institutional constellations we encounter in comparative study. The only form of typology which we can at all usefully adopt at this level of the 'total' institution is a set of ideal types, in the Weberian sense, and these in turn will depend for their usefulness on the identification of fundamental elements and principles which are embodied, in various strengths and combinations, in the institutions under investigation. Radcliffe-Brown's assertion, which I noted earlier, that the principle of the equivalence of siblings is at work in levirate is, of course, a move in this direction, and a more detailed consideration of his statement is worthwhile at this point in my discussion.

Radcliffe-Brown tells us that the levirate exhibits the principle of the equivalence of siblings because one brother replaces another in the institution. He also points out that the principle is equally well illustrated in adelphic polyandry and in 'widow-inheritance' where the inheritor is a brother of the dead man.[11] The point, as he makes it, is clearly a reasonable one, yet there is an element of paradox in this situation where such different institutions are said to be demonstrative of a single principle, and where the very differences between them appear, at first sight at least, to cast doubt on the overall validity of that same principle. Forms of widow-inheritance and levirate, for example, are often found approved in societies in which fraternal polyandry is impossible. Thus, among the Tallensi a brother's wife is not sexually accessible before her husband's death and her seduction constitutes a heinous sin which precludes her subsequent inheritance by the sinner. It is clear that Tallensi siblings are not acknowledged as equivalent in this context while they are both alive, and Fortes eloquently recognises and spells out such limitation. 'As his sexual partner' we are told 'a woman is the wife of her husband in a rigorous sense that distinguishes him from all his clansmen...' and again 'If he dies, a "brother" will have the first and strongest claim to his widow's hand. Yet these are the men who must most rigorously respect his exclusive sexual rights over his wife...'. The same point is made when he writes, with regard to siblings, of 'their social equivalence. . .in jural, ritual and economic relations, as opposed, for example, to private marital relations' and when he tells us more generally that 'Siblingship does not cancel out the uniqueness of the individual.'[12]

Again, a comparable contrast seems to underly the distinctions noted earlier between 'true' levirate and widow-inheritance. In each case, it is true, one brother may take on certain roles of the other, but what we may speak of as their individual identities, which constitute important elements of their non-equivalence, receive radically different emphases and treatment in the two forms of succession. In the case of widow-inheritance, the identity of the deceased is supplanted by that of the successor, whereas in 'true' levirate the opposite tends to take place as the story of Onan and other Old Testament material well illustrates. It will be recalled that Onan, whose name should almost certainly be linked with contraception rather than, as customarily, with self-abuse, ought to have taken the widow, Tamar, of his deceased brother, Er, in leviratic marriage. But we are told that 'Onan knew that the seed would not be his; and it came to pass when he went in unto his brother's wife, that he spilled it on the ground, lest that he should give seed to his brother.'[13] God slew Onan, but such recalcitrance is also anticipated by the provision of less violent human sanctions in the relevant text of Deuteronomy.[14] The point which emerges clearly from the story is that levirate proclaims the separate identity of individual siblings and attempts, admittedly through the medium of their potential substitutability and by virtue of the moral bonds between them, to maintain and preserve the individual identity of one beyond his normal lifespan by the sacrifice of at least part of the individuality of the other. It is this *self*-sacrifice so that another may 'live' which Onan rejects and which constitutes the very heart of levirate.

The differences between adelphic polyandry, widow-inheritance, and levirate can, then, be examined and defined in terms of differences in cultural definition of and emphasis upon the individuality of siblings. It should be clear, however, that this point should be seen as complementary and not contradictory to Radcliffe-Brown's interpretation of their similarity which appears to be reinforced by the existence of a variety of intermediate semi-institutionalised and often *sub-rosa* forms of privileged access to the wives of living kinsmen as are found among the Nuer, Tutsi and Turkana.[15] The point is that if the 'equivalence of siblings' is a general principle at work in human kinship systems, so too is the 'individuality of siblings', and it is perhaps worth emphasising that such individuality – as we have learned to understand through Fortes, and more classically through Durkheim – is as much a social and a cultural fact as is its opposite 'equivalence'.[16] Both have an 'objective' base in nature, the fact of common birth on the one hand and, once the cord has been cut, the bounded human organism born at a particular time and place on the other.[17] Both, too, receive their definition and expression in a range of customary contexts of which those under discussion here are but a few. The social equivalence of siblings is, then, not an isolated principle, but is only to be understood 'structurally' in conjunction with and in opposition to their individuality as a main component in what we may perhaps call their social ambivalence. The wider implications of a full and positive, as opposed to merely passing, recognition of this basic feature of kinship organisation are, I think, considerable. Much of the argument between substantivist and formalist economists, for example, seems to turn upon a failure to see their data in such dual terms. Moreover, within the narrower confines of the present context, such recognition can enable us to see more clearly why the categorisation of the institutions under discussion is unlikely ever to be truly typological and why the categories concerned are best thought of as ideal types, as I suggested earlier. For such institutional complexes in which ambivalence is a major variable are, more or less by definition, not to be adequately characterised in 'real' terms by categories which single out for special consideration only one *or* other of the warring elements within them.

So far I have emphasised the need to recognise the varying co-existence of individuation and equivalence in leviratic and related institutions. The ambivalence of siblings, as I have termed it here, is not, however, a phenomenon without complications and it may be useful to try to define some of its features more precisely.[18] Firstly, it seems worthwhile to distinguish analytically the cognitive from the normative elements in the situation, though these are no doubt often closely interrelated. Cognitively, all societies appear to recognise that siblings are both similar to and different from each other, though the form and symbols of such recognition vary. Similarly, all societies evaluate these similarities and differences largely through the definition of the form, extent and limits of the obligations of one sibling to another, and in this sense levirate, widow-inheritance and adelphic polyandry clearly represent different evaluations of the equivalence and individuality of siblings. The situation is further complicated by the need, which Fortes has so strongly stressed, to try to discriminate between 'internal' and 'external' aspects of the structures in question. Siblings are, for example, often more obviously equivalent to each other vis-à-vis outsiders, in situations such as those of vendetta and feud, than internally vis-à-vis each other, but it would be quite mistaken simply to characterise the distinction in these terms. For, the common positive prescription for siblings to share in the conduct and proceeds of many of their activities need not directly involve other persons, except negatively by exclusion. And again, the individuality of siblings may, of course, be at least partially defined in terms of their relationships to non-shared third parties such as affines, spouses, children and even specific sets of ancestors, and it may in fact be these third parties who insist most strongly on the differences in question. Thus in a Nyamwezi case in which a young man had seduced his elder brother's wife, the elder brother was apparently satisfied by beating up the culprit, and it was the girl's father who made most fuss and threatened to break up the marriage which, he vociferously insisted, had been contracted between his daughter and a specific, individual husband rather than a whole family. Third parties may, moreover, not only serve to demarcate and separate one sibling from another, but they may also provide resources for co-operative exchange between them, such as the sharing of the bridewealth given for a daughter, and they may additionally constitute a source and, at times, an excuse for conflict. Here I am thinking of the type of situation commonly described to me in Labwor in which the origin of conflict between brothers is ascribed, often no doubt optimistically, to quarrels between their young children who are supported by their respective mothers who in turn demand support against each other from their husbands.

The distinction just referred to between separation and co-operative or conflicting interaction needs to be complemented at this point by a discussion of a further contrast to which some reference has already been made. It is a commonplace of social structural theory that real human individuals must be analytically distinguished from the roles and statuses they play and occupy, and the idea of social structure as a system of relationships between such roles and statuses is well understood. The idea of individual identity, however, which appears to lie awkwardly across the analytic boundaries between the psycho-biological individual and the social person has received considerably less attention from anthropologists, as has the notion of conflict of, and exchange of and between, identities which I suggested earlier lies at the core of levirate.[19]

I am not claiming here that this aspect of the situation has been altogether missed by writers who have paid attention to leviratic and related institutions. Evans-Pritchard, for example, not only lays great emphasis on the continuation of the marriage of a Nuer widow to her dead husband and the ascription to him of children begotten by his successor, but he also points out quite explicitly how, in the related institution of ghost marriage, a man who marries a wife to the name of his dead kinsman may well never beget children for himself and will have to hope that his own achievement of parenthood will be fulfilled for him by a junior kinsman who will make a self-sacrifice similar to his own.[20] Again, Howell, noting that Shilluk have no ghost marriage, remarks significantly that 'in this sense the Nuer and Dinka system is perhaps more individual than that of the Shilluk'.[21] But, with the further partial exception of Howell who cites the transmission and inheritance of personal names as a comparable phenomenon, neither these nor other writers have accompanied their discussion of such institutions with a detailed account of the conception and expression of identity in the society in question and an analysis in this context of the significance of such apparently directly relevant phenomena as names, attitudes to parenthood, concepts of spirit and soul, notions of life and death and comparable elements of culture.[22] Moreover, this failure adequately to combine cultural with social structural data is compounded by the fact to which I have already alluded, that we know rather more in general about social structure itself as a system of relationships between persons than about its inevitable complementary role as a system which serves to define the individual identity of those it also links together.

Our relative ignorance of these matters stems, I suspect, fairly directly from the oversimple formula, noted earlier, which separates the social status from the human individual and proceeds to define our major field of social structural study as the system of relationships between such statuses. No-one can deny that it has been immensely fruitful to consider such a system as an autonomous social fact with a potential to continue well beyond the lifespan of the crew who man it and, in various ways, devote their lives to its upkeep. But there is, of course, an alternative viewpoint available which pays more attention to the personnel as a dominant point of reference, and looks at an institution more in terms of what it does and signifies for them rather than for society *qua* social system. It is this sort of viewpoint which appears to underly Leach's recent comment, which seems particularly apposite in the present context, that man's unique awareness of time and, with it, his awareness of death lies behind much of his ritual activity, and that society appears in this light as mortal man's challenge to and denial of the fact and power of death.[23]

The point I am trying to bring out here can perhaps be seen more clearly in contrasting relation to an important discussion of land as property in Gluckman's 'The Ideas of Barotse Jurisprudence'. Examining the widespread existence of distinctions drawn between rights in land and rights in most chattels, he advances the hypothesis 'that immovable property and chattels have different functions in the maintenance, through time, of a social system as an organised pattern of relations. Immovable property provides fixed positions which endure through the passing of generations, through quarrels and even through invasions and revolutions... Movables establish links between individuals occupying different immovable properties... The two kinds of property therefore acquire different symbolic values in the law and ritual of tribal society. This difference in social function is based on the obvious fact that all social systems...are settled on land which changes but slowly, while the living personnel of the system and their interrelations change comparatively rapidly...'[24] Gluckman then goes on to describe how the system of positional succession to offices concerned with land and arranged in a fixed hierarchy operates among the Barotse and he draws attention to the similarity between this and comparable African systems, on the one hand, and Roman 'universal' succession on the other. The emphasis in Gluckman's argument is clearly placed upon the continuity of social structure as an ordered system of relationships. 'The whole social structure' he tells us in a later passage 'is stabilised through time and change about positions on the land.'[25]

This sort of continuity of social structure which Gluckman stresses is of course real enough, but it is radically distinct analytically from the kind of continuity of individual identity which I have suggested the concept of true levirate implies. Gluckman seems to see this when he writes that 'Universal succession, among the Barotse and probably everywhere, is thus not to a person, but to a position or *persona*', though it is not quite clear to what extent he sees both persons and *personae* here as social facts.[26] However this may be, office and individual identity are two contrasting socio-cultural phenomena. They may co-exist as the well-known distinctions between personal and stool property testify; and Fortes has shown that they must often be brought into close relation with each other.[27] Continuity in one may even be accompanied by continuity in the other as in Shilluk kingship where there is both a continuing office and a conception of a continuing identity of office-holders who are all 'possessed' by the spirit of the founder-hero Nyikang'.[28] But they are not the same as each other, nor is the distinction between them the same as that between a social office and its physical incumbent.

The need for the distinction which I have tried to bring out here between the continuity of an office and the continuity of individual identity has been partially recognised by Cunnison in his analysis of social structure among the matrilineal Luapula peoples and, more particularly, in his discussion which I mentioned earlier of leviratic institutions there.[29] Moreover, his account is, I believe, particularly revealing of some of the difficulties which face the ethnographer as he tries to thread a way through the complex and confusing reality with which such institutions present him. Confronted with the fact that Luapula customs of widow inheritance do not involve an un-equivocal ascription of a widow's children to either her new or her deceased husband, Cunnison attempts to absorb his material into the general frame-work of positional succession and perpetual kinship which he has been able to apply so successfully to the analysis of offices in the area. 'Perhaps the situation may be better understood' he writes 'by considering individuals not as persons but as holders of names, positions or offices. Each man has a name. On his death, the name subsists as an attribute or possession of the lineage. After a while the lineage finds a member to succeed to the name. The member is then the embodiment of two positions, and holds two names, his own original one and the one he inherits. Of these the inherited over-rides the original name and position. . . Children in these terms are children of a position rather than of an individual. For men are mortal: a name can be inherited from generation to generation. This then is a form of widow inheritance in which the successor becomes a husband to the wife and a father to the children of the deceased. It is part of 'positional succession' and the successor adopts the *persona* of his dead kinsman'.[30] There is little to quarrel with directly in this passage as it stands in isolation, but it is, I think, fair to criticise it in the broader context of the discussion in which it is embedded for a failure to bring out clearly the distinction between office and identity which the material appears to demand. It will be noted that the main distinction drawn is that between *persona* and mortal human being rather than between forms or aspects of *persona*, and it may be added that the socio-centric direction to which the mention of office and lineage points is emphasised in much of the surrounding analysis. For this tends to concentrate on the assertion early in the relevant chapter, which is significantly entitled 'The Lineage', that the institutions in question provide the basis for lineage organisation and stability in the area.[31] It is this emphasis on structural continuity of corporations sole and aggregate which appears to inhibit Cunnison from doing full justice to the rich evidence he presents. Such evidence reveals, for instance, that names are not at all tied to the lineage but may be taken from the mother's or the father's side at birth and may be variously acquired later, for example through teknonymy. Again, he tells us that most people's names and roles and personal effects, which last he interestingly speaks of as 'tokens of identity', often continue through one successor only and no further, in contrast to the titles and statuses of major political figures which abide in structured relation to each other over much longer periods.[32] Surely there is here an element at least of true levirate's denial that an individual's identity is extinguished simply by his death.

This discussion of the distinction between office and identity among the Luapula peoples brings this paper to a close. I have attempted to show that 'true' levirate can be usefully considered as an ideal type in which there is a special and somewhat extreme form of relationship between a man's individual identity and his equivalence to his siblings and other kinsfolk. I have suggested that an understanding of this and comparable forms of widow inheritance demands a study of social structure not only as a continuing social system which binds men together, but also in terms of the way in which it demarcates its personnel as special individuals who are meaningfully different from each other. I have also suggested that an investigation of many features of culture is likely to be an essential counterpart of such social structural study. In this context, it may be worthwhile finally to say a little about attempts to correlate the incidence of leviratic institutions with other features of social structure, the best known example being Gluckman's argument that true levirate is likely to be found in patrilineal kinship systems with father-son inheritance and a house-property complex.[33] The Nuer, Zulu and Tswana cases, among others, lend support to this theory, and in general we can see that such a kinship and property system interestingly links and individuates the members of the sibling group. For, in addition to demarcating the children of one mother as a set distinct from others, it tends also to separate a man from his full brothers by virtue of his links to his own wives and children. Given this, however, and granting that the overall comparative picture is not well documented, it should be noted that not all the literature points in the same direction. For, in addition to such negative cases as the Gogo, who appear to lack levirate while possessing other requisite features, and leaving aside such 'half-way' systems as the LoDagaa and Tallensi, the ethnographic literature reports the occurrence of institutions which are apparently very close to the true levirate ideal type in such diversely structured societies as the bilateral Malagasy, the matrilineal Ashanti, the Ila whose kinship system, though imperfectly understood, is very different from that of the Nuer and the Zulu, and, if my arguments are valid, the Luapula peoples discussed earlier.[34] Closer investigation of most of the societies in question would be necessary before the true facts of the matter could be ascertained, but it is interesting that at least in the case of the Malagasy, the Ashanti and the Ila, the ties between a father and his children have in different ways been strong and prominent enough to create a debate among anthropologists about the existence or not of 'patriliny' there.[35] As my categorization of these peoples implies, the answer has been largely negative, but the debate has raised important issues concerning both the status in kinship studies of ritual and other cultural phenomena and also the extent to which forms in the 'domestic domain' of kinship are to be understood as generated by the wider kinship structure. However this may be, I would suggest that we need not be too surprised if the solution which the levirate provides to problems of human identity and mortality is found not to be confined to and derived from only one type of wider kinship and property structure.

Notes

1 Cf. Frazer, 1910, vol. IV: 139–40 and Sibree, 1880: 246.
2 Cf. Radcliffe-Brown, 1950: 64, Evans-Pritchard, 1951: 113, and Gluckman, 1950: 183 and 1971: 244.
3 Gluckman, 1971: 234.
4 Cf. Gluckman, 1950: 183, Evans-Pritchard, 1951: 112–15, and Schapera, 1950: 153, 159.
5 Cunnison, 1959: 96–7, and Gulliver, 1951: 215, 195. Gulliver here and 1955: 114, 243 appears to avoid the term 'levirate' in his account.
6 The Labwor people are a Luo-speaking group and are close neighbours of the Jie. They have a patrilineal kinship system described briefly in Abrahams, 1972a.
7 For Karimojong' and Turkana rules see Dyson-Hudson, 1966: 206, and Gulliver, 1958: 902. It seems likely that the Jie rules are similar. Cf. Gulliver, 1966: 177.

8 In addition to considerations of space, I would like to obtain further material concerning some features of Labwor culture before embarking on a full analysis of these data.

9 Radcliffe-Brown, 1950: 64.

10 Gray, 1964: 21–2.

11 Radcliffe-Brown, 1950: 64.

12 Fortes, 1949a: 113, 110, 114, 242, 243.

13 Genesis, 38, 6–11.

14 Deuteronomy, 25, 5–10.

15 Cf. Evans-Pritchard, 1951: 37, Maquet, 1961: 78, and Gulliver, 1951: 216.

16 Cf. especially Durkheim, 1952. Fortes has of course discussed these problems in many places including 1949a, *passim*, and especially 1959b.

17 The temporal aspect is of course particularly noteworthy in this context as the main basis of individuation by seniority. For a full discussion of this and also of the factor of sex difference in sibling relationships see Fortes, 1949a: 243–54. For an interesting discussion of the relation between seniority and inheritance see Goody, 1963: 314 and *passim*, and for an example of differentiation of twins by seniority see Abrahams, 1972b.

18 My account here relates mainly to full brothers and pays little attention to differences between them and classificatory brothers or other kin. This is too complex an issue to treat at length here but, briefly, I consider that leviratic institutions are archetypically full sibling institutions and that in general the inclusion in them of classificatory siblings and other kin is, in a real sense, by 'extension'. This is, of course, not to deny that such institutions may function differently when, for example, more distant kin inherit. My own material from Labwor, cited above, and the case of Ruth and Boaz in the Book of Ruth are two of many testimonies to this. See also Fortes, 1949a: 275–80. For a full discussion of the case of Ruth and other Old Testament material see Neufeld, 1944: 37–42, and Chapter 1, *passim*.

19 Fortes' work is a main exception here. For a brilliant fictional treatment of these questions see Heller's novel *Catch 22*.

20 Evans-Pritchard, 1951: 111.

21 Howell, 1953: 104.

22 Howell, 1953: 104. See also Cunnison whose material is discussed below. An interesting case in which names of the dead are given to their descendants is the Jewish custom which, in some areas at least, is significantly spoken of as 'giving the dead a name'.

23 Leach, 1972: 316.

24 Gluckman, 1965a, 116–17.

25 Gluckman, 1965a: 271.

26 Gluckman, 1965a: 125.

27 Fortes, 1962 and 1967, *passim*.

28 Cf. Evans-Pritchard, 1948: 28–9.

29 Cunnison, 1959: 96–7 and *passim*.

30 Cunnison, 1959: 98.

31 Cunnison, 1959: 83.

32 Cunnison, 1959: 86, 105.

33 Cf. Gluckman, 1971: 244.

34 Cf. Rigby, 1969: 259, Goody, 1963: 336–7, Fortes, 1949a: 278–9, Sibree, 1880: 246, Rattray, 1929: 28–9, Richards, 1950: 236, Smith and Dale, 1920: vol. I: 390.

35 Cf. Goody, 1961: 9–11, Richards, 1950: 236, and Southall, 1971: 144 and *passim*.

Polygyny, Economy and the Role of Women

Jack Goody

Many topics of interest to earlier writers have been abandoned by social anthropologists because they have involved the use of comparative rather than intensive techniques. But a whole range of problems can be dealt with only by means of comparison and the subject has been impoverished by our failure to utilise the full range of techniques available to us. And while we have lagged behind, other social scientists have tried to answer those questions in more adventurous ways.

The problem that concerns me in this paper is the relationship between plural marriage and women's position in the economy. It tries to make use of a regional comparison, using the available material from Ghana, and it attempts to set this specific comparison within a wider framework, taking into account the work of sociologists and economists as well as anthropologists.

Writing of life on the Gold Coast at the end of the seventeenth century, Bosman notes that each man marries as many wives as he pleases, but is 'commonly contented with a number betwixt three and ten' (1967: 198). The number is plainly too large for the wives of anyone but the well-to-do merchants with whom he associated. Among these rich men, two wives were exempted from labour, the chief wife who looked after the household and another who was consecrated to his god (*obossum*). The others were obliged to till the ground and plant millet and yams, 'whilst the man only idly spends his time in impertinent tattling (the woman's business in our country) and drinking of palm-wine, which the poor wives are frequently obliged to raise money to pay for, and by their hard labour maintain and satisfie these lazy wretches their greedy thirst after wines' (p. 199).

The problem raised here by Bosman, albeit in an exaggerated manner, is that of the connection between polygyny, economy and the position of women, which has recently been treated by Ester Boserup on a wider canvas. In her book *Woman's Role in Economic Development* (1970) she points to the relationship between systems of hoe farming and the predominant role of women in agricultural pursuits. This theme was earlier pursued by a number of German writers, and played a central part in Baumann's discussion of the relationship between hoe agriculture and matrilineal descent (1928). In many of the hoe economies of Africa it is women who play the major part in the growing of food crops while that of men is often confined to clearing the fields. Men also look after livestock in both mixed and pastoral economies, and they are active in other pursuits

175

such as making war and building houses. Baumann had attempted to link a woman's role in the economy with the relatively high incidence of matrilineal institutions. However, Boserup argues that because the woman produces food she also tends to trade in these commodities. And it is especially because of her role in production and distribution that she is valuable to men who try to accumulate women in polygynous marriage.

Let me turn first to the question of polygyny and monogamy. As Westermarck (1891) pointed out (and as Nimkoff and Middleton (1960) and Heath (1958) have since confirmed by more systematic investigation), monogamy has a bimodal distribution. 'Monogamy, always the predominant form of marriage, has been more prevalent at the lowest stages of civilisation than at somewhat higher stages; whilst, at a still higher stage, polygyny has again, to a great extent, yielded to monogamy' (p. 505). Monogamy is closely associated with the major societies of Europe and Asia whereas polygyny is found in virtually all the traditional societies of Africa. Of course, plural marriage also occurs in the more advanced societies of Eurasia, especially under Islam. But there is a very important difference in the rates.

Take North Africa, for instance. In discussing the situation in Morocco, André Adam notes that it is difficult to tell the extent of polygyny in earlier times; it appears to have been fairly widespread among the bourgeoisie and the middle classes, much less so among the people, 'pour des raisons économique évidentes' (1968: ii, 735). With regard to the present situation in Morocco, he claims that as in other Muslim countries, polygyny has greatly decreased. However this may be, in 1963, a rural enquiry showed that 3.1 of the population were polygynists. In Casablanca the 'proletariat' are almost universally monogynous, the rate of polygyny being about 2 per cent. However, 'la polygamie garde des positions beaucoup plus fortes dans la petite bourgeoisie, surtout traditionelle': in another survey, Anne-Marie Baron found 21 per cent of polygynous families among the members of this strata.

Similar percentages are reported from Egyptian villages at a somewhat earlier date. In Hamed Ammar's survey, carried out in 1937, 4.7 married men had more than one wife.

Number of wives	Percentage of husbands
1	96.86
2	2.95
3	1.7
4	0.02

Nor does this situation seem particularly new, despite Adam's suggestion. In the first half of the nineteenth century Lane reports that only 1 in 20 (5 per cent) of Egyptians had more than one wife. Westermarck notes that these low rates occur among many Muslim people, as well as among peripheral nomadic groups such as the Tuareg, Toda, Marea and Beni-Amer; he quotes one authority on the Indian sub-continent as saying that 95 per cent of Muslims there were monogynists, either by conviction or by necessity (p. 439).[1]

Here the difference between Eurasia and Sub-Saharan Africa is striking. Not only are systems of monogamy rare in Africa, but there is an important difference between polygynous societies in the two continents. If we look at the more extensive and systematic comparative data available in the *Ethnographic Atlas* (1967) we find that Africa is marked by 'general polygyny', and Eurasia by 'limited polygyny' (Table 1).

Table 1. *Societies with plural marriage by Continent* (percentages in brackets)

	Africa	Circum-Mediter-ranean	Eastern Eurasia	Insular Pacific	North America	South America	Total
Monogamy	2 (1)	36 (38)	20 (22)	30 (24)	30 (14)	18 (21)	136 (16)
Limited polygyny	33 (14)	25 (26)	58 (62)	64 (52)	107 (50)	46 (52)	333 (39)
General polygyny	203 (85)	34 (36)	12 (13)	29 (23)	78 (36)	24 (27)	380 (45)
Total	238 (100)	95 (100)	90 (100)	123 (100)	215 (100)	88 (100)	849 (100)

The general comparison confirms the impression gathered from specific rates from specific societies. Indeed, in Africa, plural marriage has different functions, which are related to the difference in rates. In Europe and Asia, polygyny is largely but not exclusively an heir-producing device; often it is a way of replacing a barren wife. In Africa, plural marriage is far more generalised; according to Dorjahn, about 35 per cent of married men have more than one wife. Hence a large percentage of the population is likely to be part of a polygynous unit at some point in the life-cycle. Most men will be polygynously married at some time or other; women are yet more likely to be so. And most siblings will have sets of half siblings, both because of the plural marriage of their fathers and because of the remarriage of their mothers – since polygyny inevitably involves a large differential in the age of marriage, men will be older when they beget children than women are when they bear them. Hence there will be a higher proportion of widows and fatherless children.

The figures I have quoted for Africa and Eurasia are derived from 'traditional' societies, or rather from the rural sections of developing nations. It is commonly assumed that modernisation means the decline of polygyny. Clignet's recent study in the Ivory Coast (1970) shows some surprising features if we think of urbanisation and modernisation as producing of itself a family centred on the union of one man and one woman. He examined two groups of migrants, one from a patrilineal tribe (the Bete), the other from a matrilineal one (the Abouré, who belong to the Akan family).

Polygyny is a characteristic feature of these two groups, the figures for which are given in Table 2.

Table 2. *Polygyny in the Ivory Coast* (percentages)

Type of marriage	Abouré		Bete		Total population	
	Abidjan	Hinter-land	Abidjan	Hinter-land	Abidjan	Hinter-land
Monogynous	90.9	77.8	80.7	62.4	85.3	71.0
Duogynous	8.5	18.0	16.0	25.6	12.6	21.6
Polygynous	0.6	4.2	3.3	12.0	2.1	7.4
Rate of polygyny	9.1	22.2	19.3	37.6	14.7	29.0

The Abouré are a coastal people who have been subjected to more European influence, including conversion to Christianity; they are also matrilineal, another factor which may tend to reduce the percentage of polygynous families. While the Abouré have lower rates than the Bete, the urban populations have lower rates than the villagers. But an interesting feature of the studies is that although there is a decline among urban population, the decline is less among those who have been there longest, are most successful, have most education, than it is among the newly arrived. In other words, the curve is U-shaped. That is to say, the early stage of urbanisation is accompanied by a reduction in polygyny. But the 'corresponding emergence of an autonomous nuclear family may nonetheless be a temporary phenomenon' (p. 133) and Clignet sees a successful adjustment to urban life as meaning the opportunity of returning to traditional patterns of family organisation. In fact, the patterns have never disappeared but are probably related to age differences in the population; they are associated with position in the developmental cycle (new migrants are young) and in the social hierarchy. As Clignet observes: 'Plural marriage is a privilege acquired by individuals able to reach the top positions of the social hierarchy as defined in both modern and traditional terms' (p. 133).[2]

The patrilineal Bete have higher polygyny rates than the matrilineal Abouré both in town and country. Theoretically we would expect polygyny to be more easily arranged in patrilineal societies than in matrilineal ones, which often offer special difficulties, at least where the husband is supposed to move to the wife's kin in uxorilocal residence. Nevertheless the rate of the rural Abouré, where residence is either virilocal or duolocal, remains relatively high. Bilateral societies, being found among the most and least advanced economies, would be expected to have less polygyny than patrilineal ones. According to the *Ethnographic Atlas*, this is indeed the case (Table 3).

Table 3. *Plural marriage and kin groups* (percentages in brackets)

	Bilateral	Patrilineal	Matrilineal	Double
Monogamy	68	36	29	2
	(22)	(9)	(24)	(8)
Limited polygyny	148	127	49	7
	(48)	(32)	(41)	(27)
General polygyny	90	231	42	17
	(30)	(58)	(35)	(65)
Total	306	394	120	26
	(100)	(100)	(100)	(100)

Of the town situation generally Clignet concludes, 'many observers of the contemporary African scene agree that the incidence of polygyny in cities tends to increase with the length of time spent there and with the higher levels of occupation achieved' (1970: 31). The conclusions drawn from recent urbanisation in the Ivory Coast almost certainly apply to Ghana. In 1945, Fortes found little evidence of declining rates in Ashanti (1954). It was the same conclusion I drew from the restudy of a small area in Northern Ghana (1969 *b*), though this survey was confined to the rural community. While certain elements in the population (such as civil servants) have abandoned plural marriage, there appears to be no general change in incidence. Dorjahn arrived at a similar conclusion after a wide review of the available material (1959: 101): in Africa there is no evidence of an increase or decrease in recent times.

In the longer term, the situation will no doubt change. Clignet notes that: 'Of all the manifestations of social change, schooling of the female population is the only one which has had a negative effect on polygyny. . .' (1970: 33). What will be the effects of a decrease in polygyny when it does occur? In the first place, fertility would rise; for the Temne Dorjahn has shown that monogynous marriages are more fertile than polygynous ones, a finding which is also suggested in Moni Nag's earlier survey (Nag 1962). Secondly, while monogamy may raise a woman's status in her own eyes (since it corrects an imbalance of opportunities between the sexes), it may also lower some aspects of her overall position in the social system, if indeed it is possible to draw up any balance sheet of this kind. Africa is noted for the lack of differential care meted out to male and female children, such as exists in other continents, notably India. This situation could be changed by the move to monogamy.

Finally, it is hardly necessary to add that the move to monogamy does not mean the abandonment of polycoity. Plural marriage treats women differently from men in terms of marital status, but it treats all wives the same, apart from the relatively minor differences that arise from the order in which wives were taken, i.e. the special situation of the first wife or (in some states) of the queen. Monogamy, as practised in the major Eurasian societies, raises the status of some women but lowers that of others (e.g. of concubines). The term concubinage has been used to describe certain African arrangements (e.g. by Evans-Pritchard of the Nuer and by Uchendu of the Ibo) and is sometimes employed for those Muslim spouses above the allotted four. But the differentiation between types of conjugal partner is very much less in Africa than in Europe and Asia, and concubinage in the full sense of the word[3] seems to me an attribute of monogamy rather than polygyny.

The data we have earlier cited lends support to the association between advanced agriculture and monogamy on the one hand, and hoe agriculture and 'general polygyny', on the other, an association that has been proposed by a number of writers (e.g. Heath, 1958; Goody 1969 *a*; Boserup 1970). Some of these authors have suggested an economic explanation. The desire of men to attract wives is seen as correlated with the degree of women's participation in the basic productive process, which is typical of hoe as distinct from plough agriculture. This hypothesis was tested by Heath using the World Ethnographic Sample (1957) and he found a positive correlation between simple agriculture and female participation in the economy. A similar hypothesis was put forward by Adam, Clignet and by Boserup; the latter noted that the pattern of female farming is found not only in Africa, but also among Indian and Negro groups in Latin America as well as among shifting agriculturists ('tribal farmers') in India and South-East Asia.

Some writers have seen in polygyny the assertion of male dominance, but this factor would not explain the difference in the rates and distribution of plural marriage as between Africa and Eurasia. More tenable is the suggested connection of polygyny with the value placed upon the women's contribution to the economy, and specifically upon her work in the fields.[4] There is certainly a high correlation between societies where women farm and those with high rates of polygyny (Table 4). But there are defects in the argument as far as Africa is concerned. For while it is in East Africa that

180

Table 4. *Rates of women's participation in agriculture and trade, and rates of polygyny*

	Women in agriculture[1]	Women in trade[2]	Polygyny[3]
Africa, south of Sahara			
Ghana	36	80	H
Liberia	42	35	H
Sierra Leone	42	47	H
Region of Arab influence			
Morocco	9	4	L
U.A.R.	2	6	L (< 4)
Pakistan	13	2	L (< 2)
South and South-east Asia			
India	24	11	L (< 3)
Ceylon	3	6	L
Thailand	50	56	

H = high, L = low.

[1] Female family labour as a percentage of total agricultural labour force as recorded in the most recent population census (Boserup 1970: 27–8).

[2] As percentage of total labour force in trade and commerce (Boserup 1970: 88).

[3] Percentage of polygynous marriages of all marriages (Dorjahn 1959; Boserup 1970: 48).

women's farming predominates (Goody and Buckley, 1973), it is in the west that polygyny rates are highest (Table 5).

Table 5. *Percentages of all married men who are polygynous, sub-Saharan Africa by culture areas* (after Dorjahn 1959)

Area	N	Mean	Median	Mode	Range
Khoisan	4	24.5			4–40
East African Cattle	24	24.7	21.6	15.6	5–75
Congo	38	32.6	32.1	31.1	12–48
Guinea Coast	46	43.0	41.4	38.0	24–91
Western Sudan	31	33.8	33.0	31.4	20–80
Sub-Saharan Africa	155	35.0	34.1	32.2	4–91

The figures given in Table 4 do not take into account the number of wives that each married man may have. When we do, the difference between East and West increases. In East Africa there is a mean of 124.5 wives per 100 married men; this figure rises to 159.9 in the Congo and reaches 153.7 for Africa as a whole (Table 6).

Dorjahn concludes that 'East Africa appears to lack the very large households found in the remainder of the continent' (p. 103), a finding which we have elsewhere confirmed as far as farming groups are concerned (Goody

Table 6. *Number of wives to one hundred married men, sub-Saharan Africa by culture areas* (after Dorjahn 1959)

Area	N	Mean	Median	Mode	Range
Khoisan	4	*ca.* 130.0			104–154
East African Cattle	19	124.5	129.0	138.0	107–168
Congo	29	159.9	154.0	142.2	129–211
Guinea Coast	37	153.7	158.0	166.6	131–234
Western Sudan	32	151.8	150.0	146.4	127–190
Sub-Saharan Africa	131	153.7	151.5	147.1	107–234

1972 *a*). One factor in household size is clearly the rate of polygyny, not however because of the greater number of wives per married man but because more polygyny means a greater differential in marriage age. More young men are unmarried and hence less able to break away and establish a household of their own, though in other continents they may go into service.

The case of the southern Bantu is of particular interest since the rates of polygyny are distinctly low by comparison. Plural marriage is certainly less common than it was. In Basutoland one in nine husbands had more than one wife in 1936; in 1912, it was one in 5.5 (Mair 1953: 10). Hunter calculates that in 1911 12 per cent of Pondo men were plurally married and the figure was slightly lower in 1921. In 1946, the Tswana rate was 11 per cent; according to a small sample collected by Livingstone in 1850 it was 43 per cent. The figures appear to have changed drastically over time and the reasons are interesting. 'The large household is now not a source of wealth, but a burden which only the rich can bear' (Mair 1953: 19). Not only is there a specific tax for each additional wife, but a man's wives now no longer give the same help in agriculture that they did before. One reason for this is that the fields are ploughed rather than hoed. Among the Pondo, 'the use of the plough means that the amount of grain cultivated no longer depends on women's labour'. Nowadays a man has alternative opportunities for investment, in transport and in ploughing, or he may simply keep the cash.

In this region one nowadays finds not only low rates of polygyny but low rates of divorce and a higher age of marriage for girls. These facts are clearly connected with one another. But low rates of polygyny and higher marriage age are also related to the earlier existence of age regiments and to the system of 'sweethearts'. If all girls got married at puberty, there would be no unmarried lovers available; moreover the later they marry, the less opportunity they have for polygyny and for divorce.

But the rates of polygyny, with their varying consequences, are not directly related to the role of women in agriculture, as the difference between East and West Africa shows; the women's contribution to farming is greater in East Africa where polygyny rates are lower: Boserup discusses the extent to which market trade has come into women's hands in certain regions, while in others only men go to market to sell and to buy (1970: 91). A clue to this distribution, she claims, is gained by looking at the kinds of product sold by women, which are mainly agricultural. The areas where women dominate the food trade are those where there is a female farming tradition. 'Where agriculture is a male occupation, men usually also take care of the trading, but where women are actively engaged in producing the crops, and particularly when they are farmers on their own account, they also take the crops to the market. . .' She notes as an exception some Indian communities in Latin America, where women cultivate and men trade.

However even in Africa, the hypothesis runs into difficulties. For the area most renowned for markets as well as for women's participation in them, is the West rather than the East, i.e. in the area where women contribute least to agriculture. Herskovits calls attention to the role of women in trade as a general characteristic of sub-Saharan markets. In making this point, he writes: 'The importance of women in the markets of the Guinea Coast has long been recognized' (1962: xi). But this role is not universal. In East Africa markets were certainly less common traditionally. If we take the peoples from that area discussed in the major work on African markets edited by Bohannan and Dalton (1962), namely, the Arusha (p. 432), the Masai (p. 432), the Kipsigis (p. 494), the Iraqw (p. 460), the Sonjo (p. 470), the Gusii (p. 524), the Azande (p. 537), the Lugbara (p. 560), none of these had markets (i.e. market-places) before European rule. Of Zambia, Rotberg notes that 'the concept of selling or exchanging commodities within fixed or circumscribed bounds is from all evidence a recent phenomenon' (1962: 581).[5] Writing of the marketing of staple foods in the urban situation of Kampala (Uganda), Mukwaya begins by saying, 'Those familiar with both East and West Africa have often commented on how few Africans in the East engage successfully in commerce' (p. 643). In more recent times, markets have developed in East and South Africa. And when this happens, they seem to be organised along the same division of labour as in West Africa (Herskovits 1962: xii).

The figures for Africa as a whole suggest that we need to modify the hypothesis that the rate of polygyny is directly related to the women's contribution to agriculture (or the latter to their market activities). In order to point to other factors I want to test the same hypothesis on a regional rather than a continental basis by examining the situation in Ghana. The first point to make is that there is a striking contrast within Ghana, as in other countries in West Africa, between the role of women in the savannah regions and that of women near the coast. In the latter, as Bosman noted, food production is largely carried out by women, as in much of the rest of Africa. In some forest areas, such as Ashanti, there is not very much farm work anyway, especially with crops like plantains (or bananas).

183

In East Africa the role of women in agriculture is complementary to that of men in animal husbandry. However the same situation does not exist in the coastal regions of West Africa since large livestock have rarely been kept there because of the prevalence of tsetse fly. One is led to repeat the question posed by Bosman, if the men were not involved in agriculture, what did they do? Clearly they had a large part to play in forest clearing. But they also had more time for engaging in warfare, pursuing a craft or carrying out other specialist activities. When new cash crops such as cocoa were introduced it was the men who had the leisure to grow them. It could be argued that the opportunities of the men in the army, in trade and in cash crops were made possible by the contribution made by women to food farming.

In the savannah regions of Ghana, from the Tallensi and LoDagaa in the north down to the Gonja on the southern border, it was men rather than women who engaged in agriculture. Women planted grain and helped with the harvest, but they were not concerned with yam cultivation, and did not carry out the many hoeing activities that were connected with cereal agriculture. If we follow Boserup's argument in comparing north and south, we would expect the differences in market activity and a difference in polygyny rates. Is this in fact the case?

First of all, the correlation ought to hold for contemporary as well as pre-colonial conditions. But the changes relevant to our enquiry have not been great. As far as markets go, women still do most of the trading, as they did in earlier times, and they have even extended their activities into dealing with import/export agencies. As for polygyny, the rates have not so far been greatly affected by the modern changes. Finally, women still do a greater part of the food farming in the south and men in the north.

However, the differences between north and south Ghana are not as great as the theory would predict. In the first place, what polygyny rates we have do not show any substantial difference as between northern and southern Ghana. In both areas they are high (Table 7).[6] But they tend to be somewhat lower among the Ashanti (where women produce food) than they are in the north (where men farm).

With one exception the differences are not great; in the north the Gonja (a Kwa speaking group) have lower figures than anyone in the south. Such as it is, the difference (higher in north) may be partly due to the fact that the northern peoples tend to be patrilineal (or 'bilateral') and the south matrilineal, and the latter more acculturated than the former. But it is also the case that the highest rates of polygyny are found among the peoples where men (not women) do the bulk of the farming. The highest of all occur among the Konkomba where the extent of polygyny is directly related to the pattern of infant betrothal. Men of marriageable age have to get betrothed to infant girls; all others are already engaged. Since they have to

Table 7. *Polygyny rates in some Ghanaian communities*

	Percentage of husbands polygynously married	No.	Source
North (average for Western Sudan 33.8, Dorjahn 1959)			
Konkomba (1951)	63.8[1]	96	Tait 1961: 166
Tallensi (1934)	39.6	111	Fortes 1949: 656
LoDagaba (1950)	32.7	67	J. Goody 1958: 89
LoWiili (1950)	29.0	89	J. Goody 1956: 41
Gonja: all (1966)	24.7	162	E. Goody, fieldnotes
Gonja: Buipe (1956)	18.6	59	E. Goody 1973
South (average for Guinea Coast, 43.0, Dorjahn 1959)			
Anlo Ewe (1962)	42.4	222	Nukunya 1969: 158
Ashanti (1945)	29.6[2]	473	Fortes 1954: 286
Sefwi (1970)	23.5[3]	116	Roberts, fieldnotes

[1] Wives of household heads only.

[2] Polygynously married as percentage of married men with known number of wives based on women's sample, but calculated on number of men with 1, 2, etc., wives.

[3] Higher among storekeepers and craftsmen than among farmers.

wait some fifteen years before they can get married, the age of marriage for men is late, and hence their marital career a short one compared to that of women. Moreover, they usually acquire a second wife soon after the first, often by the inheritance of widow or a fiancée. 'Gerontocratic accumulation' is a concomitant of a high rate of polygyny. In the Konkomba case, for example, the high rate of polygyny is linked with a large sex difference in marriage ages, frequent widowhood (and hence orphanhood) and considerable conflict over the allocation of women; indeed these features are always likely to increase with an increase in polygyny. But the high rate of polygyny is not directly connected with the accumulation of agricultural labour. Indeed the major difference in the sexual division of farm labour in northern and southern Ghana i.e. males as against females, is not reflected in rates of polygyny. And women's participation in the market (anyhow with regard to food crops) is vigorous in both parts of the country.

While hoe agriculture, female farming and polygyny are clearly associated in a general way, there seems little evidence directly to connect variations in rates of polygyny with differences in the role of women in farming or in trade. Indeed the attempt to relate them directly to one another appears to take a too restricted view of the 'economic' role of women. To try to measure this purely in terms of the contribution to agricultural or trading activity neglects the important role of women in food preparation, the production of children and in sexual gratification. To take the first of these, water and fuel are hardly less essential elements of human life than food and shelter. In savannah regions where water is scarce and trees scattered, their collection may make great demands on a woman's time. So too does the grinding of hard grain, in the absence of mills. In all these domestic pursuits the savannah is more demanding on a woman's time than the forest and consequently she can often make less contribution to agriculture. But the fact that she contributes less to the 'economy', in the restricted European sense of the term, does not mean that she is less necessary for basic economic purposes. We need to bear in mind the narrow range of activities that have been included in the definition of economic, a range based essentially on the standpoint of advanced industrial societies. Indeed the whole discussion of women's role in relation to the economy requires that we extend the definition of the latter. Firstly, and most obviously, a wider range of craft activities can be taken into consideration, and in some of these women play a dominant part. Secondly, many of the activities that we might classify as domestic could properly be described as economic. Indeed it can be argued that the actors themselves often see the farming and domestic activities as linked together in just such a way. I illustrate this point with a quotation from the LoDagaa myth of the Bagre. We have noted that unlike most hoe cultivators in Africa, the agricultural societies in this savannah region do not encourage women to farm. The myth explains why:

Then we came along
and also said
we would follow
the old ways.
But we did so in vain.
We followed in vain,
got together
and conferred about
the ways of our forefathers,
and then we found out
about many problems
which confront us.
What confronts us?
Don't you see farming,
which came to us?
It's a great boon
that God gave us.
Do you see that
which we feed to our children
and to the women too?
We feed them;
it's with the help of the hoe

that you feed people.
And then they asked,
'Why is it
that a girl
cannot farm?
Do you know the reason
why it is so,
that women
cannot farm?'
The little old woman
asked them
to wait a while
and keep quiet.
Then she said,
'This is the reason
why a girl
cannot hoe.
She is
the one who cooks.
She is
the one who sweeps.
She is
the lighter of fires.
She is
the fetcher of water.
She is a member
of another person's house.
That's the reason
we do not let
young girls
do any hoeing.'
The young man
asked us again,
'How is it
that girls
belong to another person's house?'
And the old woman
laughed softly
and then said,
'A young woman
is unable
to stay in your house.'
'Why is it

she can't stay
in your house?'
'She's not a man.
She gives birth
and brings increase to the house;
when she has given birth,
for two years afterwards
she sits in a room
and suffers.'

(Goody, 1972 *b*: 263)

The myth also suggests another point about polygyny, namely that the greater economic role of women could theoretically lead to their retention as daughters rather than alienation as wives. It is because they are forbidden to their natal kin as *sexual* objects that they are obliged to join another *economic* group. Looking at their role as producers of children rather than producers of food, we need to remember that in the African situation, with extensive farming and low densities, there was rarely any scarcity of land; labour becomes the dominating factor in the economy. But the critical consideration may be the labour of her (male) children rather than of the woman herself. Since the optimum strategy under these conditions is likely to be maximum fertility, a plurality of wives may be desired for reproductive purposes; at the very least, polygyny (like divorce) can counter barrenness, which may be a very significant consideration when diseases that cause infertility are endemic. Some very high figures for barrenness are reported from parts of Uganda and the Congo. In a demographic survey carried out by Audrey Richards and Priscilla Reining in Buganda in 1952, 31.6 per cent of women over 45, all of whom had had some marital experience, reported childlessness. This figure is in line with the 1948 census finding that 24 per cent of the older women in all Buganda were childless. Sterility seems to have been prevalent over a fairly long period and appears to have some relationship to the incidence of venereal disease (estimated at 10 per cent) and, according to the authors, to 'a rather high degree of instability in both areas with respect to personal marital relations. . .' (1954: 403). Note that the reported number of live births was also low: for women over 60, in Buhaya 4.08 and in Buganda, 3.21.

Apart from reproduction, sex alone must play a powerful role in polygyny. Clearly the desire for sexual gratification combined with prestige plays an important part in the establishment of hareems by princes, administrators and merchants. Moreover the attractions of polygyny do not go unconsidered even where monogamy prevails. There is much evidence that the male members of monogamous societies are attracted by the possibilities of polygyny, especially at times of play. For example, Natalie Davis reports that in 1536 one of the French Abbeys of Misrule issued a proclamation permitting all men for 101 years to take two wives. The reason given was that the Turks had put out to sea intent upon destroying Christendom (which was in fact true) and their enemies could appease them by becoming polygynous (1971: 44). In Rouen in 1541, the 'Abbot' issued a mock proclamation saying that any member of the society who had a wife confined in childbirth could provide for himself with a serving girl or neighbour woman (p. 60), the implied reason sounding very much like that given by some Africans for taking a second wife.

Of course there are also 'political' reasons for polygyny, such as the desire to extend marriage alliances. Though this factor appears to play relatively little part in Africa, it was chiefs who amassed the largest number of wives; according to Bowdich, the Ashanti king was said to have had 3,333 (see Rattray's comment, 1927: 95); though this was certainly a notion of number, chiefs did accumulate wives. One might also argue that demographic conditions in Africa are favourable to polygyny, since in some parts at least there are more girls born than boys; in any case the sex ratio is usually lower among Africans than Europeans, whether in Africa or in America (Van de Walle 1968: 43; Teitelbaum and Mantel 1971).

But these factors are of marginal importance given the high rates of polygyny found in Africa, at least among the agriculturalists. Nor is it satisfactory to explain polygyny in terms of the woman's contribution to agricultural production, especially where the productivity of labour in a largely subsistence situation is low. The contribution of women is just as great in many hunting societies where rates of polygyny are much less. What is the alternative? Because it starts from a European view of marriage and the economy, much of this discussion seems to put the cart before the horse. It is not polygyny that needs to be explained, but its absence, i.e. monogamy; the former is common, the latter rare. Here economic factors, though relating to transmission more than production, are of central importance. But that theme requires developing in another context[7] where one can examine the economic constraints on the accumulation of women. As far as the relationship of general polygyny to hoe agriculture is concerned, the economic system certainly permits a high degree of polygyny. But 'permits' is the operative word. The hypothesis that female farming is directly related to the accumulation of women does not appear to fit the facts derived from comparisons within Ghana or within Africa. The reasons behind polygyny are sexual and reproductive rather than economic and productive.

Notes

1 One of the central problems in discussing marriage is to distinguish between individuals who are married to only one wife because of the legal or jural system and those who live in a society allowing plural marriage but who happen to have only one wife at a specific time. Following Fortes I refer to the first as monogamists, the second as monogynists. The existence of a Christian church in a society that permits plural marriage creates a third type of situation, at least for some individuals.

2 It is also the case that 'individuals with a high social rank are quite likely to support a large number of dependents. In fact correlation between social rank and size of household is 0.485' (p. 127).

3 I have discussed the question at greater length in a forthcoming paper called 'Co-wives or Concubines'.

4 Mair is less specific about the kind of contribution made by women when she writes, 'Both the wealth of the group and its hopes of progeny are greater in proportion to the number of wives' (1953: 1).

5 See Colson 1951: 107–108.

6 The 1960 Census shows the national rate to be 26%.

7 For an indication of the line of argument I would develop, see Goody 1969*a*.

From Varna to Caste through Mixed Unions

S. J. Tambiah

1. Introduction: Objectives

George Gaylord Simpson in *Principles of Animal Taxonomy* (1961) describes two forms of classification, namely *hierarchy* and *key*.

Hierarchy is a systematic framework with a sequence of classes at different levels in which each class except the lowest includes one or more subordinate classes. At each level from higher to lower there is a splitting or separating off into subordinate discrete classes. The Linnaean hierarchy of dividing into seven levels – kingdom, phylum, class, order, family, genus, and species – is a classical example. Or more simply, the bear (*ursus*) subdivided into brown bear and polar bear, etc. is an example of hierarchical taxonomy.

In contrast, a *key* is an arrangement produced by the *overlap* of classes: it is a systematic framework with a sequence of classes at each level of which more restricted classes are formed by the overlap of two or more classes at the next higher level. Thus two separate classes of animals such as horned mammals and two-toed mammals can by a process of *overlap* or mixture generate the class of horned two-toed mammals.[1]

Conklin (1964) who distinguishes five methods of classification confirms the basic distinction between a taxonomic hierarchy (whose constituent taxa or entities are arranged vertically by non-dimensional class inclusion and whose hierarchic positions are *not permutable*) and a key which is a multi-dimensional and hence often *permutable* arrangement of attribute oppositions, which by their hierarchic application help to locate the entities being identified.[2]

What relevance do these two taxonomic schemes have for anthropological writings? Mary Douglas in *Purity and Danger* (1966) has in mind a classification based on a hierarchy of classes. According to her 'anomaly' or 'dirt' or 'abomination' is that which does not fit into an ordered system of categories or is an imperfect member of its class. In fact she generates a theory of impurity and taboo in terms of anomalies which interfere with the keeping of categories separate and bounded.[3] Her exegesis of the underlying logic of the Abominations of Leviticus is in terms of a hierarchical scheme of discrete classes.[4]

Edmund Leach in his seminal essay 'Animal Categories and Verbal Abuse' (1964) admits his debt to Mary Douglas, and explains the nature of taboo from a perspective similar to hers. He gives a diagrammatic representation of taboo in terms of a Venn diagram of two intersecting circles with the overlap area being the ambiguous tabooed entity.[5] Leach's exposition of English and Kachin attitudes to animals as food is based on hierarchical taxonomies; the tabooed entities being those that are interstitial to the discrete classes.

My submission is that while Mary Douglas and Edmund Leach have made an important contribution to the theory of taboo, this theory stemming from classification in terms of the logic of hierarchy is not exhaustive or comprehensive. For the *key* form of classification proceeds on the reverse principle and generates new classes by the mixing or overlapping of prior classes. The area of intersection which is tabooed in Leach's Venn diagram is precisely the new class (approved under certain circumstances, disapproved under others) generated by the *key* form. And if one pursues these implications further, one can illuminate a basis for taboo that is unexplored by the Douglas-Leach scheme and which may add to their major contribution.

From a substantive point of view an example of the generation of a classification by a systematic mixture of classes is to be found in certain portions of the Indian Dharmashastric literature dealing with *varna* and their mixing in approved and disapproved forms of marriage to generate *jati*, occupational groups etc.[6] The close study of this classificatory technique in Indian materials may actually enable us to make a substantive contribution to caste theory concerning the relation between *varna* and *jati*.

Let me explain. The relation between *varna* and *jati* though declared to be crucial by two of the most important figures in Indian sociology – Srinivas and Dumont – is never actually systematically demonstrated by them.

Srinivas (1952) has stated that the *varna* 'provides an all-India framework into which the thousands of *jati* may be fitted'; it was efficacious for the assessment of the status of *jati*-members from one region by those of another; and it provided a scale of upward social mobility for ambitious groups following the route of 'sanskritisation'. Such a weighty statement of the relation between *varna* and *jati* nevertheless fails to clarify their precise linkage.

Following Dumezil, Dumont has given us a formulation of the Indian social hierarchy in terms of the dialectical opposition and combination of the *Varna* categories: the Brahman is first defined in opposition to the Kshatriya; these two then collaborate in opposition to the Vaisya; and all three combine to form the twice born in opposition to the Sudra. Phrased differently, Morality and Religion are superior to and legitimate Politics; and Politics in turn encompasses the Economy. It is this scheme of values that Dumont sees as unique in the Indian system.

But how do the *jati* (castes) fit into the *varna* (status orders) system? Dumont sees the *varna* system and the caste order as having *homologous* structures, both culminating in the Brahmans at the apex. In fact, Dumont compares the relationship between *varna* and *jati* to that between Marx's basic dichotomisation of political classes into the bourgeoisie and the proletariat and the more complex social class systems of his historical writings.[7]

Some additional insights to the contributions of these giants can be gained by a close study of the system of ideas expressed in some of the Dharmashastric texts which have been only too familiar to students of Indian society, namely the *purusha* myth of the creation of *varnas*, and the origins of *jati* through the mixing of *varnas* (*varnasamkara*).

In some ways I am simplifying the texts and crediting them with an unwarranted clarity when I say that they contain a theory of the *generation* of castes (*jati*), occupational and other groups from the original scheme of *varna* orders. However I shall lean on Kane who holds that despite the textual complexities, the underlying import of the texts is as I have described it. Kane represents the theoretical objectives of the Dharmashastric writers such as Apastamba, Gautama, Baudhayana, Vasistha, Manu, Vishnu etc. who dilated upon mixed castes and their avocations as follows:

> The ancient writers on dharmashastra strive very hard to account for the bewildering ramifications of the caste system from the four varnas that were spoken of in the *sruti* (revelation). There is unanimity on the theory that the numerous castes actually found in the country arose from the unions of males of different varnas with women belonging to **varnas** differing from their own. The divergences (and they are many), among the several smrtikaras relate only to details (pp. 50–1).

But there is no doubt that the texts present us with certain difficulties. While the categories *varna* and *jati* (caste) are sometimes clearly distinguished (as in Yajnavalkya 11.69), very often they are confounded. In Manu for instance we find examples of *varna* being used in the sense of mixed castes (*jati*), and conversely *jati* is used for *varna* (Manu X, 27, 31, 41; III 15, 177; IX. 86).

But despite these lax usages, it is clear that *varna* and *jati* meant different things and were being brought into a scheme of correlation. As Kane informs us *varna* is known from the time of Rgveda: in its first appearance the basic dichotomy expressed by *varna* was that between Arya and Dasyu (both in terms of difference in skin colour and culture); subsequently, especially at the time of Brahmana literature the four *varnas* as we know now were differentiated, with the *shudra* probably consisting of *dasyu* subjugated and brought into the fold. *Jati* on the other hand as a concept hardly appears in Vedic literature and becomes fully developed only among the *smrti* legal writers (e.g. *jatidharma* = laws of caste). But the Vedic period though lacking *jati*, did not lack named crafts and occupational groups, and many of these names later become identified as castes in the *smrti* literature (Kane, 1941: 43 ff), and have remained so for hundreds of years afterwards.

Kane surmises that the *smrti* view of the derivation of numerous castes from the mixture or confusion (*samkara*) of the four varnas was not entirely hypothetical or imaginary, for the writers were trying to propound a social theory to account for certain facts on the ground. But the *smrti* writers could not possibly account for all the castes and subcastes in terms of mixed unions. They catalogued and gave the derivation of a limited number, merely suggesting that further numberless mixed castes arose from the repeated unions of the progeny of mixed unions.

Now it must be recognised that there is great diversity among the *smrti* writers about the actual names and status placement of progeny of mixed unions, about the interpretation of the rules of upward and downward caste mobility (*jatyutkarsa* and *jatyapakarsa*), and about the constituents of the label 'mixed castes' (*varnasamkara*) itself.[8] Nevertheless they all agree on the basic ideas of the hierarchical ordering of the *varna*, the permissibility of *anuloma* hypergamous unions and the disapproval of *pratiloma* hypogamous unions, and manifest a remarkably consistent theory of caste generation through mixed marriage.

In the fashionable language of today we can say that a few *base categories*, namely the *varna* categories, themselves arranged in a hierarchical order, are subject to combination by means of the application of certain operations or rules (such as *anuloma* (approved) and *pratiloma* (disapproved) unions, and primary marriage and secondary marriage) thereby generating a number of new ranked categories which we can identify as *jati* (castes) or their analogues.[9]

Phrased in terms of classification theory we can say that the Indian scheme begins with a hierarchical ordering of *varna* categories, and then uses the overlap (key) technique to generate further classes which derive their hierarchical value from the value attached to the prior classes that are mixed. The procedure is represented in Figure 1.

This figure is based essentially on Manu who, of all the classical writers, has the most elaborate discussion and enumeration of mixed castes. 'Manu refers to six *anuloma*, six *pratiloma* and twenty doubly mixed castes and states the avocations of about twenty-three (Kane, 1941: 57).

2. Mixed Marriage and the Generative Rules

The generative rules that I shall set out systematically are those contained in *The Laws of Manu* (particularly in Chapters III and X), supplemented by other writers wherever appropriate.

But this consideration must be prefaced with a reference to the all too

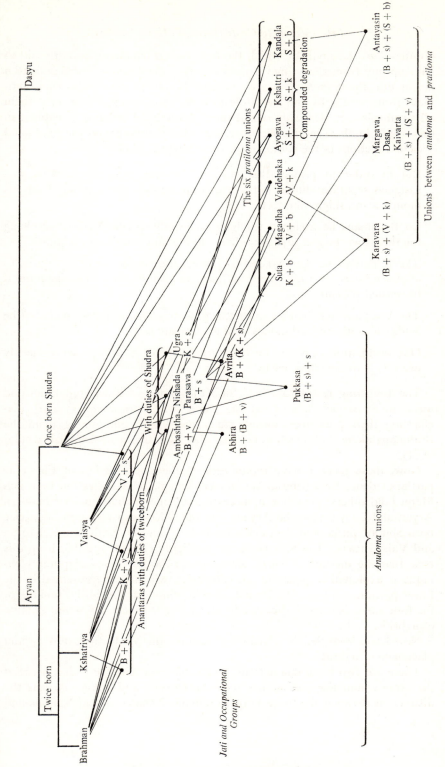

Fig. 1 From *Varna* to *Jati* through mixed unions.

familiar *Purusha* myth by which the four *varnas* (status orders) are said to have sprung from the primeval man's body – the *Brahmans* (priests) from his mouth, the *Kshatriya* (warriors) from his arms, the *Vaisya* (husbandmen) from his thighs and the *Shudras* (who are condemned to serve them all) from his feet. The *varnas* and their hierarchical ordering is explicit in this origin myth. The *shastric* texts, e.g. Manu, enumerated the graduated societal functions of the *varnas* as follows (Manu 1, 87–91):

> But in order to protect this universe He, the most resplendent one, assigned separate (duties and) occupations to those who sprang from his mouth, arms, thighs and feet.
>
> To Brahmans he assigned teaching and studying (the Veda), sacrificing for their own benefit and for others, giving and accepting (of alms).
>
> The Kshatriya he commanded to protect the people, to bestow gifts, to offer sacrifices, to study (the Veda), and to abstain from attaching himself to sensual pleasures.
>
> The Vaisya to tend cattle, to bestow gifts, to offer sacrifices, to study (the Veda), to trade, to lend money, and to cultivate land.
>
> One occupation only the lord prescribed to the Sudra, to serve meekly even these (other) three castes.

The following restriction, built into the above verses, is reiterated and made more explicit later: 'Let the three twice-born castes (varna), discharging their prescribed duties, study the Veda; but among them the Brahmana alone shall teach it, not the other two; that is an established rule' (X, 1).

Now, these ideas I have represented in the upper region of Fig. 1 as partial evidence for an initial *hierarchical* scheme of classification by which Manu (and others) postulate a successive scheme of division, first between Aryan and Dasyu, then the Aryans into the twice born *varna* and the once born Shudra varna, and then again the twice born into Brahman, Kshatriya and Vaisya *varna*. The four *varna* are explicitly ranked, and it is from this base that the mixture of *varna* according to the key or overlapping technique is exploited to generate *jati* categories, which are represented in the lower portion of Fig. 1. We should keep in mind that this initial ranking of the four *varna* is a crucial feature in the subsequent generation and ranking of hybrids.

Now let us consider the generative rules for the production, ranking and placement of hybrids.

There are two basic distinctions which the texts reiterate – that between the Aryans and the non-Aryans (e.g. the Dasyu), and among Aryans the distinction between the twice born Brahmans, Kshatriyas and Vaisyas and the once born Shudra. The Dasyus are those 'tribes' excluded from the community of those born from Brahma (i.e. the four *varnas*), and they are of that status irrespective of whether they speak the language of Mlekkas (barbarians) or that of Aryans.

Consider for instance the following rulings:

1 (a) He who was begotten by an Aryan on a non-Aryan female, may become like to an Aryan by his virtues; he whom an Aryan mother bore to a non-Aryan father is and remains unlike to an Aryan (Manu X, 67).

Thus only one kind of union – that between an Aryan male and a non-Aryan female is countenanced; for on the basis of the doctrine of male superiority, an Aryan female (who is higher in status) is polluted by mating with a non-Aryan male who stamps his qualities on the progeny (the ruling that a man can mate beneath him but not a woman beneath her is best understood in terms of the rules to be stated below).

1 (b) Marriage between the twice-born and the once-born Shudra is also discountenanced.

Twice born men, who in their folly, wed wives of the lower Shudra caste, soon degrade their families and their children to the state of Shudras (Manu III, 15).

It is particularly the Brahman (male) – Shudra (female) unions[10] that are virulently castigated as producing the consequences of hell, loss of rank upon the birth of a child, etc. (see Manu III, 16–19).

2. But this blanket condemnation is softened by the notions of 'primary' and 'secondary' marriages. The judgment in 1 (b) above applies particularly if the union of a twice born with a Shudra constitutes the only marriage. 'For the first marriage of twice born men wives of equal caste are recommended, but for those who through desire proceed to marry again the following females chosen according to the direct order of the castes, are most approved.'

'It is declared that a Shudra woman alone can be the wife of a Shudra, she and one of his own caste the wives of a Vaisya, those two and one of his own caste the wives of a Kshatriya, those three and one of his own caste the wives of a Brahmana' (Manu III, 12–13). Vishnu (XXIV, 1–4) states: 'Now a Brahmana may take four wives in the direct order of the (four) castes; a Kshatriya three, a Vaisya two, a Shudra one only' (also Baudhayana 1, 8, 16, 1–5).

Let us adopt the following notation in which the capital letter stands for male and the lower case for the female; a plus sign (+) signifies an additional spouse, and an equal sign (=) signifies the progeny of the union between man and woman.

	Male	Female
Shudra	*S*	*s*
Vaisya	*V*	*v*
Kshatriya	*K*	*k*
Brahman	*B*	*b*

Then the differential advantages of marriage or union that fall to the different statuses can be written thus:

$$S \, : \, s$$
$$V \, : \, v + (s)$$
$$K \, : \, k + (v + s)$$
$$B \, : \, b + (k + v + s)$$

The higher *varnas* have a greater range of access to women than the lower *varnas*. This differential advantage of access to lower *varna* women weighted in favour of the higher *varnas* also implies that the Brahman followed by the Kshatriya could generate more kinds of progeny (of mixed union status).

3.   There are listed some eight kinds of marriage but the two basic categories are the (1) approved or prestigious rite which involves the gift of a daughter to the bridegroom after decking her with costly garments and honouring her with jewels (as in the Brahma and Daiva rites); and (2) disapproved or non-prestigious rite which involves the bridegroom in giving as much wealth as he can afford to the bride and her kinsmen. The basic distinction is between 'gift' of a virgin together with 'dowry' and 'sale' of a girl for 'bridewealth': the first is approved for Brahmans, the second (Asura) is approved for Vaisya and Shudra, while to the Kshatriya is allotted marriage by capture (Rakshasa) (Manu X, 12–35).

Manu says: 'No father who knows the law must take even the smallest gratuity for his daughter; for a man, who, through avarice, takes a gratuity, is a seller of his offspring' (III, 51). We shall note later how in hypergamy the wife taker also profits by receiving a dowry, a fact which benefits the man of superior status.

4.   An underlying distinction which acts as an axiom in the evaluation of mixed marriage is that between male 'seed' and female 'field' or 'soil' in the theory of conception. It is declared that between the two, the male seed is *more important*, but not exclusively so for 'seed sown on barren ground perishes in it', while 'good seed, springing up in good soil, turns out perfectly well' (X, 69, 71, 72).

Now the implications of the relative statuses of male seed and female field in which it is sown are critical for caste theory; critical but also problematic, for a male's superiority cannot automatically lift his progeny from the taint of an inferior mother. Thus 'Sons begotten by twice-born

198

men on wives of the next lower castes, they declare to be similar to their fathers, but blamed on account of the fault inherent in their mothers. Such is the eternal law concerning children born of wives one degree lower than their husbands...' (Manu X, 6). 'Blamed' in the above rule which relates to men marrying women of status immediately below them is interpreted by one commentator as 'excluded from the father's caste'.

From this evaluation of 'seed' and 'field' for the status of progeny, three rules can be deduced which are of enormous importance:

4 (a) Ideally father and mother should be of the same status, and a child derives the same status bilaterally. 'In all castes (*varna*) those children only which are begotten in the direct order on wedded wives, equal in caste and married as virgins, are considered as belonging to the same caste as their fathers' (Manu X, 5).

4 (b) But since male seed is superior to female field, it is not repugnant (especially as secondary union) for a man to mate with a woman of lower status, though the child thus born is tarnished. It constitutes an act in the acceptable direction or 'with the hair' (*anuloma*).

4 (c) The reverse is repugnant and causes a contradiction in and a confusion of hierarchical categories: seed of an 'inferior' status male cannot fall on the field of a superior status female. It constitutes an act in a non-acceptable direction or 'against the hair' (*pratiloma*).

Anuloma and Pratiloma

The consequences of *anuloma* (a superior caste man uniting with an inferior caste woman) and *pratiloma* (an inferior caste man uniting with a superior caste woman), usually known in anthropology as hypergamy and hypogamy, are dramatically different and are the subject of much fine categorisation and commentary. The 'mathematical' permutations and derivations of new castes through mixed unions and the assignation of status positions to them on the basis of *anuloma* and *pratiloma* principles are worth following in detail because they exemplify a mode of formal derivation of a complex system of classification.

2 (B) Anuloma

(1) *Sons begotten on wives of the next lower ranks.* I have cited earlier (in 4 above) the rule that sons born of wives of the next lower ranks though 'similar to their fathers' are however excluded from their father's caste. Manu defines this more clearly (X, 14) thus:

'Those sons of the twice born, begotten on wives of the next lower castes, who have been enumerated in due order, they call by the name Anantaras (belonging to the next lower caste) on account of the blemish inherent in mothers.' Many commentators agree that sons of this type of union belong to the mother's caste.

The status of sons born of such unions can be represented according to our system of notation as follows:[11]

The kind of union	Valuation of sons by Manu	Valuation of sons by Baudhanya
$B + k$	K	B
$K + v$	V	K
$V + s$	S	V

But it is to be expected that sons born of wives of the next lower castes are in an *intermediate position* which can be evaluated a little differently on the basis of the superiority of male seed and the rules of hypergamy. Thus according to the school of Baudhanya (see above), sons begotten on wives of equal or the net lower caste are called Savarnas (of equal caste). However this evaluation is not confirmed by Vasishtha who supports Manu's judgment.

In sum, we may thus note that although B, K, V, S are regarded as separate *varna* categories, there is room for evaluating more or less positively the product of the union of immediately adjacent categories which are closest in status. They are ambiguous but *acceptable* intermediate categories. Further support for this will appear below.

(2) *Sons born of wives of two or three degrees lower.* Sons born of wives of two or three degrees lower are on the one hand begotten on the *anuloma* principle but on the other represent the union of *varna* categories somewhat removed in status. Hence such unions lead to the generation of *new* castes (or groups): a Brahman male begets on a Vaisya female a son called Ambastha, on a Shudra female, a Nishada or Parasava; a Kshatriya begets an Ugra son on a Shudra female.

$$B + v = \text{Ambashtha}$$
$$B + s = \text{Nishada/Parasava}$$
$$K + s = \text{Ugra}$$

These sons are distinctly downgraded (because the unions are more explicitly in violation of the law) and are said to have the 'duties of Shudras'. The principle which compares sons born of wives of one lower degree and those born of wives of two or three degrees lower is clearly enunciated by Manu thus (X, 41): 'Six sons begotten by Aryans on women of equal and the next lower castes (Anantaras) have the duties of twice-born men; but all those born in consequence of a violation of the law are, as regards their duties, equal to Shudras.'

Thus these six sons born of the following unions have 'duties of twice born':

$$B + b \quad B + k$$
$$K + k \quad K + v$$
$$V + v \quad V + s$$

But three sons born of the following unions have duties of Shudras:

$B + v$, $B + s$ (The son of a Brahman union with a Vaisya female, the
$K + s$ Ambashtha, is assigned the occupation of healing by Manu)

It is clear from the above that the twice born/once born, pure/polluted distinction applies with force to Brahman and Kshatriya unions with Shudras (Manu assigns the degrading occupations of catching fish and killing animals to their issue);[12] but the Vaisyas who are at the bottom of the twice born hierarchy, but adjacent to the once born Shudras appear to be allowed an acceptable crossing of the barrier.

But on theoretical grounds we could expect the judgment equally well to go the other way; and the *shudra* women being declared beyond the reach of all twice born men. Thus Vasishtha declares that the twice born must keep within their bounds: a Brahman is permitted three wives according to the order of castes $(b+k+v)$,[13] a Kshatriya two $(k+v)$, a Vaisya *one only* (v), and the Shudra the same (s). Vasishtha pointedly asserts that although some schools declare that twice-born men may marry even a Shudra female, 'Let him not act thus' for 'the degradation of the family ensues, and after death the loss of heaven' (I, 24–7).

(3) *Further anuloma mixed unions.* Theoretically, it should be possible for further *anuloma* unions between (pure) twice born men and the female issue of preceding acceptable mixed unions.

But the texts do not appear to be interested in multiplying these 'permutations'. Thus for instance there is no listing of the result of the union of a male Brahman with a female born of a Brahman-Kshatriya union $(B + (B + k) = ?)$, or with a female of a Brahman-Vaisya union $(B + (B + v) = ?)$ and the like $(K + (K + v) = ?, V + (V + s) = ?)$.

Curiously the texts concern themselves with the consequences of Brahman union with females who themselves were born of the union of superior males with women two or three degrees lower (i.e. women of Ambashtha and Ugra status). According to Manu, a union of a Brahman with an Ambashtha female produces an Abhira, that with an Ugra female an Avrita:

$$B + (B + V) = \text{Abhira}$$
$$B + (K + s) = \text{Avrita}$$

Another mixture which, though in the acceptable *anuloma* direction, contravenes the distinction between twice-born and Shudra, is the union of a Nishada male with a Shudra woman to produce a Pukkasa $((B + s) + s = \text{Pukkasa})$. Why the texts are more concerned with these less acceptable unions will engage us later.

The upward mobility of anuloma issue through repeated marriage. There is a truly remarkable statement in Manu (and other *shastric* writers)[14] concerning the possibilities of upward and downward social mobility (*jatyutkarsa* and *jatyapakarsa* respectively) through certain kinds of *repeated* marriage conforming to the rules of *anuloma*.

Here we are particularly interested in the rules for achieving improvement of status upwards.

If a female of the caste, sprung from a Brahmana and a Shudra female, bear children to one of the highest caste, the inferior tribe attains the highest caste within the seventh generation. Thus a Shudra attains the rank of a Brahmana, and in a similar manner a Brahmana sinks to the level of a Shudra; but know that it is the same with the offspring of a Kshatriya or of a Vaisya (Manu X, 64, 65).

According to Buhler the various schools of law essentially put two interpretations upon the question of the mechanics of upward mobility. In the one case if a female child of a Brahman male and a Shudra female, i.e. a Parasava (or Nishada) female, and her descendants all marry Brahmans, the offspring of the sixth female descendant of the original couple will be a Brahman. The second interpretation goes thus – in a Parasava son (of a Brahman male and a Shudra female) marries a most excellent Parasava female and his descendants do the same, the child born in the sixth generation will be a Brahman (see Figs. 2A and 2B).

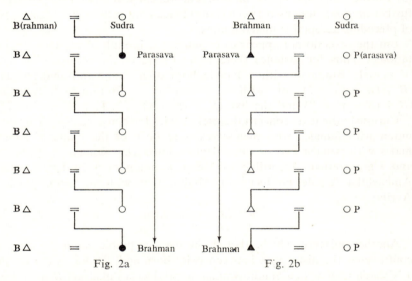

Fig. 2a   Fig. 2b

The remarkable aspect of this mechanism of upward mobility is that, as in interpretation 1, the inferior female is encouraged to consistently unite with a superior male. This of course is the blueprint for hypergamy which exists even today in India not so much across distant castes but either between ranks within a caste or between adjacent castes. Hypergamy is consistent with male superiority; it is in the right *anuloma* direction. The second interpretation promises upliftment as a result of consistently impeccable endogamy, i.e. marriage with persons of an equal status after the initial asymmetrical one. This is the preponderant rule of marriage amongst most Hindus. Thus the two interpretations can be placed within the ortho-dox hypergamy-endogamy parameter.

True to the differential evaluation of the *varna* orders, and the differential advantages accruing to them, the offspring of a Brahman and Vaisya union are promised Brahman status in the *fifth* generation and of a Brahman and Kshatriya union in the third generation if they follow the path of recommended repeated marriage on the lines discussed above.[15]

2 (C) *Pratiloma*

Unlike *anuloma* it is *pratiloma* unions which, going 'against the hair' are 'in the inverse order of castes', and therefore cause a true 'confusion of castes'. Though heavily censured, paradoxically, they are enumerated in some detail. We shall later attempt to account for this paradox and its implications for the theory of caste classification.

The aversion and moral condemnation of *pratiloma* is evidenced in this pronouncement by Manu:

> By adultery committed by persons of different castes, by marriages with women who ought not to be married, and by the neglect of the duties and occupations prescribed to each, are produced sons who owe their origin to a confusion of the castes (X, 24).

Manu lists six *pratilomas*[16] which can be placed in the following hierarchical order (from higher to lower) as gleaned from rules subsequently stated.

Son of a Kshatriya male and a Brahman woman:	$K + b$ =	Suta
Son of a Vaisya male and a Brahman woman:	$V + b$ =	Magadha
Son of a Vaisya male and a Kshatriya woman:	$V + k$ =	Vaidehaka
Son of a Shudra male and a Vaisya woman:	$S + v$ =	Ayogava
Son of a Shudra male and a Kshatriya woman:	$S + k$ =	Kshattri
Son of a Shudra male and a Brahman woman:	$S + b$ =	Kandala,
		the lowest of mortals

Vasishtha also heartily disapproves of these unions 'from the inverse order of the castes' and therefore 'destitute of virtue and good conduct' (Buhler, part II, chapter 21, 1882). It is declared that a Shudra who 'approaches a female' of the Brahman caste is thrown into a fire, and the (polluted) woman concerned is shaved, her body is anointed with butter, and then she is placed naked on a black donkey and conducted along the highroad in order to be purified. Vaisya and Kshatriya males cohabiting with a Brahman woman merit the same punishment; the only difference as far as the woman is concerned is that a yellowish and then a white donkey are correspondingly substituted (i.e. black, yellow, white are colours of decreasing impurity).

In Manu, all *pratiloma* issue are declared to be *excluded* from the Aryan community. However amongst them there is a rank order of *pratiloma* which can be listed as follows: among twice born, the *varna* statuses of the superior female and inferior male count in respect of the ordering of their *pratiloma* children – thus a Suta is superior to a Magadha who is superior to a Vaidehaka. But when there is a crossing of the twice-born/once-born barrier, and inferior Shudra males unite with superior twice-born females then there is a *reversal* in the principle of degradation, which operates by 'geometrical progression': the sons of Shudra man's union with higher females are rated *lower* than his sons by more inferior women, so that an Ayogava rates higher than a Kshattri who in turn is superior to the Kandala, who is the son of a Shudra and a Brahman female, the lowest of mortals.

Now the principle of *compounded degradation* which is truly an inversion of the ordinary *anuloma* status rules is unambiguously stated:

(1) First and foremost all possibility of *mobility* (accessible to *anuloma* issue) through successive correct and superior marriages are denied *pratiloma* issue:

> These six Pratilomas beget similar races (varna) on women of their own caste, they also produce the like with females of their mother's caste (gati), and with females of higher ones (Manu X, 27).

(2) Not only is mobility denied but a repetition of *pratiloma* unions compounds the degradation.

> These six...also beget, the one on the females of the other, a great many kinds of despicable sons, even more sinful than their fathers, and excluded from the Aryan community (vahya) (Manu X, 29).

> Just as a Shudra begets on a Brahmana female a being excluded from the Aryan community, even so a person himself excluded procreates with females of the four castes (varna) sons more worthy of being excluded than he himself (Manu X, 30).

Although a second repetition of the deprecated *pratiloma* union is denounced, the law texts however go on to state precisely the mathematical properties of such mixtures:

> Men excluded by the Aryans (vahya) who approach families of higher rank, beget races (varna) still more worthy to be excluded, low men (*hina*) still lower races, *even fifteen in number* (Manu X, 31, italics mine).

One of the interpretations given of the above rule (favoured by Buhler following Raghavananda, Narada and Kulluka: see *Laws of Manu* p. 409)[17] illustrates the simple calculation adopted. The ruling is taken to apply to the six *pratiloma* issue of wrong *varna* unions already enumerated. The lowest among them, the Kandala ($S+b$) may produce with females of the five higher *pratiloma* five *more degraded* races, the Kshattri ($S + k$) similarly with the four above him; the Ayogava ($S + v$) with the three above him, the Vaideha ($V + k$) two and the Magadha ($V + b$) one. The total of more degraded races are thus $5 + 4 + 3 + 2 + 1 = 15$.

'*More degraded races*' *born of repeated confusion of castes.* The law texts enumerate numerous castes of still other *pratiloma* mixtures which compound the error: thus men who are progeny of *pratiloma* unions unite with (a) superior women of the four *varna*, (b) with superior women who are the issue of *anuloma*, (c) with women who are themselves products of previous *pratiloma* unions, etc.

The distinctive character of these *pratiloma* progeny is that they are assigned to an infinite number of base occupations practised in general today by a varied number of polluted castes, the majority of them falling into the category called Harijans.

I give below an incomplete list of such castes (stating in parentheses the details of their mixed origin in terms of the notation adopted previously). They are all declared to be 'base born of Aryans' or produced in consequence of a 'violation of the law' (*ap-adhvamsaya*) who shall subsist by occupations reprehended by the twice born. They shall not only be known by their occupations of the most demeaning kind but also by their place of residence, food and clothing and the like:

> Let these tribes dwell near well known trees and burial grounds and in groves, known by certain marks and subsisting by their peculiar occupations (Manu X, 50).

They are to dress in garments of the dead, eat food from broken dishes, wander from place to place; they are not allowed at night in villages and towns; they are compelled to transport corpses of dead who have no relatives, and act as executioners of criminals; the most outcaste of them like the Kandalas and Svapakas are condemned to dwell outside the village, and their wealth shall be dogs and donkeys.

We can summarise the generation of degraded castes in three steps.

1. Let us first enumerate the occupations of the six archetypal *pratilomas* who derive from the confusion of the four basic *varna* categories:

	Occupation
Suta ($K + b$)	management of horses and chariots
Magadha ($V + b$)	trade
Vaidehaka ($V + k$)	the service of women (guardians in the harem)
Ayogava ($S + v$)	carpentry
Kshattri ($S + k$)	catching and killing animals living in holes
Kandala, the lowest of mortals ($S + b$)	dwelling outside the village, their wealth being dogs and donkeys

Fig. 3

205

2. Next, let us list the occupations of the heavily censured issue of *anuloma* unions which though in the right direction yet cross the barrier between the twice born and once born, a crossing which is particularly heinous according to some schools for the Brahman and Kshatriya (but not for the Vaisya). Thus

	Occupation
Nishada $(B + s)$	catching fish
Ugra $(K + s)$	catching and killing animals living in holes
Pukkasas $((B + s) + S)$	catching and killing animals living in holes

3. Third, let us enumerate the implications of still more confused unions between the progeny of *anuloma* and *pratiloma* unions.

The unions between issue of 'unacceptable' *anuloma* and despised *pratiloma*, and of double *pratiloma* unions, reproduce and frequently increase the initial degradation. Technically there can be three kinds of these unions:

(a) Male issue of (unacceptable) *anuloma* mating with female issue of *pratiloma* to produce children, e.g.

Nishada male and Vaideha female $(B + s) + (V + k)$
= Karavara, leather worker.

Nishada male and Kandala female $(B + s) + (S + b)$
= Antyavasayin,[18] employed in burial grounds, despised even by those already excluded.

Nishada male and Vaideha female $(B + s) + (V + k)$
= Ahindika, occupation not given.

Nishada male and Ayogava female $(B + s) + (S + v)$
= Margava, Dasa or Kaivarta who subsist as boatmen.

(b) Male issue of *pratiloma* unions mating with females produced by (unacceptable) *anuloma* unions to produce children, e.g. Kandala male and Pukkasa female $(S + b) + ((B + s) + s)$
= Sopaka who follows 'sinful occupation' of Kandala.

(c) Double *pratiloma* union e.g.

Kandala male and Vaideha female $(S + b) + (V + k)$
= Pandusopaka who deals in cane.

Non-Aryan Ethnic groups located in terms of confusion of castes. The Aryans in India are alleged to have encountered diverse alien ethnic groups variously called Dravida, Dasyu, etc. Here is an example of how two such alien ethnic groups – the Andhra of the Deccan and the Meda of S. E. Rajput – are placed on the margins of the classification grid by characterising them as products of sexual unions in 'the inverse order of castes'. Thus an Andhra is said to be the product of a union between a Vaidehaka male and a Karavara female (i.e. $[(V + k) + ((B + s) + (V + k))]$ = Andhra); and a Meda is described as the product of a union between a Vaidehaka male and a Nishada female (i.e. $(V + k) + (B + s)$ = Meda). Finally in this section we may include the formula that a Dasyu (i.e. non-Aryan) male unites with an Ayogava female $(S + v)$ to produce a Sairandhra who is described as living like a slave and subsisting by sharing animals.

Why so many degenerate hybrids? The social implications of the classification scheme.

We have seen in detail how a scheme of ranked castes (and analogous groups) have been generated through the systematic mixing of categories (i.e. the *key* forms of classification). But the beauty of the total scheme is that because we start with four ranked *varna* categories (derived on the basis of hierarchical taxonomy) and because the procedures for mixing are themselves evaluated as approved or disapproved etc., the categories progressively generated are themselves in turn automatically ranked. Thereby we are enabled to comprehend a whole universe of numerous castes all in principle capable of being *ranked* and *interrelated* into a single scheme.

We can also see that although several kinds of permutations and mixtures are possible in a mathematical sense, and although the classical legal theorists considered both approved hypergamous mixing and disapproved hypogamous mixing, yet paradoxically they were more concerned with the generation of castes and occupational groups through the unsanctioned and repudiated forms of intermixing. How can we explain this paradox?

It seems to me that *pratiloma* is a convenient intellectual device for generating various disapproved categories, assigning them degraded positions, and ideologically explaining and rationalising why so many groups in the caste hierarchy are placed in low or downtrodden positions. In other words the rationale of a formula which mixes the basic *varna* categories in approved and disapproved ways to produce a classificatory scheme becomes understandable in a hierarchical society which has a steep gradation of statuses. Although caste society may or may not in its actual demographic composition constitute a pyramid, its evaluation of statuses, ritual and occupational roles must necessarily be pyramidal. The pure statuses are few, the impure are legion. The economy of the distribution of purity and impurity makes this inevitable. We have now uncovered the reason why the law books show little interest in permuting the unions of the approved *anuloma* type between the twice born beyond a point (for high level positions in a society are necessarily few) and shows an unexpected preoccupation with permuting *pratiloma* type unions for these in fact though morally condemned are the vehicle for producing the lowly positions in society of which there are in actuality so many.

There is another closely related point. In the catalogue of *anuloma* and *pratiloma* unions and further derivations from their mixtures the participation of the Brahman *varna* exceeds that of the Kshatriya and Vaisya varnas.[19] From the point of view of caste theory this is remarkable, for what we have here is the purest and highest *varna* being in a sense the most lax of the twice born strata! But there is a method to this madness. The consequence of this mythical derivation of castes propounded by Brahmans is that a number of castes, many of them indeed beyond the pale, can and do relate their mythical origins to a Brahmanical ancestor male or female who was degraded. Ethnographers have reported many of these origin myths of low castes.[20] This mythical charter which the impure use to bolster their claims also implicitly and tacitly reinforces the fact that the Brahmans are – because they are the point of reference – the fountainhead of purity and the apex of the pyramid.

From the perspective of classification theory we can predict over what issues the classical lawyers would disagree or show discrepant judgments. We know that the important boundaries in the categorical system are those between Aryan and Non-Aryan, between twice-born and once-born, and between the three varna within the twice born. The phenomena which are the subject of discrepant interpretations by the *shastric* writers are precisely those mixtures which create ambiguities, as

(a) when adjacent rather than more distant categories mix: (Is the child of a Brahman male and a Kshatriya female – who is like his father but bears his mother's blemish – a Brahman or a Kshatriya?); and

(b) when *adjacency* permits union, but when at the same time the distinction between twice-born and once-born is a barrier: (Does the product of a Vaisya male and a Shudra have or not have the 'duties of the twice born'?).

3. Towards an Interactional View of Pollution Rules

I shall try and demonstrate that the two rules of *direct order and inverse order of castes* applied to the four basic *varna* categories is the underlying design of the various *shastric* formulations on pollution.

My task has been to a great extent made easy by Orenstein's three articles on ritual defilement in Hindu Sacred Law (Orenstein 1965; 1968; 1970). While Orenstein's discussion of the pollution rules is illuminating, it is my view that his labels for the three types of pollution he isolates are unsatisfactory and that he fails to see some of the logic of the underlying design.[21]

I do not pretend that I can unravel the underlying design of all the pollution rules stated by the *shastric* writers, since certain statements show inconsistencies. I merely want to show the path to an interactional view of pollution based on the 'interrelation of castes', both approved and disapproved, and to do so I shall exploit Orenstein's analyses.

Relational pollution (especially between varna/caste equals)

By 'relational pollution' Orenstein referred particularly to pollution incurred by virtue of relations of kinship on the occasions of birth and death.

Ego is polluted for a stipulated period of time irrespective of physical nearness, e.g. whether or not he has had contact with the deceased is of no account in death pollution. The graduated periods for observance of pollution depending on closeness of kinship (*sapinda*) and affinity is well known. The texts talk of pollution spreading through the group whose members are considered as being 'connected by particles of the same body'.

From a *varna* point of view Orenstein formulates the following paradigm as regards 'relational pollution':

Holding constant such factors as degree of relationship, the amount of pollution incurred is inversely proportional to the rank of the varna in which the event takes place.

The principle that the lower the *varna* the greater the birth and death pollution is well attested by the law codifiers. Thus according to both Vishnu and Manu, the impurity of a Brahman caused by the birth or death of a *sapinda* lasts ten days, of a Kshatriya twelve days, of a Vaisya fifteen days, and a Shudra a month (Manu V, 83; Vishnu XXII, 1–4).

In the 1968 essay Orenstein adds a few more details which make problematic the exposition of relational pollution he gave in 1965. There are internal differences among Brahmans which make them unequally subject to relational pollution: a Brahman who knows the Vedas and tends the Sacred Fire achieves purity in the event of birth and death pollution in one day, a Brahman who knows the Vedas but does not tend the fire achieves purity in three days, and a Brahman who does neither in ten days. A similar decreasing scale applies to the four *ashramas*: the householder is most subject to relational pollution, then the student, next the forest hermit and least of all the *sannyasi*.

The rules of pollution associated with birth and death apparently provide some sort of puzzle for caste theorists. They force even Dumont into a quite uncharacteristic explanation which he deplored in Dubois and James Mill and which he has dubbed 'voluntaristic' (1970: 23–34). This is the species of explanation which attributes certain customs and 'superstitions' to a deliberate invention by priests for their benefit. Let us allow Dumont himself to comment on certain rules which are for him 'incomprehensible from the point of view of purity':

But above all, starting from the Dharmasutras of Gautama and Vasistha, one finds illogical injunctions, which later became very widespread. These are those which prescribe, all other things being equal, an increasing period of impurity for decreasing status: in the case of death, close relations are impure for ten days for Brahmans, twelve for Kshatriyas, fifteen for Vaishyas and thirty for Shudras.

...But, going by the nature of the system, we would expect the contrary, for impurity is more powerful than purity, and the higher the degree of purity to be regained, the more severe should be the effect of impurity. Either we have not yet managed to enter into the spirit of the system, or else *the Brahmans have here transformed into a privilege what ought to be a greater incapacity* (pp. 70–1, my italics).

I believe that there is a simple and more acceptable explanation for the rules of relational pollution which reasonably follows from the requirements of 'the direct order of castes'.

Firstly we know that the higher the *varna* position, the higher the natural condition of purity (under normal circumstances). Death and birth pollution essentially refer to the bodily and therefore *kinship connection between status equals*. Death and birth pollute kinsmen by virtue of this connection alone. Hence it would be completely antithetical to the basis of *varna* status differentiation if death or birth conferred on a Brahman greater impurity than on a Kshatriya and so down the line, for this would attack the very doctrine of the sharing of 'particles of body' and kinship which makes a Brahman superior to Kshatriya, a Kshatriya to a Vaisya and so on. Hence it is clear that the normal doctrine that pollution attacks the pure more than the impure *cannot* be allowed to work here for it would *undermine the hierarchy itself*. The premises of hierarchy stem from the logic of the 'direct order of castes' and the differential dominance it implies.

Now, how do we explain the fact that the Brahman who knows the Sacred Vedas and tends the sacred fire is less prone to relational pollution in the event of birth and death than one who is less virtuous; and that a *sannyasi* is less prone than a forest hermit, who in turn is less prone than a student, who in turn is less prone than a householder. This is strictly in line with Hindu religious aspirations – the more virtuous and religious, the more removed from the chains of the physical and organic world and the physical and organic body. Therefore this detachment from the world which increases with the progressive renunciation of a gross householder's or a non-religious man's state also means *greater immunity from the bodily connections of kinship*. Thus at the highest peak of achievement we know that the true *sannyasi* renounces the world, transcends family bonds and caste status, and become a detached individual in a hierarchical group-minded society.

We thus see that birth and death within the kinship group has different polluting potencies not only for different *varna*, but also among men of different religious achievements. The more sacred the personal status the less subject to social bonds; the higher the caste status, the less polluting the bonds of kinship (particles of body) shared by that status group.

A marvellous confirmation of the thesis that pollution rules relating to death and pollution are based on the privileges of 'direct order of castes' is to be found in the following rules formulated by Vishnu (XXII; 19, 21–4).

210

19. Wives and slaves in the direct order of the castes (i.e. who do not belong to a higher caste than their lord) remain impure as long as their lord.

21. If Sapindas of a higher caste (are born or have died) the period of impurity has for their lower caste relations the same duration as for members of the higher caste.

22. A Brahmana (to whom) Sapindas of the Kshatriya, Vaisya, or Shudra castes (have been born or have died) becomes pure within six nights, or three nights, or one night, respectively.

23. A Kshatriya (to whom Sapindas of the) Vaisya or Shudra castes (have been born or have died) is purified within six and three nights, respectively.

24. A Vaisya (to whom Sapindas of the) Shudra caste (have been born or have died) becomes pure within six nights.

What verse 19 establishes is that we are dealing with *anuloma* unions, and we are particularly interested in verses 21–4 which refer to kinship between *varna* as a result of *anuloma*. How do we interpret the fact that while the superior *varna* or caste regains purity in a smaller period of time according to the degree of inferiority of the affine, the lower status affine observes pollution for his superior affine for the same duration as this superior's own caste members? For example while a Brahman achieves purity in 10 nights where a fellow Brahman kinsman is concerned, he achieves purity in 6 nights, 3 nights and 1 night respectively where the kinsman is a Kshatriya, Vaisya and Shudra respectively. But these last three achieve purity in 10 nights where a Brahman kinsman is concerned, thereby being subject to impurity for the same period as for members of Brahman status.

What this asymmetry seems to be saying is this. From the Brahman's point of view, the strength of his kinship or *sapinda* relationship to persons of inferior *varna* is *weaker* than is the case from the point of view of the lower status affine for whom it is *stronger*, as strong as it is for equals in the superior varna! This asymmetrical valuation of 'affinal' link becomes comprehensible when we see it as finding concrete expression in the Nambudiri–Nayar *tali-tying* relationship. For the Nambudiri the relationship if consummated is concubinage, for the Nayar it is marriage. The Nayar woman and child must observe death pollution when the Nambudiri male in question dies, but he does no such thing when the linked Nayar female dies. Here are differential evaluations of the strength of the same relation according to the dominance and differentiated privilege implied by the 'direct order of castes'.

There is one special sort of death pollution that I must allude to briefly. The texts minimise or curtail pollution, or declare the total absence of pollution falling on kinsmen in cases of suicide (including those who die by fasting, taking poison or hanging), and in cases of death penalty or killing administered by the king, Brahmans etc., presumably for offences or polluting actions (Orenstein 1972: 32, for textual references). Here the texts seem to be asserting that the relationship of kinship or *sapinda* does not bear the burden of sharing the blame and impurity of violent deaths, or deaths meted out for crimes which are matters of 'personal' rather than 'collective' and 'relational' responsibility, in the same way as for instance 'self pollution' induced by personal circumstances does not spread to others, if the person polluted keeps himself separate from others, and avoids social contact.

(2) The second major class of pollution rules Orenstein isolates are given the label *act pollution* (previously in the 1965 essay called transitive pollution). This kind of pollution involves some kind of interaction or contact with biological phenomena, life substance and process. Orenstein subdivides act pollution into (1) internal pollution and (2) external pollution. Let us follow him:

Internal pollution

Here 'ego as subject acts upon an object' and incurs impurity particularly through inflicting injury on living things, especially by destroying life. The pollution incurred by the sinner is proportional to the purity of the victim's *varna* or sacredness. Thus the penance imposed for killing a Brahman is heavier than that imposed for killing a Kshatriya and so on. Thus one may say that defilement is proportionate to the magnitude of the crime which in turn is measured according to the purity or sacredness of the victim. The classical acts condemned as mortal sins (*mahapataka*) under this rubric are the killing of a cow or a bullock, of a Brahman; committing adultery with a Guru's wife, theft of gold from Brahmans, drinking Sura (Manu XI, 55). Other acts condemned include reviling the Vedas, eating forbidden food, drinking spirits, incest with sisters by the same mother, intercourse with unmarried maidens, slaying kine, usury, etc. (see Manu XI): these range over a wide spectrum of injuries, crimes, sexual deviations, use of violence and the like. We may thus construe these acts as primarily signifying attacks launched or injuries inflicted by a person on other persons or objects, the most serious of which are those 'mortal sins' committed by inferiors on persons or things of a superior status.

In the light of this perspective, what Orenstein labels 'act pollution: internal pollution' is also relational in my terms, in that it deals with disapproved 'social' contact between persons and things. Orenstein further fails to see that the logic of this class of offences is based on the principle of the *direct order of castes* in two reinforcing senses: firstly, the higher the status of the person, animal or object injured, the greater the penance/punishment/impurity that befalls the offender; secondly, the higher the status of the offender usually the less severe the punishment meted out than for offenders of lower status for the same crime or offence. In this sense the scheme for calculating the degree of punishment guards the privileges of those of higher status.

External pollution

This kind of pollution is simply the reverse of the above in that a person becomes polluted by coming into contact with an inferior or a defiling object. 'The extent of ego's external pollution is proportionate to the defilement of the *varna* he contacts; for example, a Vaishya's corpse defiles more than does a Brahman's' (Orenstein 1968: 116).

The implication of these rules is that the high castes are required to undergo more thorough purification and rituals than the low castes: the paradigm of external pollution is that 'holding constant the things with which Ego interacts, he is polluted in proportion to the rank of his *varna*' (Orenstein 1965: 7).

Translating this into our idiom, we may say that these rules which punish the higher castes more than the inferior for engaging in polluting contacts appear to follow the logic of 'the inverse order of castes' in order to prevent the 'confusion of castes' and other similar consequences. The law books devote much space and verbal skill to defining the pollutions through contact against which men of caste must guard with eternal vigilance: drinking from an untouchable's cup, eating foods that have been eaten by low castes, sexual intercourse with women of low caste, living in the house of a degraded caste man; contact with a corpse, with a menstruating woman, and with polluting substances.

The familiar arithmetic is brought into operation in the stipulation of penance. If a Brahman eats the leavings of a Shudra's meal, a Vaisya's meal, a Kshatriya's meal and a fellow Brahman's meal, he must do penance by living on milk for seven days, five days, three days and one day respectively. If a Kshatriya eats the leavings of a Shudra's meal and a Vaisya's meal he does similar penance for five days, and three days respectively. A Vaisya who eats the leavings of a Shudra's meal must live on milk for three days.

The logic of these rules stems from the simple precept that the higher the purity status of a man the greater his defilement by impurity, especially that stemming from a lower level person or object. Conversely, the logic says that a lower caste person in so far as he is permanently more polluted than a higher caste person does not proportionately heap more pollution upon himself through defiling contact, and can return to his status quo ante more easily than a superior status person whose fall is proportionately steeper and the purification entailed correspondingly more elaborate. This logic is of course the precise reverse of that entailed in relational pollution resulting from birth and death.

Finally, what Orenstein calls 'self pollution', where ego pollutes himself through substances secreted from his own body, and where a man defiles himself by eating, defecating, urinating etc. naturally comes within the scope of 'inverse order of castes': the higher the status of the person in question the more elaborate the ablutions, the baths, the sipping of water. In these instances a person 'contacts' and contaminates himself. As may be expected, the severity of purification required is not only proportionate to the superiority of *varna* status but also of spiritual status. A student, an ascetic, a hermit respectively undergo more stringent purification than a [Brahman] householder.

Now in respect of 'self pollution' Orenstein faces a puzzle for which he produces a convoluted and cumbersome answer but for which perhaps a simpler one can be found. He is puzzled by the problem of 'compounded pollution' as formulated by the *shastric* writers. Why do they pay special attention to the combining of 'self pollution' with 'external pollution' (i.e. coming into contact with defiling persons or objects while suffering from self pollution) in that order, and why do they compound the resulting pollution to an extent that is more severe than the individual acts taken singly. 'In general, it appears that if one has polluting contacts with others while in self-pollution, the result is not as if one "stain" were simply added to another; rather one is much more defiled' (Orenstein 1970: 28). A final question posed by Orenstein is why the theorists deal only with 'compounded pollution' caused by the mixing of self-pollution with 'external pollution', and not by the mixing of other kinds of pollution.

The answers to all these problems are possibly already given in our previous account of the generation of mixed castes.

We saw there that while many forms of *anuloma* and *pratiloma* mixing between the *varnas* were theoretically possible, the theorists were more interested in generating the more degraded forms, and of these degraded forms the most severe 'compounded degradation' possible was the doubling of the principle of 'inverse order of castes'.[22] A good example of compounded degradation in mixed unions resulting in exclusion from the Aryan community, was the union of a man, who was the product of a Shudra father and a Brahman mother, with a Brahman woman $[(S + b) + b]$ – a case of double or repeated 'confusion' of *varnas*, or of 'inversions' of *varna* or caste order. Similarly of all the permutations of pollution possible in Orenstein's classification, there is only one mixing in which the theorists would predictably be interested, because it represents a repeated compounding of the 'inverse order of castes' (i.e. the higher the *varna*/caste status the greater the resulting defilement). This is the mixing of 'self pollution' with 'external pollution'. The other two forms, 'relational' and 'internal' pollution in Orenstein's classification, are based on the 'direct order of castes'.

The *shastras* conceived of self pollution as rendering a person vulnerable; women particularly were very vulnerable in this state; and 'external pollution' defiled a person much more in this state than in ordinary circumstances because excretions and adhesions associated with bodily processes were dangerous marginal stuff that acted as powerful conductors of impurity, multiplying or compounding the intensity of pollution.

Towards a view of Purity and Pollution

The previous discussion of the rules underlying the *shastric* theory of the generation of castes showed how far the underlying design was from a *taxonomy* which implies progressive *segmentation* into less inclusive classes that are kept separate and discrete and considered non-permutable. It was also indicated that there is a correspondence between the structure of hierarchical taxonomy and that of Douglas's approach to pollution and purity: the corollary of the keeping of categories mutually separate is the generation of marginal stuff, intermediate substances, anomalies of taboo objects, and so on.

While we must recognise the importance of this perspective and take into account the manifestation of inclusion and exclusion in caste behaviour, we must also take into account the implications of another perspective if we are to understand caste behaviour more fully. The caste system also emphasises the *rules for and consequences of the interrelation of castes*. In other words the Indian caste mentality is very much concerned with the implications of approved and disapproved contact or relation between differently valued and hierarchically ordered categories. Like all law codes, we may say that the classical Dharmashastra texts generate a grammar of 'ungrammatical' (i.e. immoral/unlawful/disapproved) conduct. They are concerned more with what ought not to be done rather than with what should be done.

It is only in this perspective that one can appreciate not only the basic rules relating to contacts that are in accordance with the direct order and the inverse order of castes, but also the fact that many of the situations against which the law codes legislate are *unrealistic*. It is as improbable for a Brahman to eat a Shudra's leavings as for a factory owner in this country to eat with his waste collector. Much of Manu's code shows the mind of a lawyer writing up rules for exigencies and emergencies rather than for everyday life. On reading these rules one might imagine that an Indian village would consist of highly exclusive groups having much less social contacts than peasant communities which are not weighed down by rules of purity and pollution. This is objectively false. Despite Srinivas's characterisation of Indian village social relations as 'back to back' rather than 'face to face', the quantitative aspects of social interaction in an Indian village are probably no different from that in other stratified societies. The interrelation between castes is best seen in the *jajmani* relationships, in ritual exchange, in graded participation of castes in temple festivals, and in the rites of passage staged by superior caste patrons. The rules of commensality and connubium can thus be seen as focussing on contact rather than segregation.

How does the picture look when we view *pollution* as disapproved contact between superior and inferior entities, or as the disapproved movement or overflow of a defiling entity onto a purer or uncontaminated entity; and when we define *purity* as signifying approved contact between entities, or as the approved withdrawal from pre-existing contact with the impure?

The difference in focus is best illustrated in relation to the notorious body substances – saliva, body hair, nail parings, urine, excreta, etc. – that inevitably make their appearance in any discussion of impurity. Rather than think of them always as marginal stuff or ambiguous substances and therefore anomalous and impure, I am inviting you to consider them somewhat differently as *boundary overflows* which threaten to flow from their sources to adjacent entities, or which conduct back to the host the condition of others, i.e. as substances that relate or join adjacent entities to produce either good or bad effects.

Boundary overflows which may connect two adjacent entities or categories can be both negatively and positively evaluated. Where negatively evaluated they constitute pollution, as exemplified by contact with body impurities, impure foods, etc. These are all overflows from beings or objects whose natural condition is one of more or less pollution, but pollution nevertheless.

But the overflows from a pure object can be eminently purifying, as in the case of the five sacred products of the cow; or less dramatically the leavings of food offered to and eaten by the pure gods; or more dramatically, the water with which a saintly guru's feet have been washed. Within the sphere of everyday caste life, the same principle is at work when the food leavings of the Brahmans are acceptable food to polluted castes, or when various categories of cooked food may pass from superior patrons to inferior clients.

The inevitable consequence of undesirable direct contact is that pure beings are polluted by the impure. There are however compensating remedial actions. Water is a primary vehicle of cleansing. Objects can be given relative values in terms of their resistance to the action of impurity. In this sense, gold is purer than silver, and silver than iron; silk is more pollution resistant than cotton; brass cooking vessels are less attacked by dirt than clay vessels. Such permanently graded objects and substances are the *wedges*, the *vehicles* and the *conductors* by which polluting contact is neutralised and purity restored. But religious acts and the acquiring of sacred knowledge are also eminently cleansing and the texts fuse 'spiritual' action with 'instrumental' action with the aid of objects. Thus Vishnu says (XXII, 88): 'Sacred knowledge, religious austerities, fire, holy food (*Pankagavya*), earth, the mind, water, smearing (with cow dung), air, the morning and evening prayers and other religious acts, the sun, and time (by the lapse of ten days of impurity and the like) are purifiers of animate objects.'

These are but the preliminary steps towards a *transactional* theory of purity and pollution, which is more in accord with McKim Marriott's analysis of the logic of food transactions between castes rather than with Mary Douglas's speculations on the same subject.[23] Mary Douglas's argument runs as follows: 'In India the cooking process is seen as the beginning of ingestion, and therefore cooking is susceptible to pollution, in the same way as eating. But why is this complex found in India and in parts of Polynesia and in Judaism and other places, but not wherever humans sit down to eat. I suggest that food is not likely to be polluting at all unless the external boundaries of the social system are under pressure' (1966: 127). She proceeds to argue: 'We can go further to explain why the actual cooking of the food in India must be ritually pure. The purity of the castes is correlated with an elaborate hereditary division of labour between castes. The work performed by each caste carries a symbolic load: it says something about the relatively pure status of the caste in question... But the point at which food is prepared for the table is the point at which the interrelation between the purity and the occupational structure needs to be set straight. For food is produced by the combined efforts of several castes... Before being admitted to the body some clear symbolic break is needed to express food's separation from necessary but impure contacts. The cooking process, entrusted to pure hands, provides this ritual break. Some such break we would expect to find whenever the production of food is in the hands of the relatively impure' (pp. 126–7).

At best this is only half the story about 'Indian pollution symbolism regarding cooked food'. For an important index of caste status arises from the *passage of food between castes*, and it is through food transactions that relative positions are demonstrated and validated. It is this *dynamic* aspect of relationship between castes through food exchange that is missing in Douglas and present in Marriott.

Marriott argues that the attributional index (the possession of qualities and the practice of customs) is not a consistent guide to the logic of ranking of castes practised by the villagers of Kishan Garhi. He finds this key in the matrix of food transactions (i.e. a transactional index). Ultimately Marriott's argument rests on social dominance and dependence deriving from the direction of giving and taking. 'Gaining dominance over others through feeding them or securing dependence on others through being fed by them appear to be comprehensive goals of actors in the system of transactions' (p. 169). Marriott's model 'is based on an implicit local postulate of the symbolic equivalence of transactions in any medium between any two castes, *high rank always deriving from the giving, low rank from the receiving of foods*' (p. 170).

While Marriott's displaying of the mechanics of mutual ranking through food transactions are revelatory, we should note that in caste relations it is not in all spheres that the giver is superior to the receiver. While this is largely so with food and other material transactions, the logic is *reversed* in marriage and sexual unions. *Anuloma* unions, hypergamy and the like rest on the principle that a woman is freely given as a gift to a superior man, and the latter honours the giver by receiving. Nevertheless although the directions of the passage of women and of food are reversed, yet they both express the same principle of dominance based on the interrelation between castes. It is now time to explore other aspects of this dominance and differential privilege according to the principle of the 'direct order of castes' as it expressed in marriage, mating patterns and sexual transactions.

4. The Direct Order of Castes, Hypergamy, and Dominance in modern India

By dominance deriving from the principle of direct order of castes I mean the privileges and immunities – material, political, occupational, sexual, and legal – that accrue to the superior varnas or castes in relation to the inferior.[24] We are here mainly concerned with the sexual/marital privileges and their consequences – which we saw right at the beginning of this essay as deriving from the notion of primary and secondary unions and the principle that the higher the *varna* status of a male the greater his access to the women of inferior *varna*. Today this differentiated privilege is reflected in India in the institution of *hypergamy* which although usually defined as women of lower status marrying men of superior status can just as well be viewed as a privilege allowing men of superior status a *greater access* to a wider range of women of his own and inferior statuses than it allows men of inferior status.[25]

While it is obvious that the classical theory of mixed unions which, as we have said before, is a rationalising theory of caste generation and fission rather than a true historical account, yet in the matter of marriage and other forms of sexual union some of the major classical premises, suitably modified, can be seen to be still operative in India.

While the preponderant rule in India is endogamous marriage between persons of the same caste or sub-caste status, yet also *hypergamous* unions of the classical *anuloma* type are widely institutionalised in different parts of India. These unions are an expression of dominance in that upper-status males have legitimate access not only to women of their own status but also to women of immediately inferior statuses; and this accessibility sometimes coinciding with lord-vassal, landlord-tenant and other hierarchical politico-economic relationships is a superb instrument within limits of political incorporation.

Hypergamy in India manifests two forms which for the sake of convenience (but not very accurately) we may call the Northern and Southern forms. While I am aware that the suffix-'gamy' implies marriage I am using the words 'hypergamous unions' and 'hypergamous concubinage' to describe certain mating patterns traditionally practised in Malabar.

The hypergamy practised by the Rajput clans of Northwest India (Blunt 1931, Tod 1832, Parry n.d.), the Patidari of Gujarat (Morris 1968, Pocock 1972), the Rarhi Brahmins of Bengal (Hutton 1951, Dumont 1970) is largely between ranked groups (clans/lineages/circles) within caste (with some crossing of caste boundaries at the lower edges in the case of the first two). In these instances in so far as the father can lift up his child to his own group's status despite the slight inferiority of the mother, the unions follow the logic of 'sons of the twice born, begotten on wives of the next lower castes' as propounded by Baudhayana (see above p. 200).

In contrast in the South Indian Malabar instances where the hypergamous union is between castes (and between sub-castes within castes) and the children are relegated to the status of the mother as the inferior partner (while merely enjoying the 'honour' of being sired by superior fathers), the logic of placement follows the interpretation as propounded by Manu (see above p. 200).

I do not wish to embark on the intricacies and implications of Indian hypergamy; the authors I have cited are better guides.[26] However a few words are in order.

Obviously the two strategies of hypergamy are connected with different institutional features. In North India where the accent is on status competition and improvement, marriage as alliance must be kept open, and these aspirations approximate *in spirit* the mechanics of social mobility stated in Manu: 'if a female of the caste, sprung from a Brahmana and a Kshatriya, Vaisya or Shudra female, repeatedly bears children to one of the highest caste, the inferior person or group attains the highest caste within certain specified generation' (see discussion above, p. 202).

In South India, the contours of the social structure are kept intact by senior sons engaging in alliance marriage with equals, while non-succeeding sons may unite more flexibly with women in a downward direction. This is consistent with ranked lineages, the core lineage at the top continuing intact through a closure best represented by prescriptive cross-cousin marriage (Dumont 1957; Gough 1961).

In the case of the intercaste *anuloma* unions in Malabar, it is clear that the relegation of children to the mother's status fits in beautifully with a situation where the patrilineal Nambudiri indulge in socially accepted concubinage while the matrilineal castes find the same unions appropriate for the placement of the progeny in the mother's matrilineage and caste or sub-caste (Gough 1961: 320; Dumont 1961).

Rather than discuss familiar and well-documented cases, I have represented in Figs. 3 and 4 the hypergamous marriages of the Rarhi Brahmans of Bengal and the hypergamous marriage and concubinage patterns among the Malabar castes in such a way as to show how men of superior status have access to a wider range of females than men of lower status, this being a statement of dominance and privilege. In Appendix 2, I quote excerpts from Morris (1968) on the ideal Patidari hypergamy scheme.

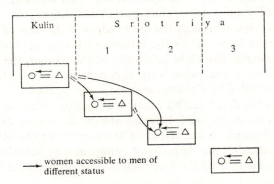

women accessible to men of different status

Fig. 3. Hypergamy among the Rarhi Brahmans in Bengal. Adapted from Dumont 1970: 120).

The spirit of *anuloma* has also been preserved in parts of India in historical times in the institutions of primary and secondary marriages, whereby the primary marriage of the male bearer of status is with an orthodox and excellent equal, and his secondary marriages are with females of lower status within the same caste, these unions in turn generating offspring of unequal status allocated according to the statuses of their mothers. This is consistent with the existence of ranked lineages, and the core lineage at the top ensuring its interests through a closure best represented by 'prescriptive' cross-cousin marriage (Dumont 1957). Another variant of this is where the children of *anuloma* unions are assigned to a third caste different from that of the parents (Karve 1961, Harper 1968).

There is no need to labour the point that Indian society guards zealously against the degradation of *pratiloma* unions whereby a woman mates with a male of inferior status (hypogamy). Practice by and large matches the

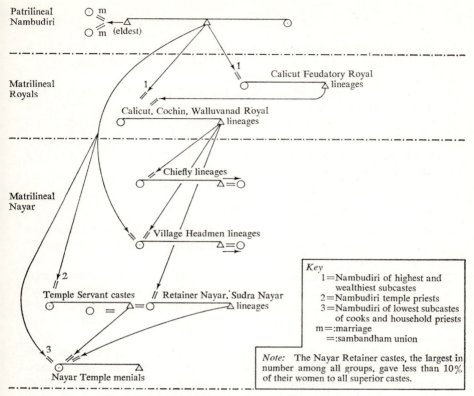

Fig. 4. Hypergamy and concubinage among the upper castes of Calicut,
Cochin and Walluvanad (based on Gough 1961: 319–22).

rule; and wherever unsanctioned hypogamous unions take place the progeny present problems of placement because they are truly 'anomalous'. They may be assigned to the father's inferior caste, or they may be considered to have no caste at all depending on the fate of the mother.

In Hindu society therefore hypergamous unions of the sanctioned and institutionalised kinds present no problems regarding the placement of children of 'mixed unions'; the soft spots in the system relate to the placement of children born of unsanctioned hypogamous mixed unions (or of unions which, though *anuloma* in direction, are still unacceptable, e.g. unions of partners of highly disparate status such as the union of a twice born male and a woman of polluting caste).

The satisfactions derived by the parties to hypergamous unions of the Nambudiri–Nayar type are crystal clear. We may therefore conclude this section by stating why, given the Indian rules and preferences, hypergamy of the North Indian type rather than hypogamy gives a 'pay off'.

(a) *Sanctioned hypergamy*

(1) From the woman's point of view: if she takes a husband of higher status, then her children take the status of their father, and her natal lineage enjoys the prestige of having affines of superior status.

(2) From the man's point of view: if he takes a wife slightly lower in status, his children still retain his status (no 'decrease' in value); he is compensated for by a sizeable dowry which his wife brings (economic advantage); and his own marriage ensures the hypergamous marriage of his sister.

Thus hypergamy is mutually advantageous to a man and his status group as well as his spouse and her natal status group.

(b) *Unsanctioned hypogamy*

(1) If a woman marries a man of lower status, her children do not enjoy her status ('decrease' in value) but are at best assigned the status of her inferior husband.

(2) If a man marries a woman of superior status, his children cannot enjoy their mother's superior status, only his own. Furthermore, he cannot expect to receive a dowry because he has no advantage of status to give in exchange. Thus hypogamous unions are disadvantageous to both men and women.

An essential feature of the caste system is that men cannot *increase* the status of their children through their own marriage, but they can increase their material assets through marriage. At the same time men cannot allow the *decrease* of the status of their children by marrying women lower than the prescribed, preferred or permitted status range. But there are indirect ways by which a man can raise the status of his group and its descendants. By strict control and manipulation of the marriages of his sisters and daughters, by successfully denying them to males of equal (and of course inferior status) and marrying them to superior males, a man can in turn aspire to marry his sons to women previously inaccessible to his own group.

Typically, hypergamy as found in certain parts of North India lends prestige to the wife givers not through the conversion of affinal bonds over time into bonds of consanguinity, but through keeping up the bonds of affinity (without repeated marriage) for three generations through prestations. After three generations the affinal obligations are dissolved, and the strategic possibilities exist for renewing marriage with the same group or for achieving marriage with a group whose females were previously inaccessible. Structurally, repetitive marriage alliance *coupled with dowry* is inimical to the spirit and aspirations of North Indian hypergamy, for it would fix and make enduring the relative statuses of wife takers and givers thus denying the possibility of social mobility. However, enduring and repeated hypergamous transactions coupled with bridewealth are possible among social groups or statuses whose positions are relatively *fixed* and unchangeable, e.g. a King taking women from Chiefs, they in turn from petty chiefs and so down the line, where political patronage is coupled with political allegiance.

In the long run hypergamy of the North Indian kind is unstable for various reasons. A primary problem is the escalation of dowry, so that the groups participating may attempt to reverse the trend and introduce egalitarian trends by forming endogamous marriage circles or legislating about dowry (Pocock 1972; Morris 1968; Parry n.d.). Furthermore there is always the problem of excess of women at the top for there are no males of higher status available to marry them; this results in female infanticide, multiple marriage like 'Kulinism' and the like, which are not enduring solutions. But despite the strong counterpressure of levelling tendencies, hypergamy fits into the general Indian aspiration for maintaining and increasing status and honour through the institution of marriage.

Marriage is thus at the heart of Hindu society. It is usually considered the most important event in a man's life; it is in the forefront of Hindu 'consciousness'; and it is a focal point of the social system. Marriage is directly integrated with caste which is the basis of a Hindu's primary status position in his society. A man's caste is first of all decided by the status of his parents, and subsequently maintained or modified by his own marriage and sexual encounters.

Final Comments: The marriage of Purity and Power

This essay is composed of several interrelated themes. It began by analysing in detail a classical Indian theory about the generation of new categories in the form of castes (*jati*) and occupational groups through the combination of the four *varnas* in socially approved and disapproved modes of mating. We were able to appreciate the intellectual scheme in which the base *varna* categories and the ordered rules of combination generated castes which were automatically ranked and evaluated.

Although this theory is fictional and non-historical, it serves to illuminate certain theoretical and substantive issues. It interests us as a classification system which, starting with a basic scheme of hierarchically arranged *varna* categories, then employs the *key* method to generate new categories by the overlapping or mixing of classes, a method of classification that is the opposite of the taxonomic hierarchy of discrete classes, which is implicitly the basis for the theories of taboo and pollution developed by Mary Douglas and Edmund Leach. We are able to supplement their contribution by demonstrating that purity and pollution in the Indian caste system can be fruitfully viewed as being grounded in the *interrelation between castes* according to two principles of participation and interaction, namely the 'direct order' and the 'inverse order' of castes. These principles are manifest in diverse spheres of caste life.

Although non-historical, the classical theory enshrines timeless truths about certain basic features of the Indian caste system. The differential privilege and dominance coded in the traditional theory in terms of the direct order of castes as regards sexual access to women of different varna status (*anuloma*) finds its modified and transformed expression today in hypergamy and concubinage in different parts of India.

But, perhaps more unexpectedly, we discovered that the rules of purity and pollution simultaneously reflected two overarching principles. The 'direct order' of reckoning ensured the *dominance* of the higher *varna* and castes over the lower by declaring them naturally more endowed with the right to use the sanction of force and to be more immune from legal and ritual disabilities. In contrast the 'inverse order' of reckoning laid the burden of more stringent purification and vigilance on the superior in relation to the inferior when in a state of self-pollution and in case of improper contact with the lower castes. What we thus learn is that the very hierarchical ordering of *varna* and caste as a social system based on inequality requires us not to separate purity and pollution from the exercise of power and dominance, for both these are intertwined in the same single theory of society which the Brahman legal ideologists propounded for their glorification. It would be totally unrealistic to think that the *shastric* writers constructed a morality and a social theory of society based solely on the principle that pollution continually attacked purity, without securing for themselves and their fellows those primary privileges which first established the dominance of the pure over the impure.

Notes

1 We should note that these analytically separate procedures can be and sometimes are combined to produce classifications. The key technique can produce a hierarchical arrangement, and hierarchical schemes such as the Linnaean in turn do exploit the key form as a result of applying multiple differentia at different levels to generate new classes.

2 Conklin goes on to say about the key: 'The selection and arrangement of dichotomous exclusions may result in a branching structure resembling a taxonomy, but the geometrical similarity is illusory' (p. 40).

The other methods of classification Conklin identifies are *index* (which in its simplest form is a sequence of entities arranged in accordance with one arbitrary dimension such as an alphabetical order (e.g. dictionary, telephone directory), *paradigm* and *typology* (both of which are multidimensional forms of arrangement by class intersection and cannot be transformed into taxonomy as is largely the case with key, but show internal differences in the manner in which they partition 'attribute space'. Over all Conklin agrees with Simpson in admitting that the basic contrast is between type as *taxon* or kind and type as *attribute combination*.

3 Consider these examples: 'Dirt is the by-product of a systematic ordering and classification of matter, in so far as ordering involves rejecting inappropriate elements' (p. 35); 'an anomaly is an element which does not fit a given set of series' (p. 37); 'any given system of classification must give rise to anomalies' (p. 39). And at one point in her exposition she exclaims: 'Surely now it would be difficult to maintain that "Be ye Holy" means no more than "Be ye separate".' When Mary Douglas does deal with the 'union of opposites which is a source of power for good' (p. 119) she has in mind *exceptional* phenomena such as the pangolin acting as a mediator for the Lele (p. 170) and the like.

4 Mary Douglas manages to make a good deal of sense of the food taboos by showing that there is an underlying three-fold division of creatures into those that belong to the Earth, Water and Firmament. The 'normal' members of the Earth category are four legged animals which hop, jump or walk; of the Water are those with fins and scales. Thus creatures which mix the attributes of the major classes are taboo e.g. four-footed creatures which fly; also taboo are creatures which are imperfect members of their class such as animals with two 'legs' and 'hands' which crawl; animals which creep, crawl or swarm or adopt a mode of propulsion not proper to any particular element (e.g. eels, worms, reptiles, etc.).

What, however, Mary Douglas entirely misses out is that the Leviticus rules derive the edible animals of the earth – the most important class by a key-type derivation! There are two initial classes posited: animals that chew the cud and animals that have cloven hooves. The edible animals are those who have both features (such as ox, sheep, goat, etc.); the inedible animals are animals that chew the cud but do not have cloven hooves (camel, hare, etc.) and animals that have cloven hooves but do not chew the cud (swine).

5 Leach's theory of taboo is based on two propositions. Firstly, the environment (which is a continuum) is perceived 'as composed of separate things by suppressing our recognition of the nonthings which fill the interstices (p. 37); secondly, these interstitial things are 'the ambiguous categories that attract the maximum interest and the most intense feelings of taboo. The general theory is that taboo applies to categories which are anomalous with respect to clearcut category oppositions' (p. 39).

6 As Fig. 1 shows, the Indian classification of *varna* and castes as embodied in Manu (and other writers) shows a combination of procedures of both *hierarchy* and *key* forms.

7 Dumont does not, however, ignore the theory of 'mixed castes' in the classical texts. He says that the texts 'described in terms of varna what must surely have been at that time a caste system in embryo' (1970: 71). Pointing out that 'the word *jati* does occur, but it is generally confused with varna...and, according to Kane, the emphasis is on birth rather than function' Dumont sees an additional inadequacy in the classical account in that no fifth varna is allowed for. Nevertheless Dumont makes a comment which we are able to take up in detail here: 'The normative Hindu texts mostly present the groups [despised castes and inferior occupations] they name as if they were products of crossing between varnas...It is generally admitted that this theory was used to refer real *jati* to the varnas...' (p. 71).

8 Kane (vol. 2 pt. 2 ch. 2) has a full and authoritative account of the differences in interpretations, contradictions and inconsistencies. Also Buhler's introduction to *The Laws of Manu* (1886).

9 As I have previously mentioned, in this scheme the groups generated are recognisable as primarily castes (*jati*) and occupational groups and less frequently as tribes and ethnic groups. The juxtaposition of castes and occupations is understandable since the distinctive feature of many low level castes are their occupations.

10 Note that what is under discussion here is union between a superior male and an inferior female.

11 Referring to the lack of unanimity among the sages as to the progeny of such unions, Kane says that three different views were expressed by them: 'The first view is that if a male of one varna married a female of the varna immediately after it, the progeny belonged to the varna of the father' (e.g. Baudhayana I.8.6 and I.9.3; also Narada, Kautiliya and Anusasanaparva). 'The second view is that the progeny of *anuloma* unions is in status lower than the father, but higher than the mother' (e.g. Manu X, 6). The third view (and this is the common view) is that the progeny. . .is of the same varna as regards its privileges and obligations as the mother's' (e.g. Visnu, Mitaksara commentary on Yajnavalkya and Aparaka). Kane misinterprets Manu for he fails to consider Manu X, 14.

12 The greatest dishonour is naturally attached to the union of a Brahman with a Shudra female. Vasishtha for example describes the condition of the son thus born – the Parasava – as 'that of one who living, is as impure as a corpse'. (XVIII, 9, 10).

13 According to Vasishtha the son by a Brahman wife shall receive three shares, by a Kshatriya wife, 2 shares and the 'other sons shall inherit equal shares' i.e. presumably one each.

14 Similar principles of caste mobility are propounded by other shastric writers such as Gautama, Yajnavalkya. The differences in interpretation relate to the number of generations to be counted before increment or loss of status is achieved. See Kane 1941: 62 ff.

15 The process of downward mobility is the inverse of that represented in Fig. 2A, e.g. a Brahman uniting with a Shudra female produces a Parasava son, and if he and his male descendants unite repeatedly with Shudra females, the male descendant of the seventh generation (counting from the first Brahman ancestor) is adjudged as being a fallen Shudra.

16 The names of the issue from these unions differ in some cases in Vasishtha whose list in corresponding order are Suta, Ramaka, Pulkasa, Antyavasyin, Vaina and Kandala.

17 See the same page for other calculations.

18 The Antyavasayin is the perfect example of the fusion of two symmetrically reversed, despised unions between Brahman and Sudra. No wonder the Antyavasayins are described as being despised even by those already excluded from the Aryan community.

19 The most frequent appearance is by the Shudra *varna* since it is the most available especially for *anuloma* type unions.

20 Berreman (1963) for instance notes how in the sub-Himalayan Pahari villages he studied, low castes claimed respectable ancestors and explained the decline of their caste status in terms of unfortunate circumstances. He writes: 'Atkinson notes that in Kumaon "the Doms like all the others, claim an exalted origin and say that they are the descendants of a Brahman named Gorakhnath and were turned out of caste for eating forbidden food". . .The blacksmiths and Bajgis of Sirkanda lay claim to relatively recent but unrecognised Rajput and Brahmin ancestry, respectively' (p. 222). Similarly, he cites Cohn as reporting that the Chamars of Senapur trace their ancestry to Rajputs or Brahmins.

21 Orenstein in his 1968 essay classifies pollution rules into (1) *Relational Pollution* (previously in 1965 called Intransitive Pollution) and (2) *Act Pollution* (previously labelled Transitive Pollution) which again he subdivides into *Internal Pollution* and *External Pollution*. In the 1973 essay he deals with *Self Pollution* as a sub-category of External Pollution.

I find these labels misleading because in my framework all these forms of pollution are 'relational', i.e. imply contact between persons and things. Orenstein fails to understand fully the underlying design of the rules because he does not place them against the framework of *varna* and caste hierarchy and interrelations as the classical writers saw them, e.g. the direct and inverse order of castes and the principles of dominance and compounded degradation they imply.

Furthermore, Orenstein has missed seeing the linkage between the base categories of *varna* and the derived '*jati*' categories as part of the thought structure of the law codes, as is attested by these words: 'The Dharmashastras speak both of caste and of *varna*, more frequently of the latter. The rules, however, are applied in the same way to both. As our concern is with ways of thinking, not the definition of social groups, we may ignore the difference.'

Orenstein clearly sees the important fact that the *shastric* writers, although they vary in details and although their treatment of subjects is not identical, yet legislated in accordance with a shared set of principles. But he fails to use the discrepancies to advantage: that these contradictions, differences in interpretation and emphases may be indicators of ambiguities inevitably generated by systems of classification.

22 This answers a fact that puzzles Orenstein: why are the theorists less interested in 'clean' women (i.e. not in a condition of self pollution) having contacts with lower castes but are only concerned with women already self-polluted?

23 Marriott has aptly stated in a recent unpublished essay: 'What unifies Indian transactional thought is assumption as to (1) the divisible or particulate nature of substance and (2) the constant circulation of divisible substance and (3) the inevitable, transformation of substance by mixtures and separations.'

24 In Appendix 1 I document the privileges in the realm of occupations granted by Manu to the *varna* according to the principle of the direct order of *varna*.

25 *Hypergamy* is not a Hindu but an anthropological concept. The *dharmashastras* speak only of *anuloma* and *pratiloma*, of 'direct' and 'inverse' order of castes etc, whose implications are as I have described them.

26 See for instance Morris's brief but perceptive discussion on the dilemmas of hypergamy (1968: 97).

APPENDIX 1. *Occupations Accessible to the Varna Under Conditions of Stress*

In the second half of Chapter X of Manu we are given the rules regarding the occupations of the Varnas during normal times (which I have already cited on p. 196) followed by those that are permissible in times of stress. The following are rules that conform to the logic of the 'direct order of castes':

(1)   The *Brahman* 'unable to subsist by his peculiar occupation. . .may live according to the law applicable to Kshatriyas *for the latter is next to him in rank* (my italics). But if the Brahman cannot maintain himself by the above, he may adopt a Vaisya's mode of life – but only the *purer aspects*. He must not practise agriculture which causes injury to many beings; and he must avoid certain types of trade such as selling condiments, cooked food, salt, cattle, human beings, dyed cloth, weapons, meat, etc. (see Manu X, 83–94).

(2)   The Kshatriya, in turn, who has fallen into distress, may adopt a Vaisya's mode of life – while he may not like the Brahman practise agriculture which is sinful, he may however practise those Vaisya trades and the sale of commodities (referred to above) which are forbidden to the Brahman.

(3)   A Vaisya may under similar conditions maintain himself by a Shudra's mode of life, avoiding however 'acts forbidden to him'.

(4)   A Shudra in turn may, faced with hunger, practise handicrafts.

The opposite process which would constitute an upward status mobility is firmly denounced for it attacks the privileges of 'the direct order of castes'. Thus neither the Kshatriya, Vaisya nor Shudra may arrogantly adopt the mode of life prescribed for his betters.

A man of low caste who through covetousness lives by the occupations of a higher one, the king shall deprive of his property and banish.

It is better to discharge one's own appointed duty incompletely than to perform completely that of another; for he who lives according to the law of another caste is instantly excluded from his own (Manu X, 196, 97).

The same jural notions are applied to property rights. A Brahman may forcibly take from a Vaisya's possession an article required for the completion of the sacrifice, and may take for the same reason two or three articles from a Shudra, 'for a Shudra has no business with sacrifice'. The reverse is heinous: stealing the property of a virtuous Brahman is like the stealing of the property of the Gods and invites heavy penance and punishment; and that sinful man 'feeds in another world on the leavings of the vultures' (Manu XI, 26). In fact 'stealing the gold of a Brahman' belongs to the class of mortal sins (*mahapataka*) (Manu XI, 55).

APPENDIX 2. *Patidar Hypergamy*

The overseas immigrants from Gujerat, Western India, to Uganda who belonged to such castes as the Patidar and Kanbi were found by Morris (1968) to have a lively idealised picture of a hypergamous scheme in their homeland to which they related their marriages.

According to Patidars in East Africa the original marriage circle apparently included families in fourteen villages. It subsequently divided into two circles of six and five villages with a few families in the remaining three villages linked to both circles. The villages in these two circles were said to contain all the 'men of family', but two other lower ranking circles of twenty-seven and twenty-one smaller villages also existed (p. 98).

In 1955 in Africa, marriages between boys and girls born and educated in Uganda were being contracted in terms of both marriage circles and prestige of lineages. Women of a circle of five villages in Gujerat still took high dowries with them when they married men in another circle of six, and their brothers were still forced to rely on finding wives among the girls in their own circle who did not marry up, or in villages outside the circle. Although in theory everybody thought the equality implicit in a mariage circle agreement most desirable, nobody was willing to forgo dowry or to consider that his family or lineage was equal to any other.

The following diagram was drawn with the assistance of an informant in Uganda to clarify the negotiations which were taking place for the marriage of his daughter.

High prestige

Circle of six villages

A. Women of all six villages nominally married into all six villages; in practice
B. women of village A tended not to marry men of village F or any below it.
C.
D.
E.
F.

Villages linked with both circles

G. Each village contained very few *kulia* (high ranking) families, all of whom
H. gave brides to the circle of six and took them from the circle of five. The
I. *Kulia* families of villages G. H and I did not usually marry their daughters into the circle of five.

Circle of five villages

J. Women of all five villages nominally married into all five villages; in practice
K. women in village N married men of village J but not vice versa except into
L. one or two 'better' households. Women of all five villages married men from
M. A to I, but the men did not not get wives in exchange.
N.

Low prestige

Villages outside the circles

Women from outside might marry into the circle of five but their brothers did not get wives in return.

The above diagram is, of course, a statement of ideal behaviour but an indication of how far it guided real behaviour can be obtained by examining marriages on genealogies and those celebrated in East Africa.

In the pedigree of a man belonging to village K in the circle of five were nine women born into his lineage whose marriages could be traced in detail. Five married up into the circle of six, four married within their own circle of five, and none married down. Of the fifteen men recorded, only one married a woman from the circle of six, eight married in the circle of five and four brought in women from lower ranking villages outside the circle. In this lineage at least, most marriages conformed to what the Patidars said was correct behaviour.

In Kampala nineteen marriages of Patidars from the Charotar district were recorded. Eight were within the two highest circles (six and five) and all were hypergamous, though one man of the lowest ranking village (N) of the circle of five had had to find a bride outside in a circle of twenty-seven villages. Of the two men in the circle of twenty-seven one married a bride from outside. No woman married down because, in the opinion of the Brahmin priest who supplied the information, all families in Africa had sufficient means to make a hypergamous marriage for their sons in India, if not in Africa. But in all nineteen recorded marriages both bride and groom in fact lived in Africa (pp. 195–6).

Bibliography of the Writings of Meyer Fortes

J. A. Barnes

1930 A new application of the theory of neogenesis to the problem of mental testing. (Perceptual tests of 'g'.) University of London, Ph.D. thesis. Typescript, 231 pp.

1932a Perceptual tests of 'general intelligence' for inter-racial use. *Transactions of the Royal Society of South Africa* **20**: 281–99.

1932b Translator. PETERMANN, Bruno. *The gestalt theory and the problem of configuration*. London: Kegan Paul, Trench, Trubner. xi, 344 pp.

1933a Notes on juvenile delinquency. *Sociological review* **23**: 14–24, 153–8.

1933b The influence of position in sibship on juvenile delinquency. *Economica* **13**: 301–28.

1936a Culture contact as a dynamic process: an investigation in the Northern Territories of the Gold Coast. *Africa* **9**: 24–55.

1936b Kinship, incest and exogamy of the Northern Territories of the Gold Coast. *In* BUXTON, Leonard Halford Dudley, ed. *Custom is king: essays presented to R. R. Marett on his seventieth birthday June 13, 1936*. London: Hutchinson's scientific and technical publications. Pp. 237–56.

1936c Ritual festivals and social cohesion in the hinterland of the Gold Coast. *American anthropologist* **38**: 590–604.

1937a Communal fishing and fishing magic in the Northern Territories of the Gold Coast. *Journal of the royal anthropological institute* **67**: 131–42.

1937b Marriage law among the Tallensi. Accra: Government printing department. 23 pp.

1938 Social and psychological aspects of education in Taleland. *Africa* **11** (4) Supplement. 64 pp. *International institute of African languages and cultures, memorandum 7*.

1939 The scope of social anthropology. *Oversea education* **10**: 125–30.

1940 The political system of the Tallensi of the Northern Territories of the Gold Coast. *In* FORTES, M., and EVANS-PRITCHARD, E. E., eds., *African political systems*. London: Oxford University Press. Pp. 238–71.

1941a Charles Gabriel Seligman, 1873–1940 *Man* **41**: 1–6.

1941b John Ranulf de la Haulle Marett, 1900–1940. *Man*. **41**: 20–1.

1943 A note on fertility among the Tallensi of the Gold Coast. *Sociological review* **35**: 99–113.

1944 The significance of descent in Tale social structure. *Africa* **14**: 362–85.

1945a *The dynamics of clanship among the Tallensi: being the first part of an analysis of the social structure of a Trans-Volta tribe*. London: Oxford University Press. xx, 270 pp.

1945b An anthropologist's point of view. *In* BRAILSFORD, Henry Noel, and others. *Fabian colonial essays*. London: Allen and Unwin. Pp. 215–34.

1948a Introduction. *In* FORTES, M., and others. *Ashanti survey, 1945–46: an experiment in social research*. Pp. 149–51.

1948b The anthropological aspect. *In* FORTES, M., and others. *Ashanti survey 1945–46*. Pp. 160–71.

1948c The Ashanti social survey: a preliminary report. *Rhodes-Livingstone journal* **6**: 1–30.

1949a The web of kinship among the Tallensi: the second part of an analysis of the social structure of a Trans-Volta tribe. London: Oxford University Press. xiv, 358 pp.

1949b Preface. In FORTES, M., ed. *Social structure*. Pp. v–xiv.

1949c Time and social structure: an Ashanti case study. In FORTES, M., ed. *Social structure*. Pp. 54–84.

1949d Sex and the family in primitive society. In NEVILLE-ROLFE, Sybil, ed. *Sex in social life*. London: Allen and Unwin. Pp. 158–73.

1949e Editor. *Social structure: studies presented to A. R. Radcliffe-Brown*. Oxford: Clarendon Press, xiv, 233 pp.

1950 Kinship and marriage among the Ashanti. In RADCLIFFE-BROWN, Alfred Reginald, and FORDE, Cyril Daryll, eds. *African systems of kinship and marriage*. London: Oxford University Press. Pp. 252–84.

1951a Social anthropology. In HEATH, Archibald Edward, ed. *Social thought in the twentieth century*. London: Watts. Pp. 329–56.

1951b Parenthood in primitive society. *Man* 51: 65.

1952 Social effects of agricultural development in Africa. *Colonial Review* 7: 164–165.

1953a The Structure of unilineal descent groups. *American anthropologist* 55: 17–41.

1953b Analysis and description in social anthropology. *Advancement of science* 10: 190–201.

1953c Social anthropology at Cambridge since 1900: an inaugural lecture. Cambridge: Cambridge University Press. 47 pp.

1953d Preface. In HENRIQUES, Fernando. *Family and colour in Jamaica*. London: Eyre and Spottiswoode. Pp. 3–8.

1933e Parenté et mariage chez les Ashanti. In RADCLIFFE-BROWN, Alfred Reginald, and FORDE, Daryll, eds. *Systèmes familiaux et matrimoniaux en Afrique*. Paris: Presses Universitaires de France. Pp. 331–72.

1954a A demographic field study in Ashanti. In LORIMER, Frank. *Culture and human fertility*. Paris: Unesco. Pp. 253–339.

1954b Mind. In EVANS-PRITCHARD, Edward Evan, and others. *The institutions of primitive society*. Oxford: Blackwell. Pp. 81–94.

1955a Radcliffe-Brown's contributions to the study of social organisation. *British journal of sociology* 6: 16–30.

1955b Names among the Tallensi of the Gold Coast. In LUKAS, Johannes, ed. *Afrikanistische Studien Diedrich Westermann zum 80. Geburtstag gewidmet*. Berlin: Akademie-Verlag. *Deutsche Akademie der Wissenschaften zu Berlin, Institut für Orientforschung, Veröffentlichung nr. 26*. Pp. 337–49.

1956a The study of society. *Listener* 55: 793–4.

1956b Foreword. In SMITH, Raymond Thomas. *The Negro family in British Guiana: family structure and social status in the villages*. London: Routledge and Kegan Paul. Pp. xi–xiv.

1956c Alfred Reginald Radcliffe-Brown, F.B.A., 1881–1955: a memoir. *Man* 56: 149–53.

1957a Malinowski and the study of kinship. In FIRTH, Raymond William, ed. *Man and culture: an evaluation of the work of Bronislaw Malinowski*. London: Routledge and Kegan Paul. Pp. 157–88.

1957b Siegfried Frederick Nadel 1903–1956: a memoir. In NADEL, Siegfried Frederick Stephen. *The theory of social structure*. London: Cohen and West. Pp. ix–xvi.

1957c A history of the millennium: an anthropological footnote. *Cambridge review* 79: 132.

J. A. Barnes

1958a Introduction. *In* GOODY, Jack Rankine, ed. *The developmental cycle in domestic groups.* Cambridge: Cambridge University Press. *Cambridge Papers in social anthropology* 1. Pp. 1–14.

1958b Thinking about society. *Cambridge review* **79**: 596–8.

1959a Descent, filiation and affinity: a rejoinder to Dr Leach. *Man* **59**: 193–7, 206–12.

1959b *Oedipus and Job in west African religion.* Cambridge: Cambridge University Press, 81 pp.

1959c Primitive kinship. *Scientific American* **200**(6): 146–57.

1959d Review: Lystad, Ashanti. *Africa* **29**: 211–12.

1960 Oedipus and Job in west African religion. *In* LESLIE, Charles, ed. *Anthropology of folk religion.* New York; Random House, Vintage Book. Pp. 5–49.

1961a Pietas in ancestor worship: the Henry Myers lecture 1960. *Journal of the royal anthropological institute* **91**: 166–91.

1961b Comment (*on* Eisenstadt, *Studies of complex societies*). *Current anthropology* **2**: 211–12.

1961c Discussion and criticism (letter to editor). *Current anthropology* **2**: 398.

1961d Radcliffe-Brown, Alfred Reginald. *Encyclopaedia Britannica* **18**: 874B–874C.

1962a Introduction. *In* FORTES, M., ed. *Marriage in tribal society*, Pp. 1–13.

1962b Ritual and office in tribal society. *In* GLUCKMAN, Max, ed. *Essays on the ritual of social relations.* Manchester: Manchester University Press. Pp. 53–88.

1962c Editor. *Marriage in tribal societies.* Cambridge: Cambridge University Press. vii, 157 pp *Cambridge papers in social anthropology* 3.

1962d Review: Rose, Kin, age structure and marriage. *British journal of sociology* **13**: 81–82.

1963a Graduate study and research. *In* MANDELBAUM, David Goodman, and others, eds. *The teaching of anthropology. American anthropological association memoir* 94. Pp. 421–38.

1963b The 'submerged descent line' in Ashanti. *In* SCHAPERA, Isaac, ed. *Studies in kinship and marriage.* London: Royal Anthropological Institute. *Occasional paper* 16. Pp. 58–67.

1963c Foreword. *In* HILL, Polly. *The migrant cocoa-farmers of southern Ghana: a study in rural capitalism.* Cambridge: Cambridge University Press. Pp. v–ix.

1964a (Contributor to) History, sociology and social anthropology. *Past and present* **27**: 102–8.

1964b Le système politique des Tallensi des territoires du nord de la Côte de l'Or. *In* FORTES, M., and EVANS-PRITCHARD, E. E., eds., *Systèmes politiques africains.* Paris: Presses Universitaires de France. Pp. 203–33.

1965a Some reflections on ancestor worship in Africa. *In* FORTES, M., *and others. African systems of thought.* Pp. 122–44.

1965b Ancestor worship. *In* FORTES, M., and others. *African systems of thought.* Pp. 16–20.

1965c (Contributor to discussion) *In* CIBA FOUNDATION. *Transcultural psychiatry: Ciba foundation symposium.* DE REUCK, Anthony Vivian Smith, and PORTER, Ruth, eds. London: Churchill. *Passim.*

1965d Brenda Zara Seligman, 1882–1965: a memoir. *Man* **65**: 177–81.

1965e Edipo e Giobbe in una religione dell'Africa occidentale. *In* LESLIE, Charles, ed. *Uomo e mito nelle società primitive: saggi di antropologia religiosa.* Firenze: Sansoni. Pp. 23–68.

1966a Ödipus und Hiob in westafrikanischen Religionen. FIGGE, Hans, trans. Frankfurt am Main: Suhrkamp. 94 pp.

1966b Religious premises and logical techniques in divinatory ritual. *Philosophical transactions of the Royal Society of London, ser. B* **251**: 409–22.

233

1967*a* Totem and taboo. *Proceedings of the royal anthropological institute* 1966: 5–22.

1967*b* Tallensi riddles. *In* To honor Roman Jakobson: essays on the occasion of his seventieth birthday 11 October 1966. The Hague: Mouton. Vol. 1. *Janua linguarum, series maior 31.* Pp. 678–87.

1967*c* Bewusstsein. *In* FIRTH, Raymond William, and others. *Institutionen in primitiven Gesellschaften,* BÄRMANN, Michael, trans. Frankfurt am Main: Suhrkamp. Pp. 93–106.

1967*d* Foreword. *In* ABRAHAMS, Raphael Garvin. *The political organization of Unyamwezi.* Cambridge: Cambridge University Press. *Cambridge studies in social anthropology* 1. Pp. ix–xii.

1968*a* On installation ceremonies. *Proceedings of the royal anthropological institute* 1967: 5–20.

1968*b* Seligman, C. G. *In* SILLS, David Lawrence, ed. *International encyclopaedia of the social sciences.* New York: Macmillan and Free Press. Vol. 14, pp. 159–62.

1969 *Kinship and the social order: the legacy of Lewis Henry Morgan.* Chicago: Aldine, xii, 347 pp.

1970*a* *Time and social structure and other essays.* London: Athlone Press xii, 287 pp. *London School of Economics monographs* on *social anthropology* 40.

1970*b* *The plural society in Africa.* The Alfred and Winifred Hoernle lecture, 1968. South African Inst. of Race Relations, Johannesburg.

1971 Some Aspects of Migration and Mobility in Ghana. *Journal of Asian and African studies* **6:** 1–20.

Works in Collaboration

FORTES, Meyer, and DIETERLEN, Germaine
  1965 Preface; I. The seminar: general review of the discussions; I. Indigenous religious systems; V. Islam in Africa; VI. Christianity in Africa. *In* FORTES, M., DIETERLEN, G., and others. *African systems of thought.* Pp. vii–viii; 1–6; 7–8; 28–30; 31–3.

FORTES, Meyer, DIETERLEN, Germaine, and others
  1965 *African systems of thought: studies presented and discussed at the third international African seminar in Salisbury, December 1960.* London: Oxford University Press, viii, 392 pp.

FORTES, Meyer, and EVANS-PRITCHARD, Edward Evan
  1940*a* Introduction. *In* FORTES, M., and EVANS-PRITCHARD, E. E., eds. *African political systems.* Pp. 1–23.

  1940*b* Editors. *African political systems.* London: Oxford University Press, xxiii, 302 pp.

  1964*a* Introduction. *In* FORTES, M., and EVANS-PRITCHARD, E. E., eds. *Systèmes politiques africaines.* Pp. 1–20.

  1964*b* Editors. *Systèmes politiques africaines.* Paris: Presses Universitaires de France. xxiv, 268 pp.

FORTES, Meyer, and FORTES, Sonia Leah
  1936 Food in the domestic economy of the Tallensi. *Africa* **9:** 237–76.

FORTES, Meyer, GOODY, John Rankine, and LEACH, Edmund Ronald
  1958 Preface. *In* GOODY, Jack, ed. *The developmental cycle in domestic groups.* Cambridge: Cambridge University Press. *Cambridge papers in social anthropology* I. P. vii.

  1960 Preface. *In* LEACH, E. R., ed. *Aspects of caste in south India, Ceylon and north-west Pakistan.* Cambridge: Cambridge University Press. *Cambridge papers in social anthropology* 2. P. viii.

1962   Preface. *In* FORTES, M., ed. *Marriage in tribal societies.* P. vii.
1966   Preface. *In* GOODY, Jack, ed. *Succession to high office.* Cambridge: Cambridge University Press. *Cambridge papers in social anthropology* 4. P. vii.
1968   Preface. *In* LEACH, E. R., ed. *Dialectic in practical religion.* Cambridge: Cambridge University Press. *Cambridge papers in social anthropology* 5. P. vii.

FORTES, Meyer, and KYEI, T. E.
1945   Unpublished field data of the Ashanti social survey.

FORTES, Meyer, and MAYER, Doris Yankauer
1966   Psychosis and social change among the Tallensi of northern Ghana. *Cahiers d'études africaines* **6:** 5–40.
1969   Psychosis and social change among the Tallensi of northern Ghana. *In* FOULKES, S. H., and PRINCE, G. S., eds. *Psychiatry in a changing society.* London: Tavistock. Pp. 33–73.

FORTES, Meyer, STEEL, R. W., and ADY, Peter
1948   Ashanti survey 1945–1946: an experiment in social research. *Geographical journal* **110:** 149–79.

References

Abrahams, I. 1924. *Studies in Pharisaism and the Gospels*. Second series. Cambridge.
Abrahams, R. G. 1972*a*. Reaching an agreement over bridewealth in Labwor, Northern Uganda: a case study. In Richards, A. I. and Kuper, A. (eds.) *Councils in Action*. Cambridge Papers in Social Anthropology No. 6. Cambridge.
  1972*b*. Spirit, twins and ashes in Labwor, Northern Uganda. In La Fontaine, J. (ed.) *The Interpretation of Ritual*. London.
Adam, A. 1968. *Casablanca: Essai sur la transformation de la société marocaine au contract de l'Occident*. Paris.
Aeschylus. *Eumenides*. In Hugh Lloyd-Jones (ed.) *Works*, 1926, vol. 2. London.
Ainsworth, M. D. 1967. *Infancy in Uganda*. Baltimore.
Ambrose, J. A. 1961. The development of the smiling response in early infancy. In Foss, B. M. (ed.) *Determinants of Infant Behaviour*. London.
Ammar, H. 1954. *Growing up in an Egyptian Village. Silwa, Province of Aswan*. London.
Anderson, J. W. 1972. Attachment behaviour out of doors. In Blurton-Jones, N. (ed.) *Ethological Studies of Child Behaviour*. Cambridge.
Aristotle. *Historia animalium*. D'Arcy Wentworth Thompson (trans.) *The works of Aristotle*, 1910, vol. 4. Oxford.
  Generation of animals, 1953. London.
Ashley-Montagu, M. F. 1937. *Coming into Being among the Australian Aborigines: A Study of the Procreative Beliefs of the Native Tribes of Australia*. London.
  1949. Embryological beliefs of primitive peoples. *Ciba Symposia* **10**: 994–1008.
Aswad, B. 1971. *Property Control and Social Strategies: Settlers on a Middle Eastern Plain*. University Museum, Michigan, Anthropological Paper No. 44.
Attenborough, F. L. 1922. *The Laws of the Earliest English Kings*. Cambridge.
Austin, C. R., and Walton, A. 1960. Fertilisation. In Marshall, F. H. A. (ed.) *Physiology of Reproduction* (3rd ed.) vol. 1. London.
Avineri, S. 1970. *The Social and Political Thought of Karl Marx*. Cambridge.
Ayoub, M. 1959. Parallel cousin marriage reconsidered. *Man* **5**.
Bailey, F. G. 1969. *Stratagems and Spoils*. Oxford.
Barnes, J. A. 1961. Physical and social kinship. *Philosophy of Science* **28**: 296–9.
  1962. African models in the New Guinea Highlands. *Man* **62**: 5–9.
  1963. Introduction. In Malinowski, B., *The Family among the Australian Aborigines*. New York.
  1964. Physical and social facts in anthropology. *Philosophy of science* A**1**. 294–7.
  1967*a*. Agnation among the Enga: a review article. *Oceania* **38**: 33–43.
  1967*b*. Feedback and real time in social enquiry. *Australian and New Zealand Journal of Sociology* 3: 78–92.
  1970. *Sociology in Cambridge: an Inaugural Lecture*. Cambridge.
  1971*a*. Agnatic taxonomies and stochastic variation. *Anthropological Forum* **3**: 3–12.
  1971*b*. *Three Styles in the Study of Kinship*. Berkeley.
Barnes, S. B. 1969. Paradigms – scientific and social. *Man* N.S. 4: 94–102.
Barth, F. 1954. Father's brother's daughter marriage in Kurdistan. *Southwestern Journal of Anthropology* 10.
  1959. *Political Leadership among Swat Pathans*. London School of Economics Monographs on Social Anthropology No. 19. London.
  1966. *Models of Social Organization*. R.A.I. Occasional Paper No. 23.

References

1972. Analytical dimensions in the comparison of social organizations. *American Anthropologist* **74**.

Baumann, H. 1928. The division of work according to sex in African hoe culture *Africa* **1**: 289–319.

Beattie, J. H. M. 1964*a*. Kinship and social anthropology. *Man* **64**: 101–3.

1964*b*. *Other Cultures*. London.

1970. *The Nyoro State*. Oxford.

Benirschke, K. 1970. Spontaneous chimerism in mammals: a critical review. *Current Topics in Pathology* **51**: 1–61.

Berreman, G. D. 1963. *Hindus of the Himalayas*. Berkeley.

Bidney, D. 1967. *Theoretical Anthropology*. New York.

Bloch, M. 1971*a*. The moral and tactical meaning of kinship terms. *Man* **6**: 79–87.

1971*b*. *Placing the Dead*. London.

Blunt, E. A. H. 1931. *The Caste System of Northern India*. London.

Bohannan, L. 1952. A genealogical charter. *Africa* **22**.

Bohannan, P., and Dalton, G. (eds). 1962. *Markets in Africa*. Evanston.

Bourdieu, Pierre. 1972. *Esquisse d'une théorie de la pratique, precédé de trois études d'ethnologie kabyle*. Geneva, Paris.

Boserup, E. 1970. *Woman's Role in Economic Development*. London.

Bosman, W. 1967 (1705). *A New and Accurate Description of the Coast of Guinea*. London.

Bott, E. 1957. *Family and Social Network*. London.

Bowlby, J. 1969. *Attachment and Loss Vol 1: Attachment*. London.

Boyer, R. M., 1964. The matrifocal family among the Mescalero: additional data. *American Anthropologist* **66**: 593.

Bronson, G. 1969. Vision in infancy: structure-function relationships. In Robinson, R. J. (ed.) *Brain and Early Behaviour*. London and New York.

Brown, P. 1960. Chimbu tribes: political organisation of the Eastern Highlands of New Guinea. *South-western Journal of Anthropology* **16**.

1964. Enemies and affines. *Ethnology* **3**.

1967. The Chimbu political system. *Anthropological Forum* **2**.

Brown, P., and Brookfield, H. C. 1959. Chimbu land and society. *Oceania* **30**.

Buhler, G. 1879. The Sacred Laws of the Aryas, Part I, Apastamba and Gautama. Muller, F. M. (ed.) *The Sacred Books of the East*. Oxford.

1882. The Sacred Laws of the Aryas, Part II, Vasishtha, Baudhayana. Muller, F. M. (ed.) *The Sacred Books of the East*. Oxford.

Burridge, K. 1957*a*. Descent in Tangu. *Oceania* **28**.

1957*b*. The *Gagai* in Tangu. *Oceania* **28**.

1959. Siblings in Tangu. *Oceania* **30**.

1960. *Mambu: a Melanesian Millenium*. London.

Carter, V. B. 1967. *Winston Churchill as I Knew Him* (1st ed. 1965). London.

Churchill, W. S. 1959. *My Early Life* (1st ed. 1930). London.

Clarke, E. 1957. *My Mother Who Fathered Me*. London.

Clignet, R. 1970. *Many Wives, Many Powers*. Evanston.

Cohen, A. 1965. *Arab Border Villages in Israel*. Manchester.

Cole, F. J. 1930. *Early Theories of Sexual Generation*. Oxford.

Collie, A. 1830. On some particulars connected with the natural history of the kangaroo. *Zoological Journal* **5**: 238–41.

Colson, E. 1951. The Plateau Tonga of Northern Rhodesia. In Colson, E., and Gluckman, M. (eds.) *Seven Tribes of British Central Africa*. Manchester.

Conel, J. L. 1939. *The Postnatal Development of the Human Cerebral Cortex*. I: *The Cortex of the Newborn*. Cambridge, Mass.

References

1941. *The Postnatal Development of the Human Cerebral Cortex.* II: *The Cortex of the One-Month Infant.* Cambridge, Mass.

1947. *The Postnatal Development of the Human Cerebral Cortex.* III: *The Cortex of the Three-Month Infant.* Cambridge, Mass.

Conklin, H. C. 1964. Ethnogenealogical method. In Goodenough, W. H. (ed.) *Explorations in Cultural Anthropology, Essays in Honor of George Peter Murdock.* New York.

Cook, E. A. 1970. On the conversion of non-agnates into agnates among the Manga, Jimi River, Western Highlands District, New Guinea. *Southwestern Journal of Anthropology* **26**.

Cunnison, I. G. 1959. *The Luapula Peoples of Northern Rhodesia.* Manchester.

Darwin, C. 1875. *The Variation of Animals and Plants Under Domestication* (2nd ed.). London.

1877. A biographical sketch of an infant. *Mind* **2**: 285–94.

Davis, N. Z. 1971. The reasons of misrule: youth groups and charivaris in sixteenth-century France. *Past and Present* **50**: 41–75.

de Lepervanche, M. 1967–8a. Descent, residence and leadership in the New Guinea Highlands, Part I. *Oceania* **38**.

1967–8b. Descent, residence and leadership in the New Guinea Highlands, Part II. *Oceania* **38**.

De Vore, I. 1963. Mother-infant relations in free-ranging baboons. In Rheingold, H. L. (ed.) *Maternal Behaviour in Mammals.* New York.

Dennis, W. 1941. Infant development under conditions of restricted practice and of minimum social stimulation. *Genetic Psychology Monographs* **23**: 143–89.

Dittrilhová, J. 1969. Social Smiling. In Robinson, R. J. (ed.) *Brain and Early Behaviour.* London and New York.

Dobzhansky, T. 1970. Heredity. In *Encyclopaedia Britannica* **11**: 419–27. Chicago.

Dorjahn, V. 1959. The factors of polygamy in African demography. In Herskovits, M., and Bascom, W. (eds.) *Continuity and Change in African Cultures.* Chicago.

Douglas, M. 1966. *Purity and Danger.* London.

1969. Virgin birth. *Man* N.S. **4**: 133–4.

Drake, St. C., and Cayton, H. B. 1945. *Black Metropolis, a Study of Negro Life in a Northern City.* New York.

Dumont, L. 1957. *Hierarchy and Marriage Alliance in South Indian Kinship.* R. A. I. Occasional Paper No. 12. London.

1961. Les mariages Nayar comme faits indiens. *L'Homme* **1**: 11–36.

1970. *Homo Hierarchicus, The Caste System and its Implications* (English trans.). London.

1971 *Introduction à deux théories d'anthropologie sociale.* Paris, The Hague. Les textes sociologiques VI.

Durkheim, E. 1952. *Suicide.* Spaulding, J. A., and Simpson, G. (trans.). London.

Dyson-Hudson, N. 1966. *Karimojong Politics,* London.

Eggan, F. 1950. *Social Organization of the Western Pueblos.* Chicago.

Eibl-Eibesfeldt, I. 1970. *Ethology: The Biology of Behaviour.* New York.

Ellingson, R. J. 1964. Studies of the electrical activity of the developing human brain. In Himwich, W. A., and Himwich, H. E. (eds.). *Progress in Brain Research, Vol. 9: The Developing Brain.* Amsterdam.

Evans-Pritchard, E. E. 1932. Heredity and gestation as the Azande see them. *Sociologus* **8**: 400–14.

1934. Lévy-Bruhl's theory of primitive mentality. University of Egypt, *Bulletin of the Faculty of Arts* **2**: 1–36.

1937. *Witchcraft, Oracles and Magic among the Azande.* Oxford.

References

1940. *The Nuer*. Oxford.

1948. *The Divine Kingship of the Shilluk of the Nilotic Sudan*. Cambridge.

1951. *Kinship and Marriage among the Nuer*. Oxford.

Farber, B. 1972. *Guardians of Virtue, Salem Families in 1800*. New York and London.

Firth, R. 1957. *Primitive Polynesian Economics*. London.

1967. Bond-friendship. In *Tikopia Ritual and Belief*. London. Originally published in 1936.

Forde, D. 1947. The anthropological approach in social science. *The Advancement of Science* **4**: 213–24.

Forge, J. A. W. 1971. Marriage and Exchange in the Sepik. In Needham, R. (ed.) *Rethinking Kinship and Marriage*. A. S. A. Monographs No. 11. London.

1972. Normative factors in the settlement size of Neolithic cultivators (New Guinea). In Ucko, P. J., Tringham, R., and Dimbleby, G. L. (eds.) *Man, Settlement and Urbanism*. London.

Formby, D. 1967. Maternal recognition of the infant's cry. *Developmental Medicine and Child Neurology* **9**: 293–8.

Fortes, M. 1936. Ritual festivals and social cohesion in the hinterland of the Gold Coast. *American Anthropologist* **38**. Reprinted in *Time and Social Structure* 1970. London.

1945. *The Dynamics of Clanship among the Tallensi*. London.

1949a. *The Web of Kinship among the Tallensi*. London.

1949b. Time and Social Structure: an Ashanti case study. In Fortes, M. (ed.) *Social Structure: Studies Presented to A. R. Radcliffe-Brown*. London.

1950. Kinship and marriage among the Ashanti. In Radcliffe-Brown, A. R., and Forde, D. (eds.) *African Systems of Kinship and Marriage*. London.

1953a. The structure of unilineal descent groups. *American Anthropologist* **55**. Reprinted in *Time and Social Structure* 1970. London.

1953b. *Social Anthropology at Cambridge Since 1900*. Cambridge.

1954. A demographic field study in Ashanti. In Lorimer, F. (ed.) *Culture and Human Fertility*. Paris.

1957. Malinowski and the study of kinship. In Firth, R. (ed.) *Man and Culture, an Evaluation of the Work of Bronislaw Malinowski*. London.

1958a. Thinking about society. *Cambridge Review* **79**: 596–8.

1958b. Introduction. In Goody, J. (ed.) *The Developmental Cycle in Domestic Groups*. Cambridge Papers in Social Anthropology No. 1. Cambridge.

1959a. Descent, filiation and affinity, *Man* 309 and 331. Reprinted in Fortes 1970.

1959b. *Oedipus and Job in West African Religion*. Cambridge.

1962. Ritual and office in tribal society. In Gluckman, M. (ed.) *Essays on the Rituals of Social Relations*. Manchester.

1966. Religious premises and logical technique in divinatory ritual. In, A discussion on ritualization of behaviour in animals and man, *Philosophical Transactions of the Royal Society of London*, Series B, Biological Sciences, 251.

1967. Of installation ceremonies (Presidential Address 1967). In *Proceedings of the Royal Anthropological Institute*. London.

1969. *Kinship and the Social Order*. London.

1970a. The significance of descent in Tale social structure. In Fortes, M. (ed.) *Time and Social Structure and other essays*. L.S.E. Monograph on Social Anthropology, No. 40. London.

1970b. *Time and Social Structure and other essays*. London.

Fortes, M., and Evans-Pritchard, E. E. (eds.) 1940. *African Political Systems*. London.

Frazer, J. G. 1910. *Totemism and Exogamy*. London.

Frazier, E. F. 1939. *The Negro Family in The United States*. Chicago.

References

Freedman, D. G. 1967. A biological approach to personality development. In Brackbill, Y. (ed.) *Infancy and Early Childhood*. New York.

Freilich, M., and Coser, L. A. 1972. Structured imbalances of gratification: The case of the Caribbean mating system. *The British Journal of Sociology* **23**: 1–19.

Freud, S. 1964. An outline of psycho-analysis (1st ed. 1940). In *The Standard Edition of the Complete Psychological Works of Sigmund Freud* **23**: 139–207. London.

Geertz, H. 1961. *The Javanese Family, A Study of Kinship and Socialization*. New York.

Gellner, E. 1963. Nature and society in social anthropology. *Philosophy of Science* **30**: 236–51.

Gilbert, J. P., and Hammel, E. A. 1966. Computer simulation and analysis of problems in kinship and social structure. *American Anthropologist* **68**.

Glasse, R. M. 1969. Marriage in South Fore. In Meggitt, M. J., and Glasse, R. M. (eds.) *Pigs, Pearlshells, and Women*. New Jersey.

Glasse, R. M., and Lindenbaum, S. 1971. South Fore politics, in Lawrence, P., and Berndt, R. M. (eds.) *Politics in New Guinea*. University of Western Australia Press.

Gluckman, M. 1950. Kinship and marriage among the Lozi of Northern Rhodesia and the Zulu of Natal. In Forde, D., and Radcliffe-Brown, A. R. (eds.) *African Systems of Kinship and Marriage*. London.

1955. *The Judicial Process among the Barotse of Northern Rhodesia*. Manchester.

1963. *Order and Rebellion in Tribal Africa*. London.

1965a. *The Ideas in Barotse Jurisprudence*. New Haven.

1965b. Introduction. In Meggitt, M. *The Lineage System of the Mae-Enga*. Edinburgh.

1971. Marriage payments and social structure among the Lozi and Zulu. In Goody, J. (ed.) *Kinship*. London.

Goldberg, H. 1967. FBD marriage and demography among Tripolitanian Jews in Israel. *Southwestern Journal of Anthropology* **23**.

González, N. L. (See also Solien and Solien de González). 1965. The consanguineal household and matrifocality. *American Anthropologist* **67**: 1541–9.

1969. *Black Carib Household Structure, A Study of Migration and Modernization*. Seattle.

1970. Toward a definition of matrifocality. In Whitten Jr., N. E., and Szwed, J. F. (eds.) *Afro-American Anthropology, Contemporary Perspectives*. New York.

Goodenough, W. H. 1956. Residence rules. *Southwestern Journal of Anthropology* **12**: 22–37.

1970a. Epilogue: transactions in parenthood. In Carroll, V. (ed.) *Adoption in Eastern Oceania*. Honolulu.

1970b. *Description and Comparison in Cultural Anthropology*. Chicago.

Goody, E. N. 1970. Legitimate and illegitimate aggression in a West African state. In Douglas, M. (ed.) *Witchcraft Confessions and Accusations*, A. S. A. Monographs, No. 9. London.

Goody, J. 1961. The classification of double descent systems. *Current Anthropology* **2**: 3–25.

1963. *Death, Property and the Ancestors*. London and Stanford.

1969a. Inheritance, property and marriage in Africa and Eurasia. *Sociology* **3**: 55–76.

1969b. 'Normative', 'recollected' and 'actual' marriage payments among the LoWiili, 1951–66. *Africa* **39**: 54–61.

1972a. The evolution of the family. In Laslett, P., and Wall, R. (eds.) *Household and Family in Past Time*. Cambridge.

1972b. *The Myth of the Bagre*. Oxford.

References

Goody, J., and Buckley, J. 1973. Inheritance and women's labour in Africa. *Africa* **43**: 108–21.

Gray, R. F. 1964. Introduction. In Gray, R. F., and Gulliver, P. H. (eds.) *The Family Estate in Africa.* London.

Grene, D., and Lattimore, R. 1959. *The Complete Greek Tragedies,* vol. 1, Aeschylus. Chicago.

Gudeman, S. 1972. The compadrazgo as a reflection of the natural and spiritual person. *Proceedings of the Royal Anthropological Institute* **1971**: 45–71.

Gulliver, P. H. 1951. A preliminary survey of the Turkana. *Communications from the School of African Studies,* New Series no. 26. Capetown.

1955. *The Family Herds.* London.

1958. The Turkana age organization. *American Anthropologist* **60**: 900–22.

1966. The Jie of Uganda. In Gibbs, J. L. (ed.) *Peoples of Africa.* New York.

1971. *Neighbours and Networks.* Berkeley.

Gusdorf, Georges. 1948. *L'expérience humaine du sacrifice.* Paris.

Habermas, J. 1972. *Knowledge and Human Interests.* London.

Hammel, Eugene A. 1968. *Alternative Social Structures and ritual relations in the Balkans.* Englewood Cliffs, N. J.

Hammel, E. A., and Goldberg, H. 1971. Parallel cousin marriage. *Man* **6.**

Harlow, H. F. 1958. The nature of love. *American Psychologist* **13**: 673–85.

1961. The development of affectional patterns in infant monkeys. In Foss, B. M. (ed.) *Determinants of Infant Behaviour.* London.

Harper, E. B. 1968. A comparative analysis of caste: the United States and India. In Singer, M., and Cohn, B. S. (eds.) *Structure and Change in Indian Society,* Viking Fund Publications in Anthropology, No. 4.

Heath, D. B. 1958. Sexual division of labor and cross-cultural research. *Social Forces* **37**: 77–9.

Herskovits, M. J. 1937. *Life in a Haitian Valley.* New York.

1941. *The Myth of the Negro Past.* New York.

1962. Preface. In Bohannan, P., and Dalton, G. (eds.) *Markets in Africa.* Evanston.

Herskovits, M. J., and Frances, S. 1934. *Rebel Destiny: among the Bush Negroes of Dutch Guiana.* New York.

1947. *Trinidad Village.* New York.

Hiatt, L. R. 1971. Secret pseudo-procreation rites among the Australian Aborigines. In Hiatt, L. R., and Jayawardena, C. (eds.) *Anthropology in Oceania, Essays Presented to Ian Hogbin.* Sydney.

Howell, P. P. 1953. Observations on the Shilluk of the Upper Nile. Customary law: marriage and the violation of rights in women. *Africa* **23**: 94–109.

Humphrey, T. 1969. Postnatal repetition of human prenatal activity sequences with some suggestions of their neuroanatomical basis. In Robinson, R. J. (ed.) *Brain and Early Behaviour.* London and New York.

Hutton, J. H. 1951. *Caste in India* (2nd ed.). London.

Jarvie, I. C. 1965. Limits to functionalism and alternatives in anthropology. In Martindale, D. (ed.) *Functionalism in the Social Sciences.* American Academy of Political and Social Sciences.

Jay, P. 1963. Mother-infant relations in langurs. In Rheingold, H. L. (ed.) *Maternal Behavior in Mammals.* New York.

Jolly, J. 1880. The institutes of Vishnu. In Muller, F. M. (ed.) *The Sacred Books of the East.* London.

Jones, E. 1951. The Madonna's conception through the ear: a contribution to the relation between aesthetics and religion. In *Essays in Applied Psycho-analysis* vol. 2. London.

References

Kaberry, P. M. 1967. The plasticity of New Guinea kinship. In Freedman, M. (ed.) *Social Organisation: Essays presented to Raymond Firth*. London.

Kane, P. V. 1941. *History of Dharmasastra*. vol. 2, Pt. 1. Poona.

Karve, I. 1953. *Kinship Organization in India*. Poona.

1961. *Hindu Society – an Interpretation*. Poona.

Keesing, R. M. 1971. Descent, residence and cultural codes. In Hiatt, L. R., and Jayawardena, C. (eds.) *Anthropology in Oceania, Essays Presented to Ian Hogbin*. Sydney.

Khuri, F. I. 1970. Parallel cousin marriage reconsidered: a Middle Eastern practice that nullifies the effects of marriage on the intensity of family relationships. *Man* 5.

Krupp, G. R. 1962. The bereavement reaction. *The Psycho-analytic Study of Society* 2: 42–74.

Kuhn, T. S. 1970. *The Structure of Scientific Revolutions* (2nd ed.). Chicago.

Kunstadter, P. 1963. A survey of the consanguine or matrifocal family. *American Anthropologist* 65: 56–66.

La Fontaine, J. S. 1962. Gisu marriage and affinal relations. In Fortes, M. (ed.) *Marriage in Tribal Societies*. Cambridge Papers in Social Anthropology, No. 3. Cambridge.

Lane, E. M. 1871. *An Account of the Manners and Customs of the Modern Egyptians* (5th edn.). London.

Langness, L. L. 1964. Some problems in the conceptualization of Highlands social structures. In Watson, J. B. (ed.) New Guinea: the Central Highlands, *American Anthropologist* (spec. public.) 66: 162–82.

1968. Bena Bena political organization. *Anthropological Forum* 2: 180–98.

1969. Marriage in Bena Bena. In Meggitt, M., and Glasse, R. M. (eds.) *Pigs, Pearl-shells and Women*. New Jersey.

Lawick-Goodall, J. van 1971a. *In the Shadow of Man*. London.

1971b. Some aspects of mother-infant relationships in a group of wild chimpanzees. In Schaffer, H. R. (ed.) *The Origins of Human Social Relations*. London and New York.

Leach, E. R. 1951. The structural implications of matrilateral cross-cousin marriage. Reprinted in Leach, 1961b.

1954. *Political Systems of Highland Burma: a Study of Kachin Social Structure*. London.

1957. Aspects of bridewealth and marriage stability among the Kachin and Lakher. *Man* 59. Reprinted in Leach, 1961b.

1961a. *Pul Eliya: a Village in Ceylon: a Study of Land Tenure and Kinship*. Cambridge.

1961b. Rethinking anthropology. In *Rethinking Anthropology and Other Essays*. London.

1961c. Golden bough or gilded twig? *Daedalus* 90: 371–87.

1964. Anthropological aspects of language: animal categories and verbal abuse. In Lennenberg, E. H. (ed.) *New Directions in the Study of Language*. Cambridge, Mass.

1966. Comments on Scheffler. *Current Anthropology* 7: 548–9.

1967. Virgin birth. *Proceedings of the Royal Anthropological Institute 1966*.

1972. The influence of cultural context on non-verbal communication in man. In Hinde, R. A. (ed.) *Non-Verbal Communication*. Cambridge.

Lévi-Strauss, C. 1966a. The future of kinship studies. *Proceedings of the Royal Anthropological Institute 1965*.

1966b. *The Savage Mind (La Pensée Sauvage)*. London.

References

Levy, M. J. 1965. Aspects of the analysis of family structure. In Coale, A. J. *et al.* *Aspects of the Analysis of Family Structure*. Princeton.

Lewis, I. M. 1961. *A Pastoral Democracy*. London.

1965. Problems in the comparative study of unilineal descent. In Banton, M. (ed.) *The Relevance of Models for Social Anthropology*. A. S. A. Monographs in Social Anthropology 1. London.

Lindsley, D. B. 1964. Brain development and behavior: historical introduction. In Himwich, W. A., and Himwich, H. A. (eds.) *Progress in Brain Research Vol. 9: The Developing Brain*. Amsterdam.

Lloyd-Jones, H. 1956. Zeus in Aeschylus. *Journal of Hellenic Studies* **76**: 55–67.

Lorenz, K. 1935. Der Kumpan in der Umwelt des Vogels. *Journal of Ornithology* **83**: 137–213, 289–413.

Lounsbury, F. G. 1965. Another view of the Trobriand kinship categories. In Hammel, E. A. (ed.) Formal semantic analysis, *American Anthropologist* (spec. public.) **67**: 142–85.

Lowman-Vayda, C. 1971. Maring Big Men. In Lawrence, P. and Berndt, R. M. (eds.) *Politics in New Guinea*. University of Western Australia Press.

Lyons, J. 1968. *Introduction to Theoretical Linguistics*. Cambridge.

Mair, L. 1953. In Phillips, A. (ed.) *Survey of African Marriage and Family Life*. London.

Malinowski, B. 1929. *The Sexual Life of Savages*. London.

1935. *Coral Gardens and Their Magic*. New York.

1963. *The Family among the Australian Aborigines: A Sociological Study* (1st edn. 1914). New York.

Maquet, J. J. 1961. *The Premise of Inequality in Ruanda*. London.

Mauss, M. 1925. Essai sur le don. *L'Année Sociologique* N.S., 1.

Mead, M. 1962. A cultural anthropologist's approach to maternal deprivation. In Ainsworth, M.D. *et al. Deprivation of Maternal Care*. Geneva.

Meggitt, M. J. 1962a. *Desert People: A Study of the Walbiri Aborigines of Central Australia*. Sydney.

1962b. The growth and decline of agnatic descent groups among the Mae-Enga of the New Guinea Highlands. *Ethnology* **1**: 158–67.

1965. *The Lineage System of the Mae-Enga of New Guinea*. Edinburgh.

1967. The pattern of leadership among the Mae-Enga of New Guinea, *Anthropological Forum* **2**.

1972. Understanding Australian Aboriginal society: kinship systems or cultural categories? In Reining, P. (ed.) *Kinship Studies in the Morgan Centennial Year*. Washington, D.C.

Meyer, A. W. 1939. *The Rise of Embryology*. Stanford.

Middleton, J. 1960. *Lugbara Religion*. London.

Middleton, J., and Tait, D. (eds.) 1958. *Tribes Without Rulers: Studies in African Segmentary Systems*. London.

Moore, S. F. 1964. Descent and symbolic filiation. *American Anthropologist* **66**.

Morris, H. S. 1968. *The Indians in Uganda: Caste and Sect in a Plural Society*. London.

Morris, T., and Blom-Cooper, L. 1964. *A Calendar of Murder*. London.

Morton, Earl of. 1821. A communication of a singular fact in natural history. *Philosophical Transactions of the Royal Society of London*.

Mukwaya, A. B. 1962. The marketing of staple foods in Kampala, Uganda. In Bohannan, P., and Dalton, G. (eds.) *Markets in Africa*. Evanston.

Mullen, R. J., and Whitten, W. K. 1971. Relationship of genotype and degree of

References

chimerism in coat color to sex ratios and gametogenesis in chimeric mice. *Journal of Experimental Zoology* **178:** 165–76.

Murdock, G. P. 1949. *Social Structure.* New York.

1967. The ethnographic atlas. *Ethnology* **6:** 109–236.

Murphy, R. F., and Kasdan, L. 1959. The structure of parallel cousin marriage. *American Anthropologist* **61.**

1967. Agnation and endogamy. Some further considerations. *Southwestern Journal of Anthropology* **23.**

Nag, M. 1962. *Factors Affecting Human Fertility in Non-industrial Societies: a Cross-Cultural Study.* New York.

Nārada, T. 1954 (trans.). *The Dhammapada.* London.

Naroll, R. S. 1964. On ethnic classification. *Current Anthropology* **5:** 283–312.

Needham, J. 1959. *A History of Embryology* (2nd ed.). Cambridge.

Neufeld, E. 1944. *Ancient Hebrew Marriage Laws.* London.

Newman, P. L. 1965. *Knowing the Gururumba.* New York.

Nimkoff, M. F., and Middleton, R. 1960. Types of family and types of Economy. *Am. J. Sociology* **46:** 215–25.

Orenstein, H. 1965. The structure of Hindu caste values: a preliminary study of hierarchy and ritual defilement. *Ethnology* **4:** 1–15.

1968. Toward a grammar of defilement in Hindu Sacred Law. In Singer, M., and Cohn, B. S. (eds.) *Structure and Change in Indian Society.* Viking Fund Publications in Anthropology.

1970. Logical congruence in Hindu Sacred Law: another interpretation. *Contributions to Indian Sociology* (n.s.) **4:** 22–35.

Parkes, A. S. 1960. The biology of spermatozoa and artificial insemination. In Marshall, F. H. A. (ed.) *Physiology of Reproduction* (3rd ed.) vol. 1. London.

Parsons, A. 1969. *Belief, Magic and Anomie, Essays in Psychosocial Anthropology.* New York.

Parry, J. Hypergamy in the hills of Northwest India. Unpublished MS.

Patai, R. 1965. The structure of endogamous unilineal descent groups. *Southwestern Journal of Anthropology* **21.**

Pehrson, R. N. 1966. *The Social Organization of the Marri Baluch.* Chicago.

Peters, E. 1960. The proliferation of segments in the lineage of the Bedouin of Cyrenaica. *J. R. Anthrop. I.* **90.**

1967. Some structural aspects of the feud among the camel-herding Bedouin of Cyrenaica. *Africa* **37.**

Pike, K. L. 1967. *Language in Relation to a Unified Theory of the Structure of Human Behavior* (2nd ed.). Janua linguarum, series major 24. The Hague.

Pitt-Rivers, J., 1968. The Stranger, the Guest and the Hostile Host. In Peristiany, J. G. (ed.) *Contributions to Mediterranean Sociology.* The Hague.

1968. Pseudo-kinship. In *Encyclopedia of Social Sciences.*

1970. Women and sanctuary in the Mediterranean. In *Echanges et Communications, mélanges offerts à Claude Lévi-Strauss,* Vol. ii, The Hague.

Ritual kinship in the Mediterranean: Spain and the Balkans. In Peristiany (ed.) *Contributions to Mediterranean Sociological Congress.* Cambridge. Forthcoming.

Ploeg, A. 1969. *Government in Wanggulam.* The Hague.

Pocock, D. 1957. Inclusion and exclusion: a process in the caste system of Gujerat. *South-western Journal of Anthropology* **13:** 19–31. 1972. *Kanbi and Patidar, A Study of the Patidar Community of Gujerat.* Oxford.

Prechtl, H. F. R. 1969a. The problems for study. In Robinson, R. J. (ed.) *Brain and Early Behaviour.* London and New York.

References

1969b. Brain and behavioural mechanisms in the human new born infant. In Robinson, R. J. (ed.) *Brain and Early Behaviour*. London and New York.

Radcliffe-Brown, A. R. 1950. Introduction. In Forde, D., and Radcliffe-Brown, A. R. (eds.) *African Systems of Kinship and Marriage*. London.

1952. The mother's brother in South Africa. *S. Afr. J. Sci.* **21:** 542–55. Reprinted in Radcliffe-Brown, A. R. 1952. *Structure and Function in Primitive Societies: Essays and Addresses*. London.

Randolph, R. R. 1964. The 'matrifocal family' as a comparative category. *American Anthropologist* **66:** 628–31.

Rappaport, R. 1967. *Pigs for the Ancestors*. New Haven and London.

Rattray, R. S. 1927. *Religion and Art in Ashanti*. London.

1929. *Ashanti Law and Constitution*. London.

Reay, M. O. 1959a. *The Kuma*. Melbourne.

1959b. Individual ownership and transfer of land among the Kuma. *Man* **59:** 109.

1967. The structural co-variants of land shortage among patrilineal peoples. *Anthropological Forum* **2**.

1971. Structural co-variants of land shortage among patrilineal peoples. In Lawrence, P., and Berndt, R. M. (eds.) *Politics in New Guinea*. University of Western Australia Press.

Rheingold, H. L. (ed.) 1963. *Maternal Behaviour in Mammals*. New York.

Richards, A. I. 1939. *Land, Labour and Diet in Northern Rhodesia*. London.

1950. Some types of family structure among the Central Bantu. In Forde, D., and Radcliffe-Brown, A. R. (eds.) *African Systems of Kinship and Marriage*. London.

Richards, A. I., and Reining, P. 1954. Report on fertility surveys in Buganda and Buheya, 1952. In Lorimer, F. (ed.) *Culture and Human Fertility*. UNESCO.

Rigby, P. 1969. *Cattle and Kinship among the Gogo*. Ithaca.

Robinson, J. 1971. *Economic Heresies*. London.

Rotberg, R. I. 1962. Rural Rhodesian markets. In Bohannan, P., and Dalton, G. (eds.) *Markets in Africa*. Evanston.

Russell, B. 1967. *The Autobiography of Bertrand Russell, 1872–1914*. London.

Ryan, D. J. 1959. Clan formation in the Mendi Valley. *Oceania* **29:** 257–89.

Sahlins, M. D. 1963. Poor man, rich man, big man, chief: political types in Melanesia and Polynesia. *Comparative Studies in Society and History* **5**.

1965. On the ideology and composition of descent groups. *Man* **65:** 104–7.

Saladin d'Anglure, B. 1967. *L'organisation sociale traditionnelle des Esquimaux de Kangirsujuaaq* (Nouveau Quebec). Centre d'études nordiques, Laval University, No. 17.

Salisbury, R. F. 1956. Unilineal descent groups in the New Guinea Highlands. *Man* **56:** 2–7.

1962. *From Stone to Steel*. Melbourne.

1964. New Guinea Highland models and descent theory. *Man* **64:** 168–71.

1965. The Siane of the Eastern Highlands. In Lawrence, P., and Meggitt, M. J. (eds.) *Gods, Ghosts and Men in Melanesia*. Melbourne and London.

Schaffer, H. R. 1963. Some issues for research in the study of attachment behaviour. In Foss, B. M. (ed.) *Determinants of Infant Behaviour: II*. London.

Schapera, I. A. 1950. Kinship and marriage among the Tswana. In Forde, D., and Radcliffe-Brown, A. R. (eds.) *African Systems of Kinship and Marriage*. London.

Scheffler, H. W. 1965. *Choiseul Island Social Structure*. Berkeley.

1966. Ancestor worship in anthropology: or, observations on descent and descent groups. *Current Anthropology* **1966:** 541–51.

1970. Kinship and adoption in the Northern New Hebrides. In Carroll, V. (ed.) *Adoption in Eastern Oceania*. Honolulu.

245

References

1972. Kinship semantics. In Siegel, B. J. (ed.) *Annual Review of Anthropology*. California.

Scheffler, H. W., and Lounsbury, F. G. 1971. *A Study in Structural Semantics. The Siriono Kinship System*. New Jersey.

Schneider, D. M. 1961. The distinctive features of matrilineal descent groups. In Schneider, D. M., and Gough, E. K. (eds.) *Matrilineal Kinship*. Berkeley.

1964. The nature of kinship. *Man* **64**: 180–1.

1965a. Some muddles in the models. In *The Relevance of Models for Social Anthropology*. A.S.A. Monographs No. 1, London.

1965b. Kinship and biology. In Coale, A. J. *et al. Aspects of the Analysis of Family Structure*. Princeton.

1967. Kinship and culture: descent and filiation as cultural constructs. *Southwestern Journal of Anthropology* **23**.

1968. *American Kinship: A Cultural Account*. Englewood Cliffs, New Jersey.

1972. What is kinship all about? In Reining, P. (ed.) *Kinship Studies in the Morgan Centennial Year*. Washington, D. C.

Schneider, D. M., and Smith, R. T. 1973. *Class Differences and Sex Roles in American Kinship and Family Structure*. Englewood Cliffs, New Jersey.

Schwimmer, E. G. 1972. *Regional Communication Systems in Papua and the Problem of Social Boundaries*. Toronto.

Scott, J. P. 1963. The process of primary socialization in canine and human infants. *Monographs of the Society for Research in Child Development* **28**: 1–47.

Scott, J. P., and Fuller, J. L. 1965. *Genetics and the Social Behavior of the Dog*. Chicago.

Seligmann, C. G. 1902. The medicine, surgery, and midwifery of the Sinaugolo. *Journal of the Anthropological Institute* **32**: 297–304.

Shapiro, W. 1969. Miwuyt marriage: social structural aspects of the bestowal of females in northeast Arnhem Land. *Ph. D. thesis*. Canberra.

1971. Patri-groups, patri-categories, and sections in Australian Aboriginal social classification, *Man* N.S. **6**: 590–60.

Sharman, A. 1969. Joking relationships in Padhola: categorical relationships, choice and social control. *Man* N.S. **4**.

Sharman, G. B. 1955. Studies on marsupial reproduction. III. Normal and delayed pregnancy in *Setonix brachyurus. Australian Journal of Zoology* **3**: 56–70.

Sharman, G. B. and Berger, P. J. 1969. Embryonic diapause in marsupials. Advances in Reproductive Physiology **4**: 211–40.

Sibree, Rev. J. 1880. *The Great African Island*. London.

Silverman, M. G. 1971. *Disconcerting Issue. Meaning and Struggle in a Resettled Pacific Community*. Chicago.

Simpson, G. G. 1961. *Principles of Animal Taxonomy*. New York.

Smith, Rev. E. W., and Dale, Capt. A. M. 1920. *The Ila Speaking Peoples of Northern Rhodesia*. London.

Smith, M. G. 1956. On Segmentary Lineage Systems. *J.R.A.I.* **86**.

1962a. *Kinship and Community in Carriaccu*. New Haven.

1962b. *West Indian Family Structure*. Seattle.

Smith, R. T. 1956. *The Negro Family in British Guiana*. London.

1957. The family in the Caribbean. In Rubin, V. (ed.) *Caribbean Studies: A Symposium*. Jamaica.

1963. Culture and social structure in the Caribbean: some recent work on family and kinship studies. *Comparative Studies in Society and History* **6**: 24–46.

1970. The nuclear family in Afro-American kinship. *Journal of Comparative Family Studies* **1**: 55–70.

References

Smith, W. Robertson. 1885. *Kinship and Marriage in Early Arabia*. Cambridge.

Solien, N. L. (See also González and Solien de González). 1958. *The Consanguineal Household among the Black Carib of Central America*. Ann Arbor.

1959*a*. The nonunilineal descent group in the Caribbean and Central America. *American Anthropologist* **61:** 578–83.

1959*b*. West Indian characteristics of the Black Carib. *Southwestern Journal of Anthropology* **15:** 300–7.

1960. Family and household in the Caribbean. *Social and Economic Studies* **9:** 101–6.

Solien de González, N. L. 1961. Family organization in five types of migratory wage labor. *American Anthropologist* **63:** 1264–80.

Southall, A. W. 1971. Ideology and group composition in Madagascar. *American Anthropologist* **73:** 144–64

Southwold, M. 1971. Meanings of kinship. In Needham, R. (ed.) *Rethinking Kinship and Marriage*. A.S.A. monographs No. 11. London.

Spencer, 1949–50. *Primitive obstetrics*. Ciba symposia 11: 1157–1188.

Spiro, M. E. 1968. Virgin birth, parthenogenesis and physiological paternity: an essay in cultural interpretation. *Man* **3:** 242–61.

1972. Virgin birth. *Man* **7:** 315–16.

Spitz, R. A., and Wolf, K. M. 1946. The smiling response: a contribution to the ontogenesis of social relations. *Genetic Psychology Monographs* **34:** 57–125.

Stevens, A. G. 1971. Attachment behaviour, separation anxiety, and stranger anxiety. In Schaffer, H. R. (ed.) *The Origins of Human Social Relations*. London and New York.

Strathern, A. J. 1969. Descent and alliance in the New Guinea Highlands: some problems of comparison. *Proceedings of the Royal Anthropological Institute for 1968:* 37–52.

1971. *The Rope of Moka*. Cambridge.

1972. *One Father, One Blood*. Australian National University Press.

Swete, H. B. 1909. *The Holy Spirit in the New Testament: A Study in Primitive Christian Teaching*. London.

Tarkowski, A. K. 1961. Mouse chimaeras developed from fused eggs. *Nature* **190:** 857–60.

Teitelbaum, M. S., and Mantel, N. 1971. Socio-economic factors and the sex ratio at birth. *J. Biosocial Science* **3:** 23–41.

Tegnaeus, H. 1952. *Blood-brothers: an ethno-sociological study of the institution of blood-brotherhood with special reference to Africa*. New York.

Tod, J. Lt. Col. 1832. *The Annals of Antiquities of Rajasthan or the Central and Western Rajpoot States of India*, vols. 1 and 2. London.

Troughton, E. 1965 *Furred Animals of Australia* (8th ed.). Sydney.

Turner, V. 1969. *The Forest of Symbols: Aspects of Ndembu Ritual*. Cornell and Oxford.

Uchendu, V. 1965. Concubinage among the Ngwa-Igbo of Southern Nigeria. *Africa* **35:** 187–97.

Van de Walle, E. 1968. Characteristics of African demographic data. In Brass, W. *et al. The Demography of Tropical Africa*. Princeton.

Vayda, A. P., and Cook, E. A. 1964. Structural variability in the Bismarck mountain cultures of New Guinea: a preliminary report. *Transactions of the New York. Acadamy of Sciences* **26:** 798–803.

Wagner, R. 1967. *The Curse of Souw: principles of Daribi clan definition and alliance in New Guinea*. Chicago and London.

1969. Marriage among the Daribi. In Meggitt, M. J., and Glasse, R. (eds.)

References

Pigs, Pearlshells and Women: Marriage in the New Guinea Highlands. New Jersey.

Warner, W. L. 1958. *A Black Civilization: A Social Study of an Australian Tribe* (rev. ed.). New York.

Watson, J. B. 1964. Introduction: anthropology in the New Guinea Highlands. In Watson, J. B. (ed.) New Guinea: the Central Highlands. *American Anthropologist* (spec. public.) **66:** 1–19.

1970. Society as organized flow: the Tairora case. *Southwestern Journal of Anthropology* **26:** 107–24.

Weber, M. 1946. Science as a vocation. In Gerth, H. H., and Mills, C. W. (eds.) *From Max Weber: Essays in Sociology*. New York.

Wegmann, T. G. 1970. Enzyme patterns in tetraparental mouse liver. *Nature* **225:** 462–3.

Weismann, A. 1893. *The Germ-plasm: A Theory of Heredity*. London.

Westermarck, E. 1891. *The History of Human Marriage*. London.

Winnington-Ingram, R. P. 1948. Clytemnestra and the vote of Athena. *Journal of Hellenic Studies* **68:** 130–47.

Wolf, Eric R. 1966. Kinship, friendship and patron-client relations. In M. Banton (ed.) *The Social Anthropology of Complex Societies*. London.

1969a. The natural history of crying and other vocalizations in early infancy. In Foss, B. M. (ed.) *Determinants of Infant Behaviour:* IV. London.

1969b. A summing-up. In Robinson, R. J. (ed.) *Brain and Early Behaviour*. London and New York.

Wolff, P. H. 1963. Observations on the early development of smiling. In Foss, B. M. (ed.) Determinants of Infant Behaviour: II. London.

Worsley, P. M. 1956. The kinship system of the Tallensi: a revaluation. *J. R. A. I.* **86**.

Yalman, N. 1967. *Under the Bo Tree: Studies in Caste, Kinship and Marriage in the Interior of Ceylon*. Berkeley.

Zirkle, C. 1935. *The Beginnings of Plant Hybridization*. Philadelphia.

1946. The early history of the idea of the inheritance of acquired characters and of pangenesis. *Transactions of the American Philosophical Society* (n.s.) **35:** 91–151.

Index

Index

Schneider, D. M., 3, 6, 8, 19, 22, 24, 29, 33, 36, 61–2, 63–4, 69, 72, 129, 130, 144

segmentary lineages, 3, 13, 24, 39, 41, 156

sex, 9, 65, 91–3, 188–9, 218; roles, 124, 127–8, 139–40

siblings, 31, 48, 101, 108, 166, 167, 178; 'equivalence of', 167–8; 'individuality of', 167; brothers, 82, 95, 166; sisters, 151

smiling, 111–12

social change, 86

social structure, 6, 21, 22, 23, 168–71, 172; models of, 5, 6

society: and culture, 22, 23

statistics, 22

structuralism, 4, 10, 123–4, 166, 169–70, 172

succession, 22, 149, 169, 171

symbol, 28, 50, 61–2, 69, 71, 72, 170, 217; mediating, 30; symbolic representations, 156, 158

taxonomy, 165, 191; hierarchical, 165, 191–2, 208, 223; key, 191, 223

terms: polysemic, 26, 27

transactional analysis, 75–6, 217–18; transactions, 22, 24, 26, 30, 48, 79

urbanisation, 178

venereal disease: and plural marriage, 188

warfare, 39, 41, 44, 147–8, 178

widow-inheritance, 166, 167, 168

witchcraft, 156–7; male/female, 157